Sally G. McMillen
DAVIDSON COLLEGE

Southern Women

Black and White in the Old South

SECOND EDITION

HARLAN DAVIDSON, INC.
WHEELING, ILLINOIS 60090-6000

Library of Congress Cataloging-in-Publication Data

McMillen, Sally Gregory, 1944–
    Southern women : Black and white in the Old South / Sally G.
      McMillen.—2nd ed.
      p. cm. — (The American history series)
    Includes bibliographical references and index.
    ISBN 0-88295-963-8
    1. Women—Southern States—History—19th century. 2. African
    American women—Southern States—History—19th century.
    3. Women—Southern States—Social conditions. I. Title. II. American
    history series (Wheeling, Ill.)

    HQ1438.A13 M36 2002
    305.4'0975—dc21

2001039212

Cover photo: Left: Detail from "planting sweet potatoes on Edisto Island,"
1862, a contraband slave. *Courtesy New Hampshire Historical Society.* Right:
Detail from "women take a moment from their sewing," farm women, Cedar
Mountain, Virginia, 1862. *Courtesy Library of Congress, LC-B8171-0502-
DLC.*

Manufactured in the United States of America
04 03 02 01 1 2 3 4 5 MG

To my mother and the memory of my father

FOREWORD

Every generation writes its own history for the reason that it sees the past in the foreshortened perspective of its own experience. This has surely been true of the writing of American history. The practical aim of our historiography is to give us a more informed sense of where we are going by helping us understand the road we took in getting where we are. As the nature and dimensions of American life are changing, so too are the themes of our historical writing. Today's scholars are hard at work reconsidering every major aspect of the nation's past: its politics, diplomacy, economy, society, recreation, mores and values, as well as status, ethnic, race, sexual, and family relations. The lists of series titles that appear on the inside covers of this book will show at once that our historians are ever broadening the range of their studies.

The aim of this series is to offer our readers a survey of what today's historians are saying about the central themes and aspects of the American past. To do this, we have invited to write for the series only scholars who have made notable contributions to the respective fields in which they are working. Drawing on primary and secondary materials, each volume presents a factual and narrative account of its particular subject, one that affords readers a basis for perceiving its larger dimensions and importance. Conscious that readers respond to the closeness and immediacy of a subject, each of our authors seeks to restore the past as an actual present, to revive it as a living reality. The individuals and groups who figure in the pages of our books appear as real people who once were looking for survival and fulfillment. Aware that historical subjects are often matters of controversy, our authors present their own findings and conclusions. Each volume closes with an extensive critical essay on the writings of the major authorities on its particular theme.

The books in this series are primarily designed for use in both basic and advanced courses in American history, on the undergraduate and graduate levels. Such a series has a particular value these days, when the format of American history courses is being altered to accommodate a greater diversity of reading materials. The series offers a number of distinct advantages. It extends the dimensions of regular course work. It makes clear that the study of our past is, more than the student might otherwise understand, at once complex, profound, and absorbing. It presents that past as a subject of continuing interest and fresh investigation.

For these reasons the series strongly invites an interest that far exceeds the walls of academe. The work of experts in their respective fields, it puts at the disposal of all readers the rich findings of historical inquiry, an invitation to join, in major fields of research, those who are pondering anew the central themes and aspects of our past.

And, going beyond the confines of the classroom, it reminds the general reader no less than the university student that in each successive generation of the ever-changing American adventure, from its very start until our own day, men and women and children were facing their daily problems and attempting, as we are now, to live their lives and to make their way.

John Hope Franklin
A. S. Eisenstadt

CONTENTS

Photos follow page 100

ACKNOWLEDGMENTS

Having attended college before women's history courses became integrated into the curriculum, I am very pleased to be able to teach such classes now. It is equally rewarding to witness the scholarly attention focused on southern women. Historians recognize that black and white women living in the antebellum South experienced a life that differed from their counterparts in the North and West. During the past thirty years, extensive research has begun to reveal the fascinating texture of southern women's lives. The advisory editors for Harlan Davidson, Inc., deserve thanks for perceiving the importance of these women by including them in their American History Series.

This volume could not exist without the excellent scholarship that preceded it. I wish to thank the scores of historians whose published writings on southern women made this effort possible. Also central to this study are the diaries, letters, reminiscences, and oral histories of antebellum southern women which provided valuable personal insights into their lives.

Individuals deserving special acknowledgment include Catherine Clinton, Suzanne Lebsock, and A. S. Eisenstadt for their insightful and helpful editorial comments, as well as the Harlan Davidson staff, including Maureen Gilgore Hewitt and Michael Kendrick in the first edition and Lucy Herz in the second edition. I am grateful to my colleague, Ralph Levering, for encouraging me to undertake this project. And I thank my most supportive and critical audience, Bruce, Blair, and Carrie, who read this manuscript word for word, offered important suggestions, challenged interpretations, and patiently endured the tensions created by a historian in the process of writing.

Finally, it is to my mother, Elizabeth Gregory, and late father, Ted Gregory, that I dedicate this book. They encouraged me to treasure the ongoing process of learning and to embrace hard work. Above all, they made possible an excellent education that encouraged me to look at the world and always ask "Why"?

Sally G. McMillen
Davidson, N.C.

An Overview of the South and Southern Women

"I find by daily experience I am of a hardier mold than I had the most distant idea," wrote Priscilla Bailey of North Carolina in 1824. This recognition of feminine strength in the context of a demanding life could have been uttered by any black or white woman living in the antebellum and Civil War South. Southern women would have understood Priscilla's statement, for most of them, whatever their status or color, endured difficult and exhausting lives. They devoted themselves to families and work, sacrificing and struggling, and made enormous contributions to the region. Southern women were, indeed, of a "hardier mold."

Unfortunately, women who lived in the Old South often remain victims of myth or exaggeration. Slave and free black southern women have been portrayed as matriarchal or profligate; white women as delicate, submissive, and idle. Farm women mostly have been ignored because their records are so few. Myths for too long have prevented an accurate assessment of southern women's contributions, sacrifices, hardships, joys, and most important, their individuality.

Yet understanding how southern women lived is becoming an easier task as historians discover the records of their lives. Women's history has received serious scholarly attention since the early 1970s, for scholars prior to that time long assumed that events defined and participated in by men were all that counted. To their thinking, history comprised a series of wars, treaties, political events, and economic crises. But with the more recent emphasis on social history, scholars have been able to disclose a hidden past, providing rich details about average citizens and neglected groups like African Americans, women, and immigrants. An understanding of how these groups functioned, how they were affected by historical events, and how they affected history provides new insights into our past.

The history of southern women has come into its own as well. Southern historians have begun to integrate women into their research and examine the influence of gender as they study the history of the South. It is essential that the tale of southern women be told. Social historians recognize that the female experience varied significantly depending on race, class, region, and time period. Until recently, historical research on American women focused on New England or urban women, consequently ignoring important regional differences. The South embodied unique American experiences. Because antebellum southern women lived in a society in which females were expected to be submissive and hardworking, they have seemed almost invisible to researchers. They participated in fewer public reforms than their northern counterparts, and thus their endeavors were less apparent. Few antebellum southern white heroines matched the achievements of northern activists like Elizabeth Cady Stanton and Lucretia Mott. Women from the South who attracted public notice such as Harriet Tubman, Mary Boykin Chesnut, and the Grimké sisters were rare. Most of the region's women lived in relative obscurity, devoted to their immediate family and other kin.

Still, it is apparent that the changes that swept the South in the decades before and during the Civil War affected black and white women. Antebellum southern white women benefited from new laws that made it easier to obtain a divorce and hold property. Education was extended to tens of thousands of southern white girls and a few free blacks who flocked to female academies. Privileged women found new avenues to assert their own authority in small but important ways through charity and church work and even political expression. Obstetrical changes begun in Europe and in the North also affected southern women, as male doctors took charge of deliveries and health problems associated with pregnancy, childbirth, and childrearing.

A thorough study of white women in the South requires an examination of new sources and a fresh look at old ones. At first glance, females scarcely seem visible. State legislative manuals, public decrees, or market statistics do not record their deeds. Yet their words and accounts of their activities can be found in myriad sources. The most fruitful of these are the diaries, journals, and letters found in manuscript libraries and historical societies throughout the South. Educated southern women were anything but silent when it came to their private world and revealed their thoughts in letters, journals, or oral histories. Family bibles, gravestones, newspapers, census records, wills and contracts, marriage records, divorce proceedings, church testimonies, archaeological findings, clothing and artifacts, medical accounts, architectural remnants, and school histories all provide additional important clues.

Understanding the lives of illiterate or poor farm women proves more difficult. But historians gradually are uncovering their lives through careful studies of manuscript censuses, county and church records, archaeological remains, travelers' accounts, and oral histories. This is a field ripe for exciting research.

For too long, the history of slavery focused solely on the male experience. That has changed. It is apparent that females experienced slavery differently from bondmen. Remarkable work has been conducted on the records of slave women, much of it based on oral histories collected during the Depression of the 1930s. Slave narratives by those who escaped to the North and archaeological findings add other perspectives. Observations by adventurous northerners or Europeans who traveled southward to observe the region's "peculiar institution," as well as plantation accounts and slave trade records, provide still more commentary on slave life. Though in many respects the experiences of southern black and white women varied significantly, they shared many similarities as well.

Though the region was populated by a variety of peoples, including Native Americans and increasing numbers of immigrants, the focus of this study is on black and white women. To this time, relatively little research has been devoted to the lives of Native American and immigrant women in the South. However, as scholars continue to unearth new facts about these two groups, the picture is growing richer and more varied.

This study examines black and white southern women from 1800 to the end of the Civil War in 1865. Although women nationwide shared many similar experiences as laborers, reformers, churchgoers, mothers, and wives, each region created unique hardships and opportunities for them. Within these regions, contrasts could be especially pronounced and lives starkly different. Today historians are undertaking scholarly efforts to reveal the variety of the southern experience for black and white men and women. Depending on where they lived—the frontier of Arkansas, a city area like Richmond or Memphis, the Appalachian mountains, a tenant farm in the Piedmont of North Carolina, or on a Deep South Louisiana sugar plantation—women's experiences varied widely. Their race and legal status, class position, marital condition, and composition of family could have a profound effect on women's daily lives.

In order to understand the particular situation of the South, an overview of the region will help put women's lives in context.

Slavery was the most distinctive characteristic of the Old South. Northern states gradually outlawed slavery after the American Revolution, and only a few slaves were to be found in the North after the 1820s. Slavery was not profitable there, since most of that region's economic success was not based on a plantation economy or the cultivation of cash crops. A growing merchant class and a nascent industrial sector pushed the North in a different direction economically during the early antebellum period. Reform and modernization came with that development.

Neither mercantilism nor industry much affected the southern states during the antebellum period; their economies were essentially agrarian. By 1860, only 4.4 percent of southerners lived in urban areas, in contrast to approximately 20 percent in the nation overall. Blessed with fertile soil and a temperate climate that were conducive to growing cash crops, the South naturally remained a rural society based on agriculture. Its earliest colonial settlements had an agrarian identity. The Chesapeake's initial settlers discovered the tobacco leaf grown by Native Americans there. It took little time for the cultivation of this plant to consume the energies of the society. At one point, early colonists became so obsessed with profits from tobacco that laws were enacted to force them to grow food in order to avoid starvation. Throughout the colonial period, southern farmers discovered other profitable crops and products including indigo, rice, naval stores (products obtained from pine trees), sugar cane, and cotton.

Cultivation and marketing of such crops demanded an enormous amount of fertile land as well as access to transportation and a huge labor supply. Coastal lowlands and river areas were highly desirable for growing crops. The need for land forced southerners to spread out their farms and plantations, far from neighbors or community. As the population expanded, soil became depleted through overuse and opportunities narrowed. So southerners pushed westward, opening new frontier areas to farming. With the invention of the cotton gin in 1793 and the gradual removal of Native Americans from the deep South by the 1820s and 1830s, southerners moved farther west, where cheap land and economic opportunities beckoned. The necessity for land precluded the formation of large cities, except along the coast or on inland transportation routes. Charleston, New Orleans, Mobile, Savannah, and Memphis became centers for shipping cotton and other products. But none of these cities rivaled the bustling northern ports of New York, Philadelphia, or Boston. Few southern towns had populations greater than 2,500 people before the Civil War. If the antebellum South could be defined by anything resembling a community, it was the ubiquitous rural village or the plantation establishment, not the city.

Desperately needing workers to raise their cash crops, white colonial settlers tried unsuccessfully to force Native Americans to work. Soon they turned to the large supply of white male and female indentured servants from Europe. However, by the end of the seventeenth century, the supply of servants decreased. Southerners observed the successful results of African slavery throughout the Caribbean and Latin America and gradually turned to blacks for laborers. Because they desired to own these servants and their offspring for life, the need to pass special laws to enforce a slave system was apparent to southern landowners. By the mid-eighteenth century, slavery and the plantation system were firmly in place. By 1860, nearly 4 million slaves were living in perpetual bondage and facing a life of oppression and hardship that brought economic rewards to slave owners but none to slaves. Planters, who had invested their wealth in slaves, considered them property, often to be treated no better than farm animals. Slaves could be bought, rented, and sold at the will of their white owners.

With the end of the external slave trade in 1808, slave owners became more conscious of their slaves' needs, while at the same time further restricting their freedom. Compared to the slaves' situation during the colonial period, food, shelter, and work requirements improved, but new state laws were enacted that forbade slaves from learning to read or from moving about freely, and it became harder for whites to manumit, or free, a slave. Marked by their color and condition, slaves were the lowest class in the South, and any degree of African heritage legally identified someone as black in nearly all southern states. In order to ensure slave productivity and prevent rebellion, slave owners maintained control of the South by exercising their political and military power. Slave uprisings, such as Nat Turner's rebellion in 1831, merely led to more restrictive slave codes that by the 1830s were in place throughout the South.

For white women, the rural composition of the South meant that the majority of them spent their lives in relative isolation, living on small farms or plantations. The region lacked the institutions and social interaction available in urban areas to middle-class northern women. With few towns or cities, the South had fewer cultural offerings, fewer opportunities for the development of female bonding and sisterhood, less social interaction, and fewer churches and charitable activities than were available in the Northeast. Home remained the center of southern women's lives. As most southern spokesmen saw it, stability was something to celebrate, and the region became identified with conservatism and a reluctance to change.

Slave women on small farms experienced similar isolation. However, slightly more than half the slave population lived on farms with more than twenty slaves; and a quarter of all slaves lived on plantations with at least fifty slaves. Thus, a good number of black women benefited from a strong sense of community. A large plantation comprised a community of several families, with opportunities for socializing, visiting, working, and attending church together. In the face of enormous hardships and lack of freedom, slave women often enjoyed a stronger, more immediate sense of community and greater opportunity for female bonding than did southern white women.

Despite slavery's considerable presence in the region, it is important to remember that the majority of southern whites did not even belong to the slave-owning class. On the eve of the Civil War, only 6 percent of all southerners even qualified as planters (those with twenty or more slaves), and the region contained two times as many women who were slaves as it did white women who belonged to families that owned at least one slave. Scholars know far less about the 6 million southerners who owned no slaves than they know about plantation and slave women.

The plantation system was anything but moribund by 1860. The 1850 federal census showed that ten of the twelve wealthiest counties in the nation were located in the South; ten years later the South could boast of having all twelve. The South marketed 75 percent of all American exports by the late antebellum period. South Carolina Senator James Henry Hammond crowed that "cotton is king," and there was truth to his assertion. The region's wealth depended on cotton. What this wealth, or potential wealth, meant to women depended on their race and class. For elite white women who benefited from their husband's wealth (or whose large dowries made such wealth possible), plantation life was often isolated and lonely. But women were hardly idle, for they had charge of most domestic responsibilities. They publicly accepted the region's institutions and its patriarchal structure. As historian Anne Firor Scott argues, white women may have complained quietly, but at the same time they enjoyed their status. They worked hard or, in rare cases, enjoyed the privilege of having others perform the drudgery. Skin color prevented any meaningful effort to overcome class consciousness by white women toward black women, and female relationships rarely crossed class boundaries. In fact, several historians have argued that elite women were probably most responsible for trying to maintain a sense of class superiority over less privileged white women.

Yeomen farm wives (who might or might not have been slave owners) worked most of their lives. They often lived among poor farmers and herdspeople like themselves, shared their labor, bartered their goods, and lived and died in relative obscurity. How actively they supported slavery and how directly the system affected them is difficult to assess since records are few. But there is some validity to the perception that up to the Civil War, slavery did not deeply trouble most yeomen farm wives. Most southern whites aspired to be slave owners. Also, the presence of slaves and free blacks allowed poor farmers to perceive that, despite their lowly status, they were not at the bottom of the social scale.

For slave women, the southern economy required of them unremitting work under constant supervision. They had to watch others benefit from their productivity. Theirs was a life defined and controlled by whites. It meant knowing that freedom was a white prerogative; that beloved family members always were vulnerable to sale; and that sexual abuse was an ever-present possibility. An owner or overseer could use the whip for the slightest infraction of rules. Slave women performed triple duty as laborers, wives, and mothers, responsible to both their owners and their own families. Some historians feel that slave women suffered more than male slaves due to their childbearing and work responsibilities. Historian Deborah White concludes that southern black women were the most vulnerable of all Americans during the antebellum period: they were blacks in a white nation;

women in a society ruled by men; and slaves in a world of the free.

Antebellum southern society has been described as patriarchal, a system in which men had ultimate control over public and private matters. Much about antebellum America also could be described as patriarchal to some degree, for white men held political, legal, and economic power throughout the nation. No woman could vote or serve on a jury. Until shortly before the Civil War, women had access to few economic opportunities, and professions in law, the ministry, and medicine were generally closed to them. As wives, women had few rights. Female power, if it existed at all, was confined to the domestic arena and to the extent a woman could influence her husband's public views. In a few instances, northern women challenged their status publicly, but southerners denounced such activity as inappropriate for southern ladies. A few outspoken or radical women in the North became active participants in antebellum reform issues and even questioned traditional assumptions about women's positions. But such challenges and public assertions were deemed unfeminine and especially threatening in the South. If a southern woman protested or criticized slavery in any setting, her presence would not long be welcomed. Involvement in reform activities rarely entered the minds of most southern white women. To confront women's status would have called into question all that the South embraced, including slavery.

The South embraced a hierarchical structure and an entrenched patriarchy where the subordination of women and slaves was essential to upholding the region's social structure. During the antebellum period, one detects southerners' growing anxiety about women's nature and their potential threat to society, especially as female reformers in the Northeast began to demand suffrage and women's rights. While much of the western world embraced ideas about women's natural mental and moral character and their secondary status, the South seemed to take these ideas a step further. As Benjamin Moore Palmer proclaimed of women, "Dependence . . . is not her degradation but her glory." White men were the ones who had to command power. Females who challenged the status quo would have jeopardized a society that prided itself on slave ownership and male authority.

According to prescriptive literature, which tried to establish (or prescribe) guidelines for ideal behavior, white women were supposed to be content with their submissive status. Men knew what was best for them. Only within the home could women excel. The exalted characteristics of antebellum women were piety, purity, domesticity, and submissiveness. Mothers were to set a virtuous example in the home and wives never to question a husband's or society's authority. How many women lived this ideal is open to question. Nevertheless, many middle-class and elite women accepted and strove to fulfill their prescribed role.

Feminine ideals persisted longer and took on greater meaning in the South. Southerners described white women as a special breed and mocked northern women who moved beyond their rightful sphere. For their part, southern women failed to challenge these ideals publicly. Perhaps they did not object to their status, or perhaps they found the odds too overwhelming to protest. They had been conditioned to accept their situation. Sometimes men emphasized their duty to protect women from whatever dangers lurked, especially alleged sexual threats to white women. Most women had little time anyway to ponder their secondary position.

Prescriptive literature and feminine ideals had little meaning for slave women. White owners wanted them to be hardworking, docile, fertile, and obedient. Yet slave women were more likely than white women to challenge their situation, despite (or perhaps because of) their lack of freedom. While group protest among antebellum female slaves was rare, many bondwomen reacted individually with surprising strength and anger, lashing out when their children were sold, running away temporarily when mistreated, fighting back, and most commonly, finding subtle means to protest their enslavement and undermine the slave system. Hardship and oppression sometimes became too much to endure.

The goal for nearly all antebellum women, black or white, was to marry and have children. Most adult women did just this, becoming wives and mothers, bearing and raising children, and devoting themselves to family concerns and productive labor. Due to high mortality and, for slave women, the constant threat of sale, family stability was often difficult to achieve. Nevertheless, most women desired the comfort and support of husband and children.

All women, regardless of color, enjoyed primary friendships with other females, including their mothers, daughters, relatives, neighbors, and friends. Men seemed to function in their own world, and women's principal emotional support came from other females. Female bonding, however, rarely crossed racial lines. Racism and oppression for blacks, and privilege and freedom for whites, were huge barriers to sisterhood. Occasional affectionate gestures between mistresses and black slaves were evident, but more often the sentiments expressed were frustration, impatience, or resentment.

Some of the most interesting recent scholarly work on the Civil War has focused on the experiences of southern women. Any war looks far different when one examines the experiences of those who were left on the home front to carry the burden of family and farm, and the Civil War was no exception. The Civil War turned the world upside down for black and white southern women. Slave women often had to take on additional tasks in the absence of black and white male laborers. They faced enormous hardships in the midst of war, and many experienced a shortage of food and clothing. But they began to sense that this war was being fought over slavery, and they anticipated that freedom would come and end centuries of bondage. Their hope for the outcome of the war was far different than that anticipated by southern whites. White women who were left without a husband, father, or son to manage the farm or plantation now had to raise their children and produce the food and raw materials needed to feed and clothe their family members as well as Confederate soldiers. Nearly all women on the home front faced shortages of basic goods, and they learned to deal with loneliness, sorrow, backbreaking work, and their fear of losing loved ones. The end of the war brought freedom to black women but a devastated world to many white women. But after 1865, both struggled to survive and determine the future of their family as well as the future of their region.

This brief history of black and white southern women focuses on their productive and reproductive lives. Whether privileged or enslaved, women spent their lives overcoming hardship and making sacrifices that are difficult for us to fathom today. A South of magnolias, mansions, and courtly gentlemen was real for only the tiniest minority of women. Far more realistic is a view of southern women as survivors, constantly facing the death of loved ones, living with poor health, enduring physical discomforts, and relishing only a few moments of joy or leisure. Raised to expect little and often finding their only strength in family and friends, they were a remarkable group, indeed, a "hardy mold."

CHAPTER ONE

Family Life and Marriage

Family

The family was the principal source of strength in black and white women's lives, but it also placed some of the greatest demands on their emotions, time, energy, and health. At its best, a family provided solace, support, love, and companionship; at its worst, it meant domestic violence, heartbreak, and pain. For many enslaved blacks, the family provided shelter against the brutality of slavery, but this institution was also most vulnerable to the whims of slave owners. In the Old South, slave marriages were never legally protected. An estimated 20 percent of all slave families were broken by sale. High mortality also affected black and white family stability during the antebellum period. Nevertheless, the family played a key role in slaves' struggle to combat oppression and gave slave women a sense of purpose. For most white women, the family was the central institution in their lives.

The emergence of a more sophisticated, stronger plantation system by the late eighteenth century fostered larger and more stable slave communities. With the ending of legal slave importation in 1808, which had brought more enslaved males than females to this country, a more balanced sex ratio emerged. Finding a marriage partner and creating a family became easier in the antebellum period, especially on large plantations. Yet slave family stability was never assured. In order to offset financial distress during a fluctuating economy, slaveholders always had the right to rent or sell a slave partner to ensure their income and minimize expenses. When planter families migrated and took only a portion of their slaves, they created rifts in some slave families.

It is important not to oversimplify the structure of slave families or to rely on a white model as their norm. By the antebellum period, many slaves did live in a nuclear family structure. Perhaps typical of those living on large plantations were nearly 160 slave families residing on sizeable Louisiana plantations. A study shows that nearly three-quarters of these slaves lived in parent-child groups. Two parents were present in half of the families studied; a single parent, usually the mother, headed 16 percent of these. Slightly less than 20 percent of all slaves lived alone, and nearly all of these were men. But being part of a family did not necessarily protect a slave. The most disruptive force to slave family stability was an owner's fluctuating financial circumstances, which might prompt the need to sell slaves. As Brenda Stevenson demonstrates in her study of slaves in Loudon County, Virginia, a downswing in the economy, a drop in the price of a cash crop, or a planter's need for cash fostered slave sales. Plantation owners sometimes sold their slaves without regard to family matters, thus splitting up partners and undermining family cohesion. The slave family was never a fixed institution, and a variety of patterns defined it. Studies of slaves on large plantations reveal a multiplicity of family forms and a wide range of household types, including nuclear, single-parent, solitary, and extended. These could change throughout an individual's lifetime and a slave family might incorporate some, or even all, of these forms. Family type also varied by plantation, depending upon slaves' economic activities, frequency of death and slave sales, the character of a plantation owner, and the type of crop produced.

Slave families usually lived in single cabins, thus fostering a sense of unity, although another family, an elderly relative, or a single person might share these quarters as well. Masters encouraged their slaves to live in family units: they perceived that this practice provided greater stability within the black community, discouraged runaways, and obviously enhanced their wealth when slave infants were born.

While the nuclear family was important, slaves received vital support from a strong extended family. Evidence of this is the fact that slaves valued the perpetuation of family names. Parents had a remarkable knowledge of genealogy and often named their children after grandparents, aunts, and uncles on both the maternal and paternal side. In the slave community, parenting could be shared as kin or family friends took charge of childrearing and education. An older slave woman or young slave girl might watch infants while parents worked in the fields. Relatives and friends often assisted single mothers with childrearing. Sometimes mothers were sold or died, leaving a slave child without a rightful parent. No slave child was truly without female affection, because aunts, sisters, grandmothers, or older women within the larger community would help raise the youngster. One slave woman recalled that because her mother lived on one plantation and her father on another; female relatives raised her. Frederick Douglass, former slave and abolitionist, scarcely remembered his mother, who had been hired out when he was an infant and died when he was only seven. Douglass, raised by his grandmother and an older woman, related that he saw his mother no more than four or five times in his life, and always at night when she could escape from her plantation.

The slave family experience varied widely. Recent research on slaves living in the Piedmont and mountain South reveals that they rarely enjoyed the support of large, stable families and communities that seemed to be more typical of slaves living on large plantations. Those in Appalachia typically resided and worked on farms or small plantations. Owners often regarded their slaves primarily as an investment, to buy and sell as needed. Operating small farms, these farmers were susceptible to the whims of fluctuating crop prices. The frequency of slave sales here exceeded the norm, fostering the disruption of slave family life and creating families in mountain areas that by the 1850s were often headed by women.

White families also depended on a broad kin network. Since white family members, of course, did not live with the threat of being sold, households were generally more stable than those of slave families. The extended family was probably less important to whites on a daily basis, but still it provided opportunities for sustenance, companionship, business ventures, socializing, and childrearing. The Petrigru (sometimes spelled *Pettigrew*) family of South and North Carolina included a wide assortment of aunts, uncles, cousins, and stepchildren. The Petrigru kin spread across two states, some living in the upcountry near Abbeville and others in Charleston or Georgetown, South Carolina, as well as Lake Phelps in North Carolina. They often summered together on Pawleys, Sullivan's and Kiawah Islands. Women in the family wrote one another frequently, sharing advice, joys, and sorrows, as well as gossip and family jealousies. They shared home-produced goods and food with one another; attended family weddings, parties, and debutante balls; and they assisted with childbirth and nursing the sick.

Most white families like the Petrigrus existed as nuclear households but often expanded to draw in kin, friends, and visitors. Mary and Charles Jones, enjoying the tranquility of middle age and an empty nest, unexpectedly became parents to their infant granddaughter when their daughter-in-law died in childbirth. Three-year-old Virginia Tunstall was sent from North Carolina to Alabama to be raised by her aunt and uncle when her mother died. Southern white families always found a place for spinsters, who typically resided with parents or siblings. When white families moved west, their migration was often in response to the urgings of a relative already settled on the frontier. Frequently, groups of families migrated together. When the Lides moved to Alabama, the extended family, including parents, six children, six grandchildren, and a number of slaves, came with them.

Family members helped to offset life's vicissitudes and provide affection and assistance in times of need. Family bonds among whites apparently helped to ameliorate class resentment, according to Wilbur J. Cash in his classic study, *The Mind of the South*. It was not unusual for rich and poor relatives to be living near one another, nor for the wealthy to assist their less fortunate relatives. For instance, Gertrude Thomas and her husband Jefferson hired a cousin as their overseer and a poor cousin as their seamstress. Letters among family members requested and offered advice, shared gossip, updated family members on children's growth and charming antics, and detailed family activities and health. At every age, southern women understood the importance of personal ties to their family. For slave women, the family often provided moments of joy amidst oppression, and home became a setting where they could function away from the scrutiny of their owner. Family associations in the South provided acceptance and some stability in a rural world where close friendships were often difficult to establish or maintain.

Despite the centrality of family, it would be wrong to assume that family relationships were always harmonious or that kin always got along well. While southern women generally were reluctant to air any side of a troubled marriage, tension and misunderstanding existed in many households. It is easy to understand how slaves, enduring oppression and hardship and living within the close confines of a tiny cabin might turn their exasperation or anger on family members. Husbands or wives might take out their frustration on a spouse or children. Members could bring shame on a family. South Carolinian Thomas Chaplin proved a continuous disappointment to his mother. Females in the Petigru family had no use for the new wife of a nephew, feeling that her common background, poor manners, and bad teeth were well below their standards, and they all but snubbed her when she came to visit. Men and women committed adultery and fathered or bore illegitimate children. Domestic violence and alcoholism in white and slave families undermined smooth family relationships.

Courtship and Marriage

Despite an antebellum married woman's limited legal standing and the challenges that marriage could bring, most southern women were eager to marry. Southern society expected them to do so. Finding a husband could become a full-time occupation, especially for a period of time during adolescence among elite white families who spent a great deal of time and money on court-ship rituals such as balls and parties. Meeting eligible men often demanded such attention, for finding a husband was not always easy, especially for those residing on isolated plantations and in rural settings.

Slave women living on large plantations usually had a rela-tively easy time finding a mate, for here, young black men and women had the opportunity to interact daily as they worked, and they often socialized on Saturday nights. Josiah Collins of Lake Phelps, North Carolina, allowed his slaves to interact with slaves on the adjacent Pettigrew plantation, giving them a choice of part-ners and frequent opportunities to socialize. At church, slaves from several plantations might gather to worship and socialize each Sunday. Young women dressed gaily, donning bright cotton dresses and clean handkerchiefs, primping to attract a man's at-tention. Finding a prospective partner on a small farm could prove more difficult, and bondmen living on nearby farms often courted these neighbor women. Some male slaves crept out at night to woo a young woman; more likely, though, they traveled once a week with an owner's permission slip in hand to visit a loved one.

Free black women living in cities had a small selection of available men because fewer free black males lived in southern cities than did females. As Dorothy Sterling points out in *We Are Your Sisters,* New Orleans had 100 free black women for every fifty-seven free black men, making marriage virtually impossible for many females. Forbidden by law to marry a white man and of-ten unwilling to marry a slave who was an economic burden, an urban black woman had limited choices. Though she could not le-gally marry a slave, a free black woman might form a liaison with one and sometimes purchase his freedom.

Courtship practices in the black community varied signifi-cantly from the casual to the ritualized. Slave courtship could be extremely romantic, with men persistently in pursuit of a comely woman. Men sometimes solicited the assistance of a conjurer to place a spell on the desired young woman in order to improve their chances of winning her. Yet many slaves had no time or use for such practices. Jane Johnson, an elderly slave woman, testified "'Dat courtin' stuff is what white folks does, no nigger knows what dat fancy thing is."

Prior to marriage, young slave women enjoyed relatively open sexual practices with black men, especially when compared to the behavior prescribed for elite southern white women. The black community did not condemn premarital sex or the birth of an infant to a single slave woman. Adulterous relationships, however, were unacceptable. Slave children born out of wedlock were incorporated into the mother's family; the parents might or might not eventually marry. Usually by the birth of a second child, a young woman had found a permanent mate.

Some slave owners did not appear all that disturbed by such behavior in the black community, despite the high standards demanded of white women. Planters could overlook slave children born out of wedlock (some of whom white men had sired) since each newborn slave increased the plantation labor pool and an owner's wealth. On the other hand, a slave owner like John Hartwell Cocke, an unusually paternalistic and concerned master who hoped to elevate his slaves and send them to the African colony of Liberia, was shocked to discover his Alabama slaves living in what he called a "state of moral depravity." He found several slave couples cohabiting without being married, mulatto children running everywhere, venereal disease rampant, and several black girls living with white men. Cocke immediately built additional slave cabins, hired a Baptist preacher, and offered the wayward slaves a choice of marriage or punishment.

Whites often accused black women of being sexually active and provocative. Deborah White suggests in *Ar'n't I a Woman?* that this accusation was used to offset white male guilt over miscegenation or was offered by white women as an excuse for their husband's wanderings. Yet sexuality in the black community was not as unrestrained as whites assumed. Black women exhibited some control over their sexuality and reproduction, for on average a slave woman bore her first child two or three years after menstruation began (which, on the average for all women at the time, started when they were about fifteen). Many concerned mothers warned their daughters about the predatory nature of black and white men. Nevertheless, bearing children was a rewarding experience for the black woman, within or outside of marriage, proving her ability to have children, confirming her identity as a mother and sexual being, and giving her a baby whom she could love.

Meeting eligible young men might be difficult for white women in the rural South. With the exception of girls living in urban areas like Charleston or New Orleans, where young men and numerous activities created a social whirlwind, contacts with single men were infrequent. Young people met at church, at a party or ball, or at the home of school friends or relatives. Such locations were safe meeting grounds; they attracted young men and women from the same social class who understood proper social boundaries and behavior. Mary Boykin's future husband, James Chesnut, was the brother of a schoolmate, and they met in Charleston when she was only fourteen. Though James's wealth and social standing made him an excellent suitor, Mary's parents became so concerned about the relationship developing between the couple that they pulled Mary out of school and sent her to their Mississippi plantation.

Marrying a first cousin or someone from the same county was common among southern white families. Such relationships developed naturally, since social interaction with extended family and neighbors was the norm. Most southern white women, whether privileged or poor, had little opportunity to meet a man living outside their county unless they went away to school or traveled to visit friends and family. In the South at least, cousin marriages were legal and made sense, for they cemented future family and business ties and could consolidate land holdings. There was undoubtedly something comforting about marrying a man you knew well. Mary Jones married her first cousin, Charles Colcock Jones, creating a family tied by land, tradition, common relations, and deep affection. Three of the eight children in the Thomas Lenoir family of North Carolina married their first cousins. Isabella Fraser of South Carolina married her first cousin, and when he died, she wed her second cousin. Jane Turner Censer's study of North Carolina planter families asserts that one in ten marriages among that state's elite took place between first and second cousins; other southern states may have exhibited a similar pattern.

Several marriages might occur between two white families, such as two brothers in one family marrying two sisters in another. When Thomas Chaplin of St. Helena Island, South Carolina, married Mary McDowell, her sister Sophy moved in to live with the couple. Mary was bedridden after bearing four children, and Sophy became a surrogate mother to these children as well as companion to Thomas, accompanying him to church and on shopping trips and listening to his endless woes. Ten months after Mary died at the age of twenty-nine, Thomas and Sophy married and remained united for forty years. Marrying the sibling of a deceased spouse could arouse widespread criticism as happened when Moses Mordecai of North Carolina, whose wife Margaret died in childbirth, married her sister Ann.

Courtship rituals varied significantly among white women, depending on the individual, family status, religious principles, and degree of parental control. Young men and women, after interacting closely and playing together as children, separated during adolescence and schooling and pursued their own activities or work. Reuniting during courtship among those within their same class often led to intense interaction between the sexes. For wealthy women, especially those living in or near southern cities, courtship became the stuff of myths that still persist about the Old South. Debutante balls, horse races, parties, and teas contributed to endless social activities and dozens of eligible suitors for urban girls. In such formalized courtship among the elite, southern women had learned their lessons well and knew how to appeal to men. This was probably a rare moment in their lives when women held some power over men, especially among females who were rich and attractive and thus highly desirable as future wives. Visitors to the South often remarked that southern belles were true coquettes. Competing for a man's attention could resemble medieval courtship, as men clamored for a beautiful girl's affection. Young women measured their success by the number of proposals they received. In such cases, courtship was almost a battle of the sexes, with women briefly in control. Such an exhilarating experience was short lived, however, for once married, society expected southern wives to be compliant and sedate.

Although information about yeoman farm girls is sparse, what little there is indicates that fewer courtship rituals surrounded them, and apparently many country girls enjoyed freer sexual behavior than did elite women. The number of scantily clad young women openly parading the street of a North Carolina village startled one visitor. Yet parental and religious constraints may have imposed limits on their behavior. Like privileged women, most farm girls married men from their local area whom they met through church or community activities.

Despite the importance of marriage in southern women's lives, some girls expressed trepidation about the institution and professed a desire to remain single. It was not unusual for adolescent girls to share their fear of marriage and childbirth and announce a preference for female companionship. When seventeen years old, Martha Crawford of Tuscaloosa County, Alabama, wrote, "I am continually haunted with the idea of <u>being married</u>." One can imagine impressionable teenage girls noticing the unending work undertaken by married women and how childbearing and rearing and domestic chores circumscribed their lives and fostered exhaustion and poor health. Compared to an adolescent's more carefree life and the joy that many girls found in female friendships, marriage might not have seemed all that appealing. However, as scholars have shown, most young women like Crawford who expressed such fears eventually wed. She married in her twenties and accompanied her missionary husband to China.

Not all courtship was coquettish and frivolous for the well-to-do, for religious precepts often encouraged submissiveness and piety. Frances Webb met the scholarly Rev. Samuel Bumpass when he heard her read for her final exams in school and apparently was charmed by her mastery of Greek literature. However, as an itinerant minister, he was too poor to marry. Two years passed, and Bumpass received an appointment to a Raleigh church, a stable position that also promised him an adequate salary. He then wooed Webb by sending her a white leather New Testament which he marked with relevant passages. He asked for her hand a year later, and she accepted. Another example of restrained behavior was a courtship related by Steve Stowe in *Intimacy and Power in the Old South*. Bessie Lacy met Thomas Dewey through one of her schoolmates, and they became engaged in 1851. Theirs was a distant courtship, both geographically and emotionally, carried out essentially by correspondence. Bessie's letters reflected the various phases of the relationship. During the initial stage, Bessie's penmanship, elegant stationery, and formal diction reflected her concern with proper behavior. A second period became more casual and intimate as she revealed more about her personal character and daily activities. In the final stage, Bessie expressed uneasiness about their forthcoming wedding but adopted a submissive and somewhat helpless demeanor as she realized that the man she had chosen could not match her dreams for lifelong happiness and close companionship.

Bessie was not alone. Many antebellum white women dreamed of a companionate relationship, expecting that in marriage, they would find a friend, lover, and soulmate for life. Yet companionship, then as now, implies equality. Men ordinarily possessed greater physical strength and held economic and legal control over their wives. It is doubtful that men willingly acquiesced to female equality once married, for it would have demanded enormous sacrifices and created a change in well-entrenched ideas about proper gender relationships.

Perhaps women like Bessie worried, knowing that their choice of a husband was the most important decision they would make. A good man could lead to a lifetime of happiness and fulfillment; a bad one, to violence and misery. Most marriages undoubtedly fell in between the extremes. Few women ever found the perfect man, but prescriptive literature and the profusion of romantic novels now being published offered them that fantasy. Because divorce was a virtual impossibility for southern women, and because their future life would be consumed with home and family, women knew their choice of a mate was critical.

Parents played a limited role in the selection process. The characteristics they sought in a proper mate did not necessarily parallel their daughter's desires. From a father's or mother's perspective, wealth, family, and status helped determine a man's eligibility. Young women would have included romantic love as well. Parents rarely influenced their daughter's choice directly, though cases of elopement show that some must have tried. Parents had a more subtle impact on a daughter's marital selection through the manner in which they raised her, including the characteristics they taught her to value, the way they responded to a suitor, and what gifts they bestowed on the newlyweds. Parental consent was not a necessity for marriage, though men often went through the motions of requesting a woman's hand from her father as a gesture of courtesy.

Though it would have been unseemly for a woman to discuss a suitor's wealth openly, a man's financial well-being influenced his chances to woo and win the woman of his choice. An elite woman might turn down a suitor because he evidenced no sign of his ability to support her in the manner to which she was accustomed. But important to a man was the dowry or inherited wealth that a young woman could bring to her marriage. For slave women and poor farm women who had no dowry or wealthy relatives, money had little or nothing to do with their appeal as a future mate; they were evaluated on their character, appearance, behavior, and ability to work hard.

Some southern white men improved their economic status significantly by marrying a wealthy woman who brought substantial land holdings or slaves to a marriage. James Henry Hammond, whose father was a South Carolina schoolteacher, had ambitions that far surpassed his middle-class background, and he purposely courted wealthy women. He set his sights on Catherine Fitzsimmons, a homely young woman with important family connections who was sole heiress to a wealthy Charleston merchant's fortune. Hammond pursued her relentlessly and finally succeeded, despite strong objections from her relatives who correctly recognized a fortune hunter. On the other hand, the lack of a sizeable dowry could bring disappointment. Sarah Williams, a New

York woman who married a North Carolina planter, felt the unending disapproval of her mother-in-law, who blamed Sarah for not bringing her son slaves as part of her dowry.

Miscegenation and Sexuality

Proper courtship rituals were meaningless when white men raped or threatened black women or forced slave women into marriages or relationships against their will. A slave woman was always sexually vulnerable to both black and white men, whether married or not. Miscegenation, or sex between different races, was common throughout the South and proved one of the system's greatest injustices against black women. Owners and slaves lived in close, physical intimacy. A Mrs. Douglas of Virginia denounced miscegenation as the "one great evil hanging over the Southern Slave States," and she claimed that "the practice is more general than even the Southerners are willing to allow." Historians estimate that by the Civil War, approximately 10 percent of the southern black population was mulatto, a result primarily from forced relationships between white men and black women. Slavery meant ownership, and to many southern white men, that implied the right to force sex on black women. Undoubtedly, too, there existed same-sex relationships between the races, though this topic has received little scholarly attention, in part because such relationships were generally hidden from public record and thus difficult to document.

In some instances, however, interracial sexual liaisons reflected affection and even true love between a black woman and a white man (and in rarer cases, between a white woman and a black man). Scholars debate whether a slave system could foster relationships of real affection when power between a black and white partner was so uneven. Yet some former slave women spoke or wrote lovingly of a close relationship with a master or white man. Plantation owners sometimes fell in love with a bondwoman, and such feelings could have been reciprocated. The existence of meaningful relationships is evident in wills, especially those in Louisiana where miscegenous relationships were legal until the 1850s. Some men openly admitted the paternity of off-spring from these relationships and freed their mulatto children or willed them a portion of their estate. A man sometimes left a be-loved slave woman money or land and sometimes set her free.

Though southerners knew that miscegenation was common, it defied the honor code for white men publicly to acknowledge this activity. Most men wisely conducted such relationships discreetly. As related by Adele Logan Alexander in *Ambiguous Lives,* Susan Hunt, a free woman of black, Cherokee, and white heritage appar-ently had a long, presumably affectionate relationship with Judge Nathan Sayre of Alabama. In his beautiful plantation home, Pomegranate Hall, he built an apartment for Hunt and their three children. For twenty years, he appeared as a bachelor in public, a "husband" and father in private. Federal census takers never noted the presence of either Hunt or her children. But family legend and documentation suggest that these two shared a private and mean-ingful life together. A white male like Sayre could cross the South's sexual boundaries of color as long as he did not flaunt it.

Couples like Sayre and Hunt never married because marriage between different races was illegal. Occasionally a common-law marriage existed when a biracial couple lived together for several years. These relationships usually involved a poor white farmer or woman and a former slave or free black. These relationships com-plicated the status of any offspring, especially those born to a slave father and a free white mother. Because children legally fol-lowed the condition of their mother, the mulatto children in these cases were free. What is surprising is that antebellum white soci-ety, like Sayre's neighbors, apparently evidenced a degree of tol-erance or indifference toward these interracial relationships, un-like the violent responses that would be more common in the postbellum South.

As recent scholarship reveals, the color barrier in the Old South was less absolute and rigid than we might think, even though whites usually condemned interracial relationships and several states had passed laws making these partnerships illegal. As historian Martha Hodes argues in her book, *Black Men, White Women,* some white communities tolerated interracial partnerships, especially when they were not flaunted or when the couple resided in the black community. Responses from the white community to these situations could vary considerably, depending on the circumstances. In court cases challenging these relationships, a white owner might defend his male slave involved with a white woman, for he would not want him jailed or killed because of the investment he had made in him.

Though rare, husbands and wives engaged in adulterous interracial relationships. Several divorce petitions from Virginia show a husband or wife who sued for divorce by charging a spouse with both adultery and sexual intercourse with a black partner. A few individuals who presented their cases received a complete divorce based on accusations of interracial adultery. Such behavior challenged the social, racial, and gender order of the South—and the institution of marriage. Because of society's double standard toward interracial sex (it being more acceptable for a white man to engage in such behavior than a white woman), a woman's chances of gaining a divorce were not enhanced by her merely charging her husband with interracial intercourse. On the other hand, it was usually adequate for a man to charge his wife with interracial adultery since this behavior was a grave threat to male honor. A woman had to present a litany of charges, such as physical and verbal abuse, his inability to support her and their children, and interracial intercourse. Despite the serious charges, judges and the General Assembly did not always agree with the supplicants; nearly half of all Virginia cases did not win a divorce. In one case, a white Virginia woman in 1824 was accused of carrying on an adulturous relationship with a black man for several years. Her white husband demanded a divorce. But because he had behaved violently toward her, the court showed little sympathy and refused to grant him one. Apparently, upholding the marriage was more important to the court than punishing her transgression.

Nevertheless, most troubling to southern whites was the coupling of a white woman and a black man. A white woman could not easily hide a resulting pregnancy or explain away the birth of a mulatto infant. (Sometimes, however, a woman claimed rape to protect her reputation or marriage.) In the Old South, the image of

a black "buck" eager to attack a white woman became a carica-
ture. The irony, of course, was that black men rarely forced white
women to have sex, for the consequence was usually a cruel
death. Such relationships, though rare, usually occurred because
white women desired them.

Some black women knowingly used their sexuality to foster
relationships with white men to improve their situation, whether
or not affection entered into the equation. Some slave women became predators and seductresses and used their feminine charms
to gain what they could. Sexual favors with a white owner or
overseer could be traded for articles of clothing, better food, and
perhaps freedom for her children. Slave women, who otherwise
had little power over white men, could achieve momentary control through sexual attraction.

Despite these relationships, rape defined most miscegenous
relationships between white men and slave women, often initiated
by a plantation owner, his son, an overseer, or a stranger. One
wealthy planter, David Dickson of Hancock County, Georgia,
raped a slave girl, Amelia, when she was only fourteen years old.
The child of that momentary, forced union, Amanda America, was
raised in the Dickson home and married her father's nephew in
1865. Her father willed her his fortune when he died, leaving
Amanda a wealthy woman. In a case related by Pauli Murray in
her family history, *Proud Shoes,* the wealthy Smith family of Orange County, North Carolina, purchased Harriet, a fifteen-year-
old slave, in 1834 to serve as maid to their daughter Mary. Five
years later, Harriet married a free black, Reuben Day, and in
1842, bore a son. But tragedy intervened when Mary's two brothers, Frank and Sidney, returned from college. They both openly
pursued and competed for Harriet, despite her married state and
the horrified reactions of the rest of the Smith family. In 1843, the
brothers severely beat and threatened Reuben, and he fled the
county, leaving Harriet unprotected. One evening, Sidney broke
into her cabin and raped her. This soon became a nightly ritual,
and despite Harriet's cries for help, there was little anyone could
do. Frank's jealousy intensified, and one night he attacked Sidney
and left him unconscious in the yard. Sidney suffered a severe

head injury, began to drink heavily, and never again bothered Harriet. Harriet bore a mulatto daughter, and Frank took his brother's place, eventually fathering three daughters over the next eight years. Harriet's anguish and helplessness must have been profound. Their mulatto children were raised in the Smith household (they were, after all, family members), and all the Smiths suffered deep embarrassment. Neither Mary, Sidney, nor Frank ever married. Interestingly, in later years, Harriet spoke with pride about her white relations.

The experience of another Harriet, Harriet Jacobs, detailed in her highly edited account, *Incidents in the Life of a Slave Girl,* is one of the best known cases of sexual harassment. Born around 1813, Harriet became the slave of Dr. John Norcom, a prominent physician of Edenton, North Carolina. Norcom apparently subjected Harriet to unrelenting sexual threats, eager for a physical relationship with the attractive mulatto woman. Harriet resisted his advances and turned to a prominent white congressman living nearby for protection, establishing a liaison with him. She eventually bore him two children. Norcom continued his pursuit, threatening Harriet and her children if she did not submit. Harriet feared for her children and finally fled, hiding for nearly seven years in an attic, at least according to her dramatic and emotional account. Eventually she escaped to the North and secured the freedom of her two children.

Another incident, related by historian Melton McLaurin, occurred in the 1850s and involved a fourteen-year old slave girl, Celia. Robert Newsome, a sixty-year-old Missouri farmer, purchased her as a domestic servant and concubine. Celia eventually bore two children by him. But she developed a relationship with George, a slave on the farm, and George apparently urged her to end the relationship with Newsome. One night when Newsome appeared at her cabin to claim what he saw as rightfully his, Celia struck him with a stick and killed him. Burning his clothing and body parts in her fireplace and burying the large bones outside, Celia hoped to avoid detection. Apparently George implicated her, probably to save himself, and Celia was brought to trial. Defended by two white lawyers, she naturally was found guilty.

While white women could use the law to defend themselves against this type of predator, a slave woman like Celia lacked that same right. Ultimately she was hanged in 1855.

Though the real victims were slave women, miscegenation had an impact on white women and on white marriages as well. Harriet Jacobs perceived that she aroused the jealousy of her mistress, especially when her master requested that she sleep in his bedroom under the pretense of caring for his four-year-old daughter. James Henry Hammond of South Carolina had relations with a slave woman and her twelve-year-old daughter, Louisa. Catherine Hammond discovered her husband's involvement with the young girl. Hammond pushed his wife to the brink by bringing the adolescent into their home to share his bedroom. Catherine, who had been extremely patient over the years with her husband's sexual indiscretions, protested, packed up their children, and went to reside with relatives near Charleston. Divorce was not an option for women in South Carolina, and without her own resources (her extensive wealth now belonged to her husband), Catherine had few choices. After two years of separation, Henry finally agreed that Louisa would leave, but only if Catherine's family found the slave girl a position in Charleston. Catherine and the children returned, but within a few months, so did Louisa. The ultimate resolution and Louisa's feelings are unknown.

Miscegenation deeply troubled white women, even those who were not directly affected by it. Rachel O'Connor criticized her brother for punishing one of his slave women for having sex with the overseer, Mulkey. Rachel's sympathies lay with the young woman. "She was a good girl before that villain came here," Rachel claimed. Yet steeped in racism and feelings of superiority, few white women could escape ambiguous feelings, including a sense of antipathy and even jealousy toward the real victims. Rachel continued, "I scarcely think there is one Negro woman in existence that is not guilty of the same wickedness. They are poor ignorant beings, born to serve out their days, and are led astray by such vile wretches as Mulkey." To O'Connor, all slave women were possible victims, but she concluded that ignorance, not powerlessness, governed their behavior.

Of course, many men also disapproved of miscegenous relationships and never succumbed to temptation. Some ministers tried to curb the widespread practice. The impact of evangelical Christianity on the South in the early antebellum period may have imposed some restraints, or at least heightened a sense of guilt in those men who took advantage of black women. Preachers decried the prevalence of sexual misconduct and criticized parishioners who indulged, seeing it as a negative reflection on the region and their own church. Expressed fears were sometimes racist; some critics detected a "bleaching" of the black race, raising concern that physical differences between black and white someday might become indiscernible. Others expressed outrage. Charles Colcock Jones, a Presbyterian minister and wealthy Georgia slave owner, was livid when he discovered that a man who had visited his plantation had fathered a child by one of his slaves. Many southern men were never tempted and maintained faithful relationships with their wives. Slave owner Rachel O'Connor was cautious about hiring a new overseer, for many earned a bad reputation for their liaisons with slave women. But she was relieved to learn about the personal life of Germany, the man who applied for the position. "There would be no danger of Germany's behaving as overseers commonly did amongst the Negroes; that he was too fond of his wife to behave in that way," she wrote. Her assessment was accurate; the man proved to be an excellent overseer.

Southern states began to legislate against miscegenation, though how actively they enforced such laws is unclear. White family members who hoped to benefit from family fortunes resented the mulatto offspring, fearing that they might be left out in the cold when men willed gifts and wealth to black women and their mulatto children. The civil code in Louisiana was the most supportive in allowing white men to leave their money and possessions to a slave mistress and children. But growing pressure from whites urged the legislature to restrict slave inheritances. By the 1850s, mulatto children in that state could receive no more than a quarter of a deceased man's fortune.

The double standard of fidelity victimized black women and white women alike. Though rarely the victims of sexual assault, white women perceived themselves every bit as injured as slave women who suffered the assaults; sometimes out of jealousy they accused slave women of welcoming forced physical intimacy. White men were not always discreet about their liaisons. Some, like Hammond, challenged the marital relationship by bringing a black woman into their home. Unfortunately, black and white women did not, and probably could not, unite to denounce the perpetrator. Because men held power and for the most part accepted and upheld the double standard, wives and slave women were helpless to protest the situation publicly. Occasionally, white women confided their despair in private writings. Most slave women dared mention a liaison outside the family circle only years after the fact. Mary Boykin Chesnut, a wealthy plantation mistress, observed widespread miscegenation on her father-in-law's South Carolina plantation. "Like the patriarchs of old our men live all in one house with their wives and their concubines," she wrote, "and the mulattoes one sees in every family exactly resemble the white children." Miscegenation fostered tension, jealousy, and suspicion between white women and female slaves, but this translated into little more than resentment and anger toward the men involved. Neither white nor black women had the power to protest effectively, though some women, like the two Harriets and Celia mentioned above, tried to resist male advances. Aside from the oppression inherent in slavery, miscegenation was an issue that inhibited bonding between white and black women.

Incredible as it may sound, some spokesmen regarded miscegenation as beneficial to the South. In 1853, William Harper, a proslavery advocate, concluded that the availability of black women saved the region from the pernicious effects of prostitution so prevalent in the North by affording "easy gratification of the hot passions of men." Through liaisons with black women, a man apparently expended his sexual appetite, and white women preserved their virtue and delicacy. Harper believed that black women placed little value on their chastity and were, by nature, sexually provocative. It is doubtful that any southern women, black or white, saw it this way, but such an argument justified male behavior and assuaged men's guilt. Also, Harper was misinformed, since prostitution in southern cities like New Orleans, Charleston, and Richmond, was common.

Forced sex affected slave marriages, for no bondman could protect a wife or daughter against rape without risking his own life and perhaps further endangering hers as well. Some scholars argue that miscegenation may have been an unconscious but nonetheless real means by which white men increased their power over black men. White men had access to both black and white women; black men only to black females.

A more unusual type of relationship involved white men and young mulatto women, the "fancy girls," of New Orleans and other port cities. This practice, often referred to as "plaçage," was condoned in the Crescent City. Plaçage evolved from a tradition during the French colonial period when European settlers established relationships with black women in the Louisiana territory. These "quadroons" (defined specifically as women with one-fourth black blood but more generally applied to a light-skinned mulatto woman) typically had a free mulatto mother and a white father. Many such females were so light complexioned that they were hard to distinguish from white women. New Yorker Frederick Law Olmsted, during his travels to New Orleans, described many of these women as educated, accomplished, well-dressed, and attractive. But he also predicted that "crime and heart breaking sorrow" could result from the system of plaçage. Planters, gamblers, merchants, and visitors desired these beautiful, well-mannered young women as mistresses or concubines. Not being allowed to marry them, a white man supported two lifestyles, as husband and father to his white family and protector of a particular octoroon woman (having one-eighth black blood), often supporting her and her offspring for years or even a lifetime. Some men living in or near Charleston kept colored or mulatto mistresses, a system tolerated there as long as the situation was not openly flaunted. Some quadroons, seeking a life of ease and prestige, knowingly traded sexual favors and companionship for decent housing, fine clothing, gifts, and money.

Annual quadroon balls, or *bals masqués,* were events where men could meet these women. After paying an entrance fee, a man could socialize and dance with eligible young women. Though these dances became highly romanticized in film and fiction, apparently they were often bawdy, at times even violent events, with drunken men displaying unbecoming behavior. Advertisements warned participants that they would be searched for weapons. If a man and young woman discovered mutual attraction, the man would pursue her, sometimes signing a contract whereby he would promise to support her and any offspring. Despite their material advantages, quadroons were still defined as free blacks, forbidden to gather in public places when white women were present, punished like slaves for committing certain transgressions, unable to interact publicly with whites, and forbidden to travel freely throughout the city.

Marriage

A southern white woman generally married at a younger age than her New England counterpart. Studies show that the average age for first marriages among elite southern white women was between eighteen-and-one-half and twenty years old, while on the average, northern women married at twenty-four. Southern women married men approximately six years older than they were, similar to the age of typical New England husbands. However, among the Moravians in North Carolina, the average age at marriage for females was twenty-seven; for men, thirty-six. These were the exception; the many southern women who married as teenagers is noteworthy. It is not unusual to discover southern girls marrying at fifteen or sixteen, though parents usually discouraged their daughters from marrying any younger. And there were exceptions for men as well. Thomas Chaplin of South Carolina married just before his seventeenth birthday, perhaps because his mother wanted to rid herself of responsibility for him. In second marriages, an older man often courted a younger woman, and they created another family. Slave women tended to be a year or two younger than elite white women when they married, though as noted, they may already have borne children.

Although slave marriages were not recognized as legal by whites, in the black community, relationships were fully sanctioned and legitimate. The failure to have their unions considered legal by whites brought advantages and disadvantages to the slave woman. Slave owners encouraged black couples to live together and bear children. They often held a wedding ceremony and celebration for the couple. Planters believed that slaves who married and had a family tended to be more responsible and less likely to run away. One might conclude then that legalizing these relationships would have made sense. But if marriage had been legally sanctioned, laws would have prevented its dissolution, thus interfering with an owner's right to sell those slaves who were married. Slave relationships could not supersede a planter's economic needs. By the late antebellum period, however, some owners allowed black or white ministers to marry slave couples, creating a union at least sanctioned by God. Gertrude Thomas of Georgia mentioned attending several slave marriages performed by ministers, and her mother baked cakes for the celebration that followed. But even with a religious ceremony, owners retained the right to dissolve a slave marriage if necessary, and apparently few ministers protested.

Slaves developed their own customs to symbolize their unions, based on African traditions or rituals adapted from white culture. Sometimes the couple laid two blankets next to one another as a symbol of their unity. Others jumped over a broomstick; in some instances, they merely moved into the same cabin together. But no slave marriage was secure, whatever the ceremony.

Some slave owners determined whom a slave could marry. They might forbid their slaves from "marrying abroad" (finding a partner on another plantation) because of possible disruption to their work and the time involved in traveling to and from another plantation. Furthermore, masters who owned the male lost any potential increase to their slave population since children automatically belonged to the owner of the slave woman. Owners encouraged their bondmen to marry on the plantation or farm whenever possible. Some slaveholders apparently played an active role in selecting a marriage partner for their slaves. West Virginian Lizzie Grant recalled that she was seventeen when her master put her together with the man he wanted her to call husband. "They never cared or thought about our feeling in the matter," she related.

Two of the most dreaded practices that slave women endured were forced marriages and the owner's use of a stud for procreation. Mary Gaffney, a Texas freedwoman, had no choice in selecting her husband while she was enslaved, and this left her with bitter feelings about marriage. "I just hated the man I married, but it was what Maser said do," Mary recalled years later. Bondwomen knew that owners encouraged slave marriages to serve their own economic benefit. Oral testimony by former slaves confirms that the desire of plantation owners to increase the size of their labor force was more important than the feelings of the black couple. In a few instances, a primitive kind of eugenics evolved in which owners selected strong young men and women for mating. The case of Rose Williams reveals such practices. Mr. Hawkins of Texas purchased Rose and her parents. Hawkins was apparently a relatively kind master, providing adequate food, limiting his slaves' work hours, and giving them some freedom. But Hawkins insisted that sixteen-year-old Rose share a cabin with Rufus, a large field hand. Initially, Rose failed to understand the implications of this living arrangement. The first night Rufus startled Rose by trying to get into her bed. She pushed him onto the floor and then hit him with a poker when he persisted. Rufus finally left but attempted the same thing the next night. Rose again rebuffed him and then appealed to her mistress. She was told that Mr. Hawkins wanted these two portly slaves to produce children. Hawkins warned Rose that she would be whipped if she failed to cooperate. Realizing that she had no choice and feeling some gratitude for her master's relative kindness, Rose complied. But she subsequently soured on marriage, "'cause one 'sperience am 'nough for this nigger. After what I does for the massa, I's never wants no truck with any man. The Lord forgive this colored woman, but he have to 'scuse me and look for others for to 'plenish the earth."

Rare was the use of stud men whom owners encouraged to impregnate several slave women. Such men had no family ties or responsibilities. The children of such liaisons often were unaware of their own father's identity. One North Carolina woman stated that, "I specks dat I doan know who my pappy wuz, maybe de stock nigger on de plantation." One male slave reported that his father had more than fifteen women and fathered at least 100 children.

Black Women and Marriage

The marital relationships of slaves differed from those of southern whites because of the tenuous status of black husbands and the fact that sales could split apart a slave family at any time. While planters encouraged slave marriages, they were also the prime cause of marital dissolution, selling their slaves in order to pay off their debts. A bondman, without economic and political power, was denied traditional male ways of asserting control over his family. Slave husbands could not protect their wives and children against mistreatment, punishment, rape, or sale. Many tried to improve family living conditions by building furniture, chinking their cabin, and gathering or hunting extra food to supplement a monotonous diet, but husbands were not the ultimate family providers. The white master gave his slaves food, shelter, and clothing, limited though they might be. The diminished role of the male within the slave family helps explain the relationship that evolved between slave men and women.

The issue of matriarchy frequently arises when studying slavery. Some sociologists and historians have concluded that the African American family was and still is matriarchal, based in part on the husband-wife relationship that evolved during slavery. The controversial Moynihan Report, released in 1965, asserted that modern African American families were unstable and disorganized. Households headed by females, the report argued, seemed to symbolize the troubled state of black families. Some scholars looked to the past to explain this situation. They observed that slave fathers seemed to be either absent or powerless, causing enormous problems within families and the wider community. They concluded that slavery, by weakening marital bonds, seemed to presage twentieth-century problems.

More recent studies have argued that the concept of matriarchy is an inappropriate one for defining the structure of African

American families. Researchers have pointed to the egalitarianism between black men and women, a discovery worthy of attention because it did not parallel the white experience. The power and strength of black women were striking, especially in comparison to antebellum white women who held so little power. Like many others, historian Suzanne Lebsock, in her book *Free Women of Petersburg,* argues that "matriarchy" improperly describes slave families and a black woman's role:

It needs to be understood from the beginning that the term "matriarch" would never have been applied to black women in the first place were it not for our culture's touchiness over reduced male authority within the family. It is a telling fact that matriarchy has most often been used as a relative term. That is, women are called matriarchs when the power they exercise relative to the men of their own group is in some respect greater than that defined as appropriate by the dominant culture. Given this standard, women need not be the equals of men, much less men's superiors, in order to qualify as matriarchs.

Because white women had so little power over men, situations in which bondwomen seemed powerful, or at least the equal of their husbands, resulted in misapplication of the term. Scholars prefer to use the term "matrifocal" when describing slave families in which the mother had primary responsibility for the children.

Deborah White's study of slave women further explains how black women became resilient and strong and, according to her, lived free of the dominance of black men (though they were always dominated by white men). According to White, slave women's strength derived, in part, from African tradition. Lineal descent was often traced through the mother's side of the family in African cultures, and women customarily played an important role in family survival. In some cases, fathers were rarely present. On southern plantations, black girls and boys interacted from infancy, playing together and performing odd jobs around the plantation until old enough to work in the fields. They rarely were separated as adolescents, for both slave men and women labored in the fields, and black women were expected to be strong and hardworking. While gender defined some tasks, especially on large plantations, the overseer or master expected slave women to perform almost any job. Black mothers often had no choice but to be tough. Many raised their children alone if a husband lived elsewhere or as single women if they had been raped or had borne babies out of wedlock. Also, White shows that prices for fertile young slave women could be nearly comparable to those demanded for brawny young men. Within the slave community and in the eyes of their owners, black women were highly valued, often on a par with men.

Recent scholarship by historians Leslie Schwalm and Brenda Stevenson paints a less rosy picture of female slave power within the black family. They argue that slave families lived under an inordinate amount of stress, and that black men and women resented the constant oppression and servitude they endured. Men might take out their frustration and anger on those closest to them: their wives and children. A mother might lash out at her children after a particularly bad day. But complaints of domestic violence were not shared with others. Black women usually suffered in silence, not wanting to expose their fragile lives to additional stress. They internalized such behavior and carried on with their lives.

Slave women, despite their strength and position within their family and community, were the most powerless group in the nation. They had no legitimate right to keep their children, to remain married, or to prevent physical or sexual abuse by black and white men. They faced discrimination, as women, as slaves, and as blacks. They could be punished and sold at whim. Yet slave women were not pawns, and they found means to protest their oppression without the aid of men. They also knew when to comply with a "Yes, Massa" and when to play dumb. Within the black community and in their personal relationships, black women could wield influence comparable to men. Their strength and resilience passed on to subsequent generations.

The degree of satisfaction and happiness in slave marriages can only be suggested. Some relationships must have provided the support and affection missing in a life of oppression and hardship. But it is important not to over-romanticize the quality of these marriages, however central they were in black women's lives. Some involuntary—and even voluntary—marriages must have been difficult and filled with tension and antipathy. Marriages under the best of circumstances require compromise, patience, and understanding. Slaves probably had little opportunity to forge an ideal union. Exhausted and powerless, both husband and wife must have taken out some of their frustration on a spouse or child. One Alabama slave recalled, "I 'members dat de overseer use ta whip mammy an' pappy, 'ca'se dey fight so much." Slave unions sometimes ended due to quarreling and violence. While marriages could be supportive and affectionate, to declare that most couples achieved deep marital happiness would misrepresent reality.

Slaves could, however, easily dissolve their marriages, a freedom denied nearly all southern whites. Since the marital relationship had no legal basis and since slave communities condoned marital dissolution, the couple merely parted if the partners were unhappy. If distance interfered with the marriage and visitation proved impossible, white owners encouraged slaves to remarry in their respective slave communities. A Georgia freedwoman, Amanda McDaniel, related that her mother had married and borne two daughters while a slave in Virginia. When she was sold to a Georgia planter, she married again and bore more children. The ease of dissolution could be empowering for black women in one respect, for they did not have to endure a difficult relationship. But the ease of such dissolutions also reflected an owner's ultimate control over his slaves, a situation that could break up happy marriages.

Though there is little information about free black women, we know that most of them resided in cities. Suzanne Lebsock's study of women in Petersburg, Virginia, shows that a surprising percentage of them remained single and that a high incidence of female-headed households existed among free blacks. As autonomous females, they usually worked a paid job and sometimes owned property. Many were mothers as well. Free black women were forbidden to marry white men (although they sometimes cohabited together as noted), and in most southern cities, there were not enough black men to go around. Some free black women lived with a slave mate, hoping to earn enough money to free him.

But, as the most impoverished of all free urban dwellers, many of these women could not afford to marry, much less purchase land or the freedom of a slave. Marital statistics may be deceiving, however. For some freed blacks, "marriage" could mean merely living together, without a formal union. Other free black women recognized the benefits of being single and preferred this status. They could retain control of their property and remain legally autonomous by not marrying.

Some free black women enjoyed successful marriages and a meaningful family life. Ann Battles Johnson was freed when she was eleven years old and later married William Johnson, a free black man who established a thriving barber business in Natchez, Mississippi. Her life centered around their ten children and managing the nine slaves the couple owned. Ann earned money with her skilled sewing and by selling and trading goods. The Johnsons made additional money in real estate. Yet tragedy struck this family. A white man killed William, and Ann then had to run the family businesses, raise their children, and manage the slaves on her own.

White Women and Marriage

White marriages in the Old South varied according to a couple's status and personal situation and reflected customs much like those of today. Engagements were usually brief, providing enough time to gather a trousseau or belongings, plan the ceremony, and establish a household (although some couples lived with their parents for a while). Weddings could be extravagant affairs for the elite, involving the hiring of a female "consultant" to take charge of every detail. Hand-delivered invitations might be distributed to more than 200 guests. A sumptuous dinner and all-night party marked these nuptial celebrations. More commonly, marriages were simple ceremonies, performed by a judge or minister for family members and a few close friends and followed by a simple supper. For men and women on the frontier or those who did not want to bother with a ceremony, couples might live together for several years and become legally united through common-law marriages. For some, getting to a justice of the peace or minister was almost impossible; others apparently didn't care.

The level of satisfaction that white women found in their marriages is easier to detect than that for black women. Expectations had risen by the nineteenth century, and more women began to anticipate the ideal of a truly companionate marriage. Yet these high expectations outpaced social change, especially in the South where the hierarchical, patriarchal social structure made such equality in the home difficult to achieve. As Anya Jabour's study of Elizabeth and William Wirt shows, this Virginia couple entered marriage with a commitment to achieve such an ideal relationship, but the reality of children, the demands of the household, and Wirt's professional career and personal goals made companionate marriage impossible to maintain. On the other hand, a pious Martha Hancock married a man who shared her deep religious convictions. Apparently she found her soul mate, and in their harmonious marital relationship, she wrote him affectionate poems for at least the next twenty years.

Personal writings, legal documents, and divorce proceedings reveal additional clues. Some marriages were troubled by violence, heartbreak, alcoholism, and adultery. Despite their wealth and the privileged rituals of courtship that they enjoyed, the Petigru women achieved little success wedding a loving companion. Several of the Petigru marriages involved husbands who fell victim to alcoholism, engaged in adultery, or exhibited an insensitivity or indifference to female needs. Letters between many husbands and wives, though, also reveal affection between loving mates. Then, as now, the vitality of a marriage varied with each relationship. Some were harmonious and affectionate; others filled with tension and sadness; the majority fell somewhere in between. Neither men nor women were saints; some engaged in behavior that exacerbated family tension. Charges of adultery sometimes were drawn against southern wives; others ran away from a husband in order to live with another man; a few wives beat their husbands. Any bad behavior exacted a high social cost, especially among elite whites who had a family name to uphold.

As related by Elizabeth Fox-Genovese in *Within the Plantation Household,* Sarah Haynesworth Gayle married her husband before her sixteenth birthday; he was a dozen years her senior. Sarah's writings express her adoration and respect for her mate. After seven years of marriage, she wrote him on their anniversary:

It was our wedding day, and they are talismanic words, to wake up all that is precious and hallowed in memory. Dear, dear period—if I had been asked to single out from the whole earth, a being exempt from care, and in possession of perfect happiness, I would have laid my hand on my own bounding heart, and said, "she is here."

As ill health and hardships aged Sarah beyond her young years, she feared losing her husband's affection and dreaded the day when death would end their loving relationship. But she counted her blessings, pitying female friends who endured adulterous or alcoholic husbands. Unfortunately, Sarah's premonitions of death proved true, for she died suddenly when only thirty-one, contracting tetanus after a dentist operated on her teeth. Her last message, written on her deathbed to her absent husband, stated, "I testify with my dying breath that since first I laid my young heart upon his manly bosom I have known only love and happiness."

The paucity of divorce petitions in the antebellum South is no indication that this was a golden time or place for marriage. For southern white women, divorce was difficult and options few. South Carolina made marriage indissoluble, placing virtually no limits on men's authority over their wives. As Judge Glover of South Carolina declared, the state could not permit a "divided empire in the government of the family." The sense was that if families fell into disorder, so too might the government. Even in those southern states where a husband or wife could petition for a divorce, few did so. During the antebellum period, white women who legally tried to end a marriage were usually bold or desperate. Divorce carried a stigma, and the process in many states of appearing before a state legislature or male judge was intimidating. Also, during a period when men and women were accustomed to accept stoically their choices in life and to complain little, few considered an alternative to the selection they had made. Most women counted their blessings if they had an honest, respectable, and kind husband. Marriage was not expected to bring romance, eternal devotion, and daily excitement into a woman's life. In many cases, marriage was a practical response to offset loneliness, a means to create a family, and a way to gain a partner for protection and household or farm help. Unlike Sarah Gayle, the majority of southern women had little time, before or after marriage, to ponder life's joys or sorrows or how to retain a husband's affection. They worried instead about family survival.

A woman prone to romantic dreams about marriage would likely encounter disappointment. Rebecca Haywood Hall was a case in point. Rebecca met her future husband, Albert Hall, while visiting Raleigh and apparently became sexually involved with him before their marriage. Despite warnings about his questionable character and behavior, Rebecca thought she was in love. They married and went to live on his plantation in rural North Carolina. Albert found little to praise in his wife and frequently was absent from the home. Rebecca's pathetic letters to her sister reveal the difficulties of her lonely and demanding existence as she coped with young children, plantation management, and a husband with a wandering eye. Albert managed to be absent during her childbirth confinements. When one of their daughters accidently fell into a fire and Rebecca severely burned her hand trying to rescue the youngster, Albert berated his wife for her carelessness. It is not surprising to learn that Rebecca died at a relatively young age. Virginian Laura Wirt married a man eleven years her senior, and the couple then moved to Florida, far from her family and friends. Giving birth to three babies in three years and experiencing poor health, Laura became dependent on opium and laudanum and died the next year following the birth of her fourth child.

The personal quality of most antebellum marriages remains hidden to historians who often have to extrapolate beyond documentary evidence. For instance, Gertrude Thomas's detailed journals, which she kept for more than forty years, never stated directly that her husband was an alcoholic and perhaps sexually involved with a slave woman for as long as twenty-five years. In fact, she rarely even mentioned him affectionately (often referring to him as Mr. Thomas, a formality not all that unusual) and focused more attention on her daily activities, children, health, and personal reflections than on her husband's activities. After the Civil War, Jefferson Thomas squandered the family fortune, much of it from Gertrude's family, creating tension among her siblings and forcing the Thomases to sell much of their property.

What held antebellum relationships together is just as mysterious as what holds marriages together today. Economic considerations were a primary bond, since free women lost legal rights and access to their own property when they married and were dependent on their husband's farming skills or income for survival. A couple's public appearance did not necessarily correspond to private conduct. The Hammond marriage is a good example. Catherine's relatives had correctly pegged James Henry Hammond as a fortune hunter. Once married, Hammond took control of his wife's 1,500 acres of river land, 137 slaves, and farm equipment and with them made a substantial fortune. Catherine's husband's miscegenous relationship with the slave girl Louisa was merely one instance of James's infidelity. Several years prior to that discovery, scandal had threatened Hammond's political career and marriage. Catherine learned that her husband was involved in sexual improprieties with four of their nieces, the daughters of her brother-in-law, Wade Hampton, Jr., a member of one of South Carolina's most powerful and wealthiest families. Hammond's indiscretions ended his political dreams when Hampton threatened public revelation, but Catherine apparently stood by her husband and bore him another child a few years later. When Hammond died in 1864, Catherine spoke lovingly of her husband and defended him to her death. Perhaps her affection was so deep that she could overlook his transgressions; perhaps she recognized that she had no choice but to accept the situation because they lived in a state that forbade divorce; or perhaps she found happiness through other channels.

How much power wives achieved in the home is difficult to assess, for individual circumstances varied significantly. Some historians feel that by the nineteenth century, as the idea that men and women commanded separate spheres took hold, wives made significant gains toward achieving power in domestic matters. They had charge of household management, their children's upbringing, and the moral behavior of family members. According to this idea, as men became busy in their public world, they relinquished control over the household. Proof of this argument comes in part from the significant decline in fertility throughout the nineteenth century, implying that a number of women took greater control of their biological destiny. But this theory has dubious validity when applied to the Old South because separate spheres were less distinct for southern farm and plantation women; it had no relevance at all for slave women. Also undermining this theory of growing power in the domestic sphere, at least as applied to southern women, is that fertility rates in the South remained higher than the national norm, suggesting that women there did less than northern women to control their fertility. Southern women experienced years of unending childbearing and caretaking.

In such an agrarian society, the roles of men and women often overlapped. Some southern fathers bridged the gap in stepping into the domestic sphere and were surprisingly attentive in helping to care for and raise their children. They often helped to nurse a sick infant, and many fathers paid strict attention to their sons' and daughters' education. Women often undertook more traditional male roles, working alongside their husband in the fields, gardening, tending orchards and livestock, and selling goods they produced to help sustain the family. A few women undertook specific male tasks, such as Elizabeth Wirt who called herself "a woman of business." Though married women could not legally hold property or make contracts, Wirt negotiated the sale of slaves and of the family's Richmond home in order to purchase a more expensive one. She was well versed in family finances and expenditures, and her husband William depended on her financial expertise. Such skills could prove useful to women, especially widows who often had to administer their late husband's estate and run the farm or plantation.

Migration may have negatively affected southern marriages, at least according to historian Joan Cashin. She argues that men usually made the decision to move the family to a new territory or state like Alabama, Mississippi, or Tennessee. Such a move could foster unhappiness; women tended to be reluctant participants, not wanting to leave behind family, friends, and everything they held dear. According to Cashin, young men living on the frontier, now freed from social and parental restraints, might test their manhood, acting in a wild, unrestrained manner. Patriarchal behaviors may have increased, for women were more isolated and less powerful, and fewer social constraints held white men in check.

Nevertheless, marriage was desired. An indication of the importance of marriage and mothering was the disdain and pity shown toward unmarried women in the Old South. Michael O'Brien, who has studied single women in the South, estimates that during the antebellum period, some 25 percent of all women never married, indicating that a significant percentage of females fell into this category. A woman's identity derived from her husband and family. Society accepted widows without disapproval, for they had proven their worth by marrying at least once. But some single women who never married found it difficult to establish a comfortable role in a society where family was so central to everyday life. Spinsterhood was a kind of social death, at least according to prescriptive literature, and perhaps some white women decided that it was better to compromise on a partner than never to marry. Spinsters usually lived with parents or siblings and often moved from family to family, making themselves useful by assisting with domestic chores and caring for nieces and nephews. A few became governesses or teachers, though they often elicited condescending reactions. Remaining single and falling into the category of spinsterhood was not desirable for most white women in social terms.

Barren women, too, were objects of gentle gossip. Whether the husband or wife was infertile, a woman invariably was blamed if the couple had no children. Mary Boykin Chesnut, the celebrated Civil War diarist, felt a sense of pity from her husband's family and her friends because she could not bear children. She bitterly referred to herself as a "childless wretch." Despite her active life as the wife of a South Carolina senator and aide to the Jefferson Davis administration during the Civil War, her condition brought lifelong sorrow. Fortunately, Mary found a substitute for her maternal needs in her nieces and nephews whom she showered with affection.

Laws and Marriage

Despite the desirability of marriage, the sacrifices were great when antebellum women married, just as they had been during the colonial period. Married women lost their status as independent beings and, based on the precedents of British common law, became legally bound to their husbands. It was considered desirable and proper for a woman to be married, but the institution restricted them legally. A woman lost her *feme sole* status upon marriage and became a *feme covert*. The law stripped married women of property rights; everything they owned automatically became the husband's property, including slaves, land, and furnishings. Any wages a wife earned became her husband's, and in the rare instances of separation or divorce, the children usually belonged to him. Married women could not make independent contracts. By contrast, single women, whether spinsters or widows, retained their own property and earnings as *feme sole* and could sign binding agreements.

Common-law precedents did protect widows, ensuring them a dower for their support upon a husband's death of at least a third of his estate. Generally dower was held only during a widow's lifetime, but state laws varied, and sometimes a woman could use the property as her own and sell or will it upon her death. Such provisions were not intended to foster female independence or reward wives for their contributions to the marriage, but rather to ensure against the family falling into poverty and becoming dependent on the public dole.

Fortunately for some women, equity courts softened the rigidity of common law. Equity courts were an alternative system of justice also developed in England and carried to the colonies, but they exercised more flexibility than common-law courts. Judges considered the spirit, rather than the letter or precedent, of the law. In other words, equity courts considered each case on its own merit, though a set of principles gradually developed. Courts of equity were kinder to women than were common-law courts, for they were more likely to challenge the concept of "unity of person" (the legal doctrine that considers a married couple as being one person, with the wife's rights subservient to her husband's); common-law courts rarely made any exceptions. Equity courts offered better odds to women, and those who sought redress or greater access to property were successful in some cases. Under equity rulings, a written conveyance (a document identifying assets and transferring them from one person to another) gave individual women the right to own, manage, and convey property. While this can be seen as an important legal advance for women, conveyances were granted women only on an individual basis. There were no statutes or legislative acts that conferred this right on all women living in a state.

State legislatures moved ahead during the antebellum period to create new laws that brought about significant legal changes for southern white women. These statutes, primarily concerning property rights and divorce, reflected a national spirit of reform but also a concern over a volatile economy. Eventually, the new laws made it easier for women to obtain divorces, although even by 1860, few women took advantage of these statutes where they existed. In a region of the country that valued tradition and frowned on change, it is particularly surprising that some southern states and territories made the earliest and most significant alterations in property laws affecting married women.

In Petersburg, Virginia, according to Suzanne Lebsock, the number of separate estates (the practice of legally separating a wife's estate from her husband's, thereby allowing a woman to keep control of her property) retained by women mushroomed during the antebellum period. At first glance it might appear that husbands became more willing to relinquish control of a wife's property, a seeming contradiction to traditional nineteenth-century male behavior. However, the appearance of more separate estates in Petersburg was not a liberating or humanitarian gesture to aid women; it was a step taken to counter the uncertainties of a fluctuating economy. If creditors closed in, demanding payment on debts during a period of declining fortunes, a separate estate guaranteed that a wife's property could not be seized, only her husband's. Thus, the couple's losses could be minimized—and perhaps more financial risks could be taken—without the family losing everything.

An increase in the number of "fee simple" estates (estates assigned to individuals without condition) awarded to Petersburg widows gave more women absolute control over the dower from their late husband. Women could sell the property as needed, rather than merely living off the profits, and not worry about whether it eventually came to their husbands' children from a previous marriage or their children in entirety. With greater frequency men also named their wives as executors if their estates were small. Those with large inheritances tended to name a male relative or trusted friend.

One of the most significant changes in women's legal status was the movement of southern states to pass laws giving wives greater control over their own estates and over property that they brought to their marriage. Rather than relying on individual appeals to an equity court for exceptions, states considered the possibility that all women with property should retain rights to it even when married. In 1835, the Arkansas territorial legislature passed two bills relating to women. The first permitted married women to carry on independent legal action; the second proposed to "secure the property of females." The legislation stated that real property (land) and personal property (such as slaves) owned by any Arkansas woman at the time of her marriage or willed or given her before the ceremony could not be used to pay debts incurred by her husband prior to their wedding. The intention of this law was to discourage the most blatant forms of fortune-hunting. This law, however, failed to secure a woman's property if a husband acquired debts during the marriage. Further, any property that she received after the wedding, such as an inheritance from a deceased parent, automatically became her husband's and could be seized by creditors.

The Louisiana Civil Code was unique, for it allowed married women more control over property they brought to the marriage than did laws in other states. Louisiana's laws, based on the

Napoloeonic Code, were exceptionally liberal in protecting married women's separate estates. Here, wives could sell, mortgage, donate, and will their personal and real property, assuming they had the approval of their husbands. A widow's dower rights usually were half of her husband's estate, rather than a third.

The Mississippi Married Women's Property Law of 1839 granted more expansive rights than the Arkansas law and was significant as the first state law in the nation to allow wives the right to hold property in their own name. Mississippi, a Deep South cotton state, was an unlikely site for such a seemingly liberal statute. It made sense, however, when one considers the legal and economic reasoning behind such efforts to protect women's property. Mississippi, even in the 1830s, was still a frontier state but one profiting enormously from the cotton boom. It was a place to make a fortune, but also a place where failure could hit suddenly, especially in the boom-and-bust economy of antebellum America. There was much land speculation, and some extraordinarily wealthy men lived within Mississippi's borders. The fact that the Women's Property Law passed the state legislature only two years after the Panic of 1837 was no coincidence. Mississippi's "Act for the Protection and Preservation of the Rights and Property of Married Women" became law in 1839. Subsequent acts in 1846 and 1857 expanded women's legal rights so that by the Civil War, Mississippi's married women could retain profits earned from their property, sign contracts and deeds relating to their property, and operate their holdings alone without their husband's consent.

Other states followed. In 1851 Arkansas expanded the protection of its territorial law of 1835 by preserving a woman's property even if her husband incurred debts during marriage. In 1845 the Republic of Texas created a provision allowing married women rights to their own property. Although Georgia relied on the common law, the state demonstrated an increasingly generous spirit toward women, allowing married women in 1847 the right to establish separate estates by conveyance or by prenuptial trusts or agreements. After 1851, married women could apply to the state legislature for "relief" to carry on an independent business as free traders.

The legal changes for women varied by state, but overall the South made major adjustments to protect married women and their property during the antebellum period. Nevertheless, these legalities failed to translate immediately into greater power for women. It still took a bold or determined individual to address the state legislature or local judge to seek her rights. Few women bothered because they were timid, indifferent, fearful of a husband's wrath, ignorant of changing laws, or unable to pay the cost involved in redressing her situation.

The more intriguing question is why southern states showed such concern in protecting married women's property. Historians posit that during the colonial period, southern women may have had more legal rights than their New England counterparts, in part because their limited numbers increased their value to southern society. This precedent may have made it easier for southern women to gain property rights at an earlier date than women living elsewhere. Also, in the antebellum South, property had special meaning, and a woman's holdings, like those of Catherine Hammond, could represent a considerable portion of the marital estate.

On the other hand, such laws to protect women also reflected male paternalism. Male legislators often saw women as helpless and dependent. Perhaps some concluded that male wisdom was required to assist those women who were ignorant of financial and legal matters. Hence these laws were designed not so much to benefit women as to protect families. Because economic reversals could be disastrous and thereby threaten a family's entire fortune, protecting a woman's property was essential to prevent the family from becoming destitute. In addition, fathers worried about protecting a daughter's property from an unscrupulous fortune hunter or spendthrift son-in-law who might waste a family fortune. Under *feme covert* laws, nothing could prevent a husband from selling everything that his wife had brought into the marriage. Thus, in some southern states, married women gained control over their property, not to enhance their independence or uphold their rights, but to protect the estate their fathers or relatives had accumulated. Gaining such power, however limited, aided women in the long run. New York and Massachusetts became the first northern states to pass similar legislation several years after Mississippi took action. Other protective statutes followed nationwide.

Prenuptial agreements also ensured a woman's access to her own property. Yet contracting a prenuptial agreement was rare in first marriages. Women who had been married before, had children, or owned substantial property that they wished to protect were more likely to seek such agreements, knowing how restrictive their *feme covert* status was.

The South had the lowest divorce rate of any region in the antebellum period. As noted earlier, this was not because marriages were necessarily so happy but mostly because obtaining a divorce was so difficult. In part, this reflected the South's concern with the family, which many felt deserved protecting at almost any cost, even at the expense of the individual. If a white woman was miserable in her marital relationship, she might live separately from her husband while remaining legally married (a "bed and board" divorce). Equity courts in some states sometimes granted alimony to an impoverished wife if her husband abandoned her, though legally she was only separated and could not remarry. Legislators were, however, sympathetic to removing the worst abuses of marriage, and some states such as Tennessee in 1799 and North Carolina in 1814 passed more liberal divorce statutes. On the other hand, South Carolina did not allow divorce for any cause until 1868 when the state revised its constitution.

Stephanie McCurry, in *Masters of Small Worlds,* offers a provocative interpretation on the importance of the southern family and its hierarchical relationships, helping to explain why divorce was so difficult in the South and forbidden in South Carolina. She detects a parallel between the struggle to maintain slavery and efforts to preserve gender hierarchy within the family. McCurry finds that proslavery defenders equated the subordination of women with that of slaves, investing "the defense of slavery with the survival of customary gender relations." Every white man, whatever his station, had a stake in the defense of slavery. In the South, a woman's natural and social role assumed political significance. Southern society glorified women's sphere and their secondary position and vilified anyone who stepped beyond its boundaries. "The legitimacy of male authority over women in the household was a cornerstone of the slavery edifice," argues McCurry. Slaves and women had to fit into their subordinate position, and white men had the inherent right to command those presumed to be naturally subordinate. Social relations in the private sphere thus affected political ideas and institutions in the public sphere. Anything, such as divorce, that might upset what seemed to be the natural order of the family threatened the southern social order. In South Carolina, where slaves comprised a majority of the population, this hierarchy was especially important to uphold.

During the antebellum period, nevertheless, it did become somewhat easier for white women to gain a divorce, and more women than men sought redress. Frontier states were the first to liberalize their divorce laws. All southern states except South Carolina broadened the causes for redress, which by the Civil War usually included consanguinity (marrying a blood relative such as a sibling or parent), insanity, impotence, bigamy, adultery, cruelty, and desertion. A few states added alcoholism, and many shortened the time required to establish desertion. States enlarged the meaning of cruelty to include not just the endangering of life but mental cruelty as well. Louisiana and Texas had community property clauses, but nearly all states awarded children to their father because men were more likely than women to be able to meet their offspring's financial needs. But a few southern judges even chipped away at this precedent and occasionally awarded children to the mother, especially if the husband was incompetent or violent.

The number of divorce petitions increased over time, but success was never assured. According to historian Jane Turner Censer, wives who were most successful in pleading their cases before state legislatures tended to be ladylike and wealthy, in part because these women had the self-confidence and financial resources necessary to seek a divorce. Strong-willed or poor women had less success. Judges sympathized with a virtuous, delicate, and refined woman, feeling that it would be best to remove her from a degenerate husband. (Apparently the less ladylike woman could stand almost anything.) However, few poor women could afford a divorce or had the time or energy to consider their legal options. Unhappy couples were more likely to separate and live apart, often without any legal decree.

In one instance, Evelina Gregory Roane was able to win an absolute divorce against her husband Newman B. Roane after less than two years of marriage. Both were from prominent King William County, Virginia, families. Married when she was nineteen and he twenty-six, she bore a child ten months after the wedding. According to her account and corroborated by several witnesses, seven months later he brutally beat her while she was pregnant again, which may have caused her to miscarry. She accused him of cruel, violent conduct, of denying her access to her family and church, and threatening her life. He had made a slave woman, Biney, mistress of their home, and Evelina was forced to undertake the work of a slave. Evelina won not only an absolute divorce but also the rights to their child. The absolute divorce allowed her to remarry, which she did three more times, and for each, she wisely drew up a premarital contract.

Despite changing laws, most unhappily married women did not achieve Roane's success; winning a divorce was extremely difficult. Bertram Wyatt-Brown's description of divorce proceedings in his book *Southern Honor* attests to that difficulty in the early antebellum period. Margaret Ramsay, for instance, sought a divorce in 1821 in Tennessee, a state that had more liberal divorce laws than most of the South. She claimed that for four years, her husband had whipped her during his drunken sprees. He had held a knife to her throat, brought prostitutes into their home, and refused to let her visit friends. He provided her with only a single dress, had taken up with a prostitute, and contracted a venereal disease. The legislature refused her plea. In Virginia, a more conservative state, Lucy Dabney pleaded to end her marriage, claiming that her husband had beaten her, her mother, and younger siblings, and he had become so threatening that he had to be thrown in jail. Rumors suggested he had another wife and children in Pennsylvania. Lucy's plea also was rejected.

The most intolerable situations sometimes had to be endured. Women had little choice but to remain dependent on their husband, sometimes living under extraordinarily difficult marital circumstances. Many southern men tended to drink; some resorted to violence; and most maintained their patriarchal authority over the family. Women lacking economic independence, political power, and sometimes living far from home or supportive relatives, had to cope on their own.

CHAPTER TWO

Reproduction and Childrearing

Fertility

Married women's lives were largely concerned with the bearing and rearing of children. Being a mother was a fulfilling goal for married women in the nineteenth century. Prescriptive literature, sermons, maternal advice books, novels, and school lessons encouraged white women to pursue their "sacred occupation" as mothers. For obvious reasons, planters encouraged their slave women to bear children. Motherhood held special meaning in the South, where family and kin were the foundation of the region's social and economic structure. Few other options provided women with more satisfaction or gained them a greater degree of public recognition than their maternal role.

Pregnancies, confinements, suckling babies, and nurturing infants were unceasing and demanding activities for black and white women. Many began bearing children in their late teens and continued to do so almost unabated until ill health, menopause, or death interceded. One slave woman, May, bore nineteen children, though only four lived. Mrs. Rhea, at the age of thirty-seven, had borne sixteen offspring, and one friend observed wistfully, "Her family may yet be much larger." John Ball, Jr.'s first wife bore eleven children in twelve years of marriage, and when she died, he remarried and began another family.

American women proved to be extremely fertile, more so than their European counterparts. The first national census in 1790 showed that white women of childbearing age bore, on the average, 7.1 children. But most married women were pregnant more than seven times; the tabulated birthrate was lower than the actual number of pregnancies and births due to the frequency of miscarriages and infant deaths. Throughout the antebellum period, fertility decreased nationwide, declining to an average of 5.4 children by 1850 and 4.6 by 1860. However, regional variations existed, and the number of live births was higher in the Old South than in the North.

There were many reasons why southern women bore more children than women in the Northeast. While some northern middle-class couples apparently recognized the advisability of restricting family size, there seemed little reason to limit the number of children in southern families, aside from the health concerns of the women who bore them. Instead, there were positive arguments for large families. For farm women, each child became a potential worker to assist with agricultural production and contribute to family survival. For families living in isolated circumstances, children became the principal source of companionship and socializing. Ann Holmes Blank of Leesburg, North Carolina, was a lonely young mother, writing in 1846 that "if my dear little Henry would talk so that I could have someone to talk with me, I would not mind it so bad but to stay morning until night and no one to say a word to you is lonesome." Within a few years, her home would be bustling. Anna Page King, living on a St. Simons Island, Georgia, plantation, turned to her ten children as her companions since her husband Thomas was absent for months and years at a time.

Limited land and economic constraints often unconsciously induced a family to control its size. But these restrictions were hardly relevant in the South, where opportunities beckoned the bold and aggressive. Overcrowding, which also discouraged larger families, especially in urban areas, was an alien notion to antebellum southerners who had plentiful land available, especially on the frontier. By the 1840s some middle-class couples in the Northeast were practicing birth control, but southern women rarely did, at least judging by large southern families and the frequency with which white and slave women bore children. Religious constraints may have affected white southerners' reactions to birth control, though this issue was not discussed publicly. According to Anne Firor Scott in *The Southern Lady,* sometimes the only effective means for women to delay another conception was abstinence, and they might leave home for extended visits with parents and childhood friends.

By marrying a few years earlier than northern women, southern women might bear two or more additional children. And with the positive attention heaped on motherhood and the personal achievement associated with childrearing, there was little reason, other than enormous health risks and high maternal mortality, to limit family size. Perhaps the major constraint against unlimited childbearing was the fact that so many women suffered gynecological problems and ongoing ill health due to childbirth, such as a fallen uterus or a torn perineum. In this period of limited medical knowledge, these health problems were poorly understood and poorly administered by doctors. Nevertheless, Virginia Meade Gordon placed herself in the hands of one. She was so uncomfortable after the birth of one baby that she checked into the Holmes Infirmary near Jackson, Mississippi. Dr. Holmes was reputed to be an "expert" in female illnesses, and she, along with some twenty other patients in residence, hoped to find a cure. Gordon wrote her sister, "Pray for me that I may be renewed in soul and body." Yet it is unusual to find a southern husband who paid heed to such debilitating problems arising from a wife's constant childbearing. He might sympathize with his wife's immediate suffering, but for a man, a large family reflected positively on his status, his masculinity, and his ability to support several dependents. For farmers, each child promised another laborer as well.

For slave women, bearing an infant was a mixed blessing, evoking love for the child, the thrill of creating a blessed and helpless being, but also the realization that the child could be sold at any time and might never know any life beyond slavery. Yet many slave women continually held out hope that they could purchase their children's freedom. Statistics suggest that slave women may have borne slightly more children than southern white women, probably because they started two or three years earlier. Still, slave families ultimately were smaller than southern white families due to higher infant mortality and overall ill health. In addition, slave women experienced frequent miscarriages, and such health risks apparently increased during the late antebellum period due to worsening conditions and greater work demands.

The high fertility rates among slave women appear to counter what one might expect under an oppressive system. It would seem that these women might not want to bear children in a society where hardships were ever-present and their future dim. Anthropologists know that in societies that are overly repressive or where living conditions prove difficult, couples both consciously and unconsciously limit family size. Fertility declines because of poor diet and bad health, overwork, a shortage of men, or a conscious desire not to have children. But southern slave women actually bore more children than their counterparts on Caribbean plantations. The natural increase of the southern slave population was enormous, leaping from around 1.5 million in 1820 to almost 4 million by 1860. At least after 1820, the slave population here was largely native-born, making it quite different from the situation in the Caribbean and Latin America. The high proportion of women in the slave population in this country helped to ensure a large number of births, as did a relatively healthy climate. The absence of tropical diseases meant that more slave children survived here than they did in the Caribbean or Latin America.

Another explanation for this population surge was the encouragement to bear children that slave women received from their masters. Each additional child enhanced a master's wealth. One owner reported happily that a twenty-two-year-old bondwoman had already borne five children. Slave owner Rachel O'Connor congratulated her sister on her luck in having five black babies born in a two-month period, with two more slave women expecting. Owners may not have considered such attitudes as opportunistic or profit-minded, but slave women saw it otherwise. "You see dey raised de chilluns ter make money on jes lak we raise pigs ter sell," stated a Tennessee woman. How significantly such encouragement fostered high birth rates cannot be assessed, but it certainly did not inhibit fertility. Slave women knew that their value increased with their ability to bear children and that their fertility often protected them against willful sale. Plantation owners might express their approval by rewarding a new mother with a dress, a small amount of cash, a trinket and, of course, time off during pregnancy and after delivery. Commented one Louisiana mistress who promised dresses to each new slave mother, "I am now in debt to four that has young babes, and fine ones too. They do much better by being encouraged a little and I have ever thought they deserved it."

A slave owner's financial situation, the crop he grew, and the region where he lived may have affected his views on his slaves' bearing children. As Maria Jenkins Schwartz explains in *Born in Bondage,* slave owners in the upper South tended to see their slaves principally as investments, to be bought and sold as needed in order to maximize their personal fortune—or pay off debts. Thus, each new slave baby meant an additional source of revenue. In the lower South, where enormous profits could be made from cash crops like cotton, rice and sugar, plantation owners depended on hard-working, dependable laborers. Here, a plantation owner's fortune was made on profits from agriculture. While each newborn slave promised a future worker, each pregnancy meant time off for a pregnant slave woman, as well as a month's respite after the birth of her baby. All of this deprived the owner of an adult worker and ate into potential profits.

While white women rarely did anything to limit their own fertility, slave women may have been more comfortable with the idea, though how often they aborted fetuses or resorted to infanticide is unknown. Certainly some bondwomen had cause to contemplate such action, considering widespread miscegenation and the problems associated with raising children as slaves. Occasionally bondwomen found ways to end a pregnancy. One slave seamstress, Jane, successfully aborted every baby she conceived, even as late as six months into one pregnancy, causing her mistress tremendous sorrow. Jane may have felt discouraged before she became a mother and did not want to face possible heartache. Being single may have created problems for her. Plantation and medical accounts sometimes recounted cases of infanticide in which dead infants were discovered in the woods or behind a barn. Nevertheless, considering the high fertility rate among southern blacks, it is evident that most slave women desired children, whatever the risks of bearing and rearing them, and rarely interfered with their pregnancies. Most important, like all mothers, they discovered immense joy in a baby's birth and found fulfillment that was otherwise absent in their bleak existence as farm laborers.

Pregnancy

Pregnancy was a time of anxiety and ill health for many southern women. While one might imagine that mothers joyfully anticipated the birth of an infant, the months preceding confinement were filled with fears about the upcoming event. Poor health was also a common complaint among pregnant women as they struggled to remain vital and useful, and, if possible, follow judicious behavior to ensure a healthy infant.

The single greatest health problem that expectant white women endured was malaria, a disease endemic in most areas of the Old South. During the antebellum period, malaria was the major health concern of all Americans outside of New England, but it was pervasive in the Old South. Nearly everyone suffered "fever and ague" during the summer and early fall, experiencing symptoms that included high fever, chills, and debilitation. Some elite families migrated temporarily to higher elevations or to the North to avoid annual bouts of sickness. This disease was spread by the anopheles mosquito, the carrier of the malaria protozoa. No one during the antebellum period correctly understood its cause. Most southerners, including physicians, deduced that a miasma, or "bad air," caused the disease, for it seemed to affect those southerners living near marshy or damp areas. Southerners never understood that such damp areas were prolific breeding grounds for mosquitoes. Lucy Shaw, living in the frontier town of Galveston, Texas, found the mosquitoes overwhelming. She wrote her mother: "If you wish to know what will thrive best in a climate like this, I can tell you that I know of nothing quite equal to the fleas and mosquitoes. . . . [They are] double the size of New England mosquitoes." Lucy repeatedly described the swarms of mosquitoes that made life intolerable, but she had no idea that these bothersome insects also caused frequent bouts of malaria.

Families like the Shaws living in lowland coastal areas, along rivers, and in delta regions where cotton and sugar cane flourished, were most vulnerable. Ironically, the wealthy seemed to be most affected by incidents of malaria, for poor farm families who often lived in higher, drier elevations encountered fewer mosquitoes and thereby suffered less than plantation families. It may be that farm women had healthier pregnancies, fewer miscarriages, and easier deliveries since they were less likely to suffer from malaria.

Pregnant women were more susceptible to malaria than most southerners because their immune systems weakened during the last trimester of pregnancy. They lost their partial resistance acquired over years of exposure. The alternating chills and fever (up to 104 degrees), anorexia, and anemia of malaria created major health problems in pregnant women. Miscarriages were common in areas where malaria was endemic. The accompanying high temperature in the womb created an environment too uncomfortable for the fetus. In addition, quinine, the most effective cure for malaria during this time period, was a known abortifacient, but expectant women took it, desperate to offset the disease's symptoms. Malaria also inhibited fertility rates by raising a male's scrotal temperature and creating infertile sperm during the disease's duration.

Antebellum women (and physicians as well) had little scientific understanding of conception. Americans were naive about the process of pregnancy, believing that women were most fertile immediately before and after menstruation. Prenatal visits to a physician were not regarded as necessary, except to treat severe health problems such as hemorrhaging or convulsions. But as medical books of the period indicate, doctors exhibited increasing interest in the mysteries of pregnancy. They began to recognize the prenatal period as an important time in the infant's development and encouraged expectant mothers to take proper care of themselves in order to bear a healthy child.

For literate women, medical literature like *Gunn's Domestic Medicine, or Poor Man's Friend,* or *Buchan's Domestic Medicine* provided helpful advice for home treatment. Many southern white families, especially those living on the frontier and far from a doctor's care, found a medical advice book an essential item. Expectant farm and slave women secured wisdom and support from family members and female friends. Many women used herbal cures or folk remedies and collected recipes in notebooks. Southern women knew that various teas eased heartburn. Gentle exercise such as walking, riding in a carriage, or brushing the skin stimulated the body. A bland diet and immature, rather than mature, meats (such as unseasoned dishes and lamb rather than mutton) apparently were believed to be most pleasing to the developing fetus. Reading books that would not provoke passion or excite the mind was highly recommended. Nevertheless, women shared not only information but also explicit, often scary, details about childbirth, fueling fears among friends who would have benefited from a state of calm before their forthcoming confinement.

Whatever advice they may have read or heard, nearly all healthy southern women carried on a normal routine while pregnant, continuing to work, care for children, labor in the fields and around the house, visit, and attend church. However, many slave owners exhibited concern about the health of their expectant slaves and provided them extra days off as needed, especially during the last trimester. Researchers have noted a relationship between the number of days off slave women received and the success of their confinement and health of their infant. Some expectant bondwomen moved from field work to less strenuous chores, such as sewing or weaving. Some received lighter punishments when pregnant (although a common practice was digging a hole in the dirt for a pregnant woman to lie face down in to receive her lashes).

Horizontal rest was a rare privilege for pregnant women, except for the truly privileged or those who were ill. Expectant mothers had little choice but to maintain their daily routine, for what southern family could have survived with a wife and mother who chose to lie down throughout her numerous pregnancies? Although the medical profession classified pregnant women as ill and childbirth as a disease, few southerners saw this as cause for easing the female work load. Pregnancy was a normal condition (especially true for those women who bore eight, ten, or fourteen children) that did not warrant a change in routine. Older children still needed watching, feeding, and nurturing; gardens and orchards required weeding and picking; food had to be prepared; houses needed occasional cleaning; and field work demanded extra hands. Southern women carried on as long as their health and energy held out.

Expectant mothers spent their months of pregnancy in a state of anxiety for good cause. Women in their childbearing years experienced a higher mortality rate than did men of comparable age. In the South, women had much to fear. As Sally McMillen relates in *Motherhood in the Old South,* statistics from the 1850 federal census demonstrate that southern white women were twice as likely to die in childbirth as women in the Northeast. An unhealthy climate, the prevalence of malaria, improper medical practices, and the comparably frequent childbearing of southern women all contributed to the grim statistics. The medical profession was not yet proficient at delivering babies, for medical misperceptions about proper treatment and unsanitary practices persisted. A midwife depended on luck and nature to bring a woman safely through her delivery.

Today, walking through an old southern cemetery sadly reminds one of the tenuous existence of the many who died during or shortly after bearing a child. The health risks were enormous, and expectant southern women put their faith in God and shared their worries with friends and family. As their diaries and letters reveal, nearly all women entered each confinement expecting it to be their last moment on earth. A period of pregnancy was not a joyous time, however much mothers loved their children. Many expressed a desire for longer intervals between each birth and for fewer confinements.

Childbearing

Birthing practices varied by race, class, and individual need. In the antebellum period, new medical practices also affected the process of childbearing. Who was present during the birth and where it occurred could reflect practical considerations or a conscious choice. Slave women generally gave birth in their cabins, though on large plantations a slave hospital might be available for birthing. Most farm women remained at home, having little means to travel elsewhere. Poor white and free black women living in cities might use a charity hospital, such as those associated with medical colleges in New Orleans, Charleston, or Lexington. Urban women who were destitute or who lived alone often delivered their babies in a hospital. Unfortunately, these institutions served as teaching facilities for medical students and were not known for quality care or cleanliness. Doctors who performed multiple deliveries and failed to wash their hands and instruments might unknowingly infect prospective mothers. Puerperal fever, an infection that could develop in the womb following birth and was usually spread by physicians unaware of proper sanitary procedures, was more common among those women who bore babies in hospitals, though it occurred less frequently in the South than in the Northeast and Europe.

Unless ill or weighed down by family responsibilities, some women traveled home to their mothers to bear their infant in familiar surroundings. Southern women were eager to have their mother present, especially with the birth of a firstborn. A surprising number of females made the effort to travel to their family home, even those living far from civilization or hundreds of miles from their parents. In a familiar setting, expectant women could bask in the attention of doting mothers, friends, and a trained medical assistant. Sometimes expectant women left their husbands three to four months before the infant was due (and usually accompanied by an escort, for southern women were not supposed to travel alone). Others arrived only a day or two before the infant emerged.

During the antebellum period, male doctors began to assume obstetrical duties traditionally handled by female midwives, reflecting a change that had begun in Europe and spread to America by the late eighteenth century. Since physicians classified childbirth as a disease, medical assistance was considered desirable. Medicine was not yet an elite occupation or a particularly lucrative one, and doctors wanted to generate more income by acquiring new patients. Because of a growing emphasis on education and scientific inquiry, the educated and elite began to regard female midwives and traditional domestic medical practices as old fashioned. Increasing numbers of men attended medical college as these institutions opened, but women and midwives were not admitted (at least until 1846, when Elizabeth Blackwell graduated from Geneva Medical College in New York, but her admission was apparently considered a joke by the students who voted to accept her).

Men would gradually come to dominate obstetrical care, for they possessed the latest medical instruments, access to medical education, anesthetics, scientific testing, and professional literature. Antebellum doctors embarked on a campaign to denigrate the skills of female midwives, making them appear rather suspect to potential patients and drive them out of a specialty that men wished to control. Yet despite their education and training, there is little evidence during this time period that doctors improved the survival rate of mothers and newborns, and, in fact, they may have made confinements even riskier. Physicians were not particularly well prepared to deliver a baby, for medical education and knowledge were rudimentary. Then too, medical schools were not very discriminating, and any white male who could afford the fees could attend medical college. Medical students did not receive actual training in delivering babies since demonstrating on a woman was not considered suitable. Training was by lecture, not through experience. Therefore, most physicians finished school with little actual experience and delivered their first baby on the job. Doctors did their best to gain the confidence of female patients, though an advertisement by a Louisville physician in 1836 stating that "in cases of obstetrics, will be attended to without mutilation or instruments" could not have been too reassuring. Doctors proliferated in the South, taking advantage of the region's sickly population and its cheap land and economic opportunities. By 1860, the region had a higher proportion of physicians than the Northeast.

Doctors sometimes delivered slave babies; this practice reflected not as much the woman's choice as the desire of her owner. Plantation masters often contracted with a doctor to tend all slave and family health problems, and delivering babies was included in the list of responsibilities. Owners believed that such measures provided slaves with good medical care. Also, a number of slave owners had attended medical school and a cotton planter like John Bratton of upcountry South Carolina also served as a part-time physician. Some southern fathers apparently regarded a medical education as excellent training for a son's future, giving him skills that would serve well on a plantation. Thus, medical care, however questionable in quality, was available in many rural and frontier areas during the antebellum period, for many ambitious young professionals migrated to such states as Alabama, Mississippi, Texas, and Arkansas seeking a livelihood.

Yet it was more common for slave women to depend on midwives, friends, or a slave mistress rather than on a physician. Financial considerations often took precedence over professional care. Planters who had no doctor on contract preferred to hire midwives, since their delivery fees, ranging from $1 to $4, were far less than the $5 to $25 that doctors charged. Rachel O'Connor wrote that she paid a black midwife $4 for each of four deliveries of slave babies, commenting that "it is better to pay that than to run any risk." A doctor was usually reserved for a medical emergency or prolonged confinement. Moreover, physicians who attended slave women were more inclined to experiment on them with drugs or radical surgery than they did on elite white women. Caesareans, which had been attempted for hundreds of years, were rarely successful because physicians knew little about proper suturing, cleanliness, or controlling blood flow. Still, a doctor might attempt to operate on a slave woman if her life was endangered and the fetus still viable. Since anesthesia was not used until the late antebellum period, the woman suffered excruciating pain. Invariably the woman and infant died, though apparently a handful of Louisiana doctors had a few successes during the antebellum period. Dr. J. Marion Sims of Alabama, who became one of the most respected gynecological physicians of the nineteenth century, developed a successful surgical cure for vesico-vaginal fistula (a tear of the vaginal tissue during birth) by experimenting on thirty slave women over a four-year period. Despite bondwomen's value to plantation owners, they were regarded as more expendable than white women when it came to medical experimentation.

Health conditions influenced slave women's ability to bear children. Considering the extent of female ills and poor diet, the high fertility rate among bondwomen is all the more remarkable. Inadequate nutrition weakened pregnant and lactating slave women and their infants (as it did impoverished white farm women who ate a poor diet). A typical slave diet of corn meal, pork, and molasses, supplemented by seasonal vegetables and an occasional helping of fruit or fish, provided women with adequate calories but insufficient nutrients. Some slave and poor white women ate clay or dirt (a practice known as geophagy) to gain supplemental nutrients not available through their diet. No physician—or any American for that matter—yet understood the importance of vitamins and balanced meals. Slave women could only eat what their masters provided and any food they grew that supplemented a monotonous diet.

Slave owners encouraged early childbearing among their slave women. James Madison apparently expressed his desire that every slave girl would be a mother by the time she was fifteen. The average age for bearing a first child among all slave women in the South was twenty-one years old. But this varied by region and living conditions. The average slave woman in Loudon County, Virginia, bore her first child at twenty years of age, while for Appalachian slave women, the majority bore a first child before turning nineteen years old.

Burdened by poor nutrition and heavy work demands, slave mothers often bore infants of low birth weight. In one sense this was positive, for a small baby led to shorter and less painful deliveries. (White southerners often misread the situation and concluded that slave women's apparent ease in bearing children was due to their vigorous activity as plantation laborers rather than poor diet and overwork.) Nevertheless a mother's nutritional deficiencies contributed to poorly developed bones and small pelvises which could foster difficult confinements. In one respect, slave women were healthier than pregnant white women, for they were less likely to suffer from malaria and rarely experienced stillbirths caused by the dreaded disease. The sickle cell trait, found almost exclusively in blacks, helped them resist the most common forms of malaria. Yet this same trait increased the risk of chronic anemia and fostered their susceptibility to other diseases. Inadequate nutrition, heavy work demands, harsh treatment, and overall poor physical condition interfered with slave women's ability to reproduce as quickly as white owners might have wished. In general, while white women in good health typically bore a child every two years, the spacing between slave children was usually two-and-a-half years.

White women who used doctors usually did so by choice, and according to Sally McMillen, by the Civil War probably about half of all elite women in the South depended on a male attendant for their confinements. Some white families planned ahead, estimating what they assumed to be the correct due date and then scheduling the doctor. Other white women, both rich and poor, preferred midwives. Some mothers-to-be were sensitive about a male's presence in the birthing room. Tradition, expense, or a desire to depend totally on female support were other considerations. In many cases, women used whomever they could find, and family members often scrambled to locate an assistant when the baby arrived unexpectedly.

Considering the number of babies born in the South and the many families who could not afford a physician or preferred not to use one, midwives still had a thriving business, despite doctors' efforts to denigrate their skills. Some women purposely avoided physicians, fearing their dramatic cures and use of instruments and drugs. And however critical male doctors were of midwives, the two attendants often worked side by side to deliver an infant. Rarely did midwives interfere directly with what they regarded as a natural process, except to turn the baby or pull on the placenta to dislodge it after delivery. Female midwives, both black and white, calmed the patient, understood the importance of keeping her upright as long as possible during contractions, administered soothing teas, pushed on the abdomen, and occasionally gave a medicine like ergot to enhance contractions.

Doctors may have identified childbirth as a disease, but like midwives, most hoped that nature would prove kind and ease the patient's delivery. Physicians, however, altered traditional procedures. They preferred that a woman lie horizontally in order to ease the use of medical instruments. They introduced scientific technology into the birthing chamber, speeding the process along artificially if necessary by assisting the infant's delivery with forceps, cathartics, and hooks. If the fetus was impacted, they might perform a craniotomy in which they used scalpels to chop up the baby's head inside the womb to remove it, sacrificing the infant to save the mother. Apparently, fewer southern doctors employed obstetrical instruments than their northern counterparts, perhaps because few felt competent enough to use them. Yet doctors still depended on heroic procedures during delivery, including an aggressive form of therapy to balance vascular tension. They bled women before and during delivery, lancing an artery or placing leeches on the temples or vagina to foster relaxation and lessen pressure. Purging a woman's system with calomel, a mercury chloride, was often deemed essential, and physicians also relied on ergot to hasten contractions. These techniques were performed in the name of science to balance the body's fluids, decrease blood pressure, and enhance relaxation.

By the 1850s, some doctors in the Northeast had successfully used ether and chloroform during confinements, allowing women a less agonizing experience by deadening most of the pain during delivery. But prior to the Civil War, few southern doctors used either anesthetic. Many were cautious or unfamiliar with the drugs, fearing the dangerous effect they could have on the mother and infant if administered improperly. Others believed it morally wrong to intervene by using painkillers. They upheld the biblical dictate, "In sorrow thou shalt bring forth children." For these physicians, the intensity of maternal pain corresponded to the depth of maternal love, and many believed that if a mother had an easy or painless delivery, she might ignore her newborn.

The ritual of childbirth fostered female bonding. Confinements could last for several hours or even a couple of days, as women watched, encouraged, and provided loving assistance to the birth mother. Male doctors changed this atmosphere with their presence, although most left the female support unit intact, recognizing it as too powerful and essential to ignore. But medical literature urged the professionalization of the entire process, insisting on such details as a darkened room to preserve female delicacy, a horizontal birth position, proper bedclothing, and an absent husband. Doctors probably regarded female friends as necessary nuisances, but they were not secure enough to dismiss them entirely and needed women to run errands and provide emotional support. Husbands were encouraged to be present in the home but never in the delivery room.

In the South, black and white women were often together during childbirth. If women of the two races ever shared any intimacies, it was during this important event. Childbirth was a rare time of mutual sharing, understanding, gratitude, and even affection. The meaning of birth, its pains and joys, drew common responses, whatever one's race or class. Many black women were highly skilled midwives, and they often delivered white babies. In one instance, a white Virginia woman was left in critical condition after two physicians struggled unsuccessfully for hours to deliver her baby. Her husband finally called Mildred, a black midwife, despite the doctors' objections. Mildred worked for the next seven hours. "I did ev'ything I knowed an' somethings I didn' know," she recalled, and successfully delivered a five-pound infant. The white mistress was extremely grateful, and even the attending physicians grudgingly acknowledged Mildred's skills. White women often were present when their slave women delivered babies and assisted with these births.

Four weeks seemed to be the prescribed recuperative period for white and slave women following delivery. Of course, many required a much longer period to regain good health, and some were ill for months following a confinement. A particularly profit-minded or mean-spirited master such as Pierce Butler of Georgia allowed his slave women only three weeks to rest and tend to their newborn before returning to the fields.

Despite similar recovery periods, the subsequent activities of white and black women following childbirth were markedly different. For slave women, the end of their month marked the resumption of plantation duties with little time to nurture their newborn. It was expected that elite white women at the end of their recuperative period would appear downstairs, dine with the family, stroll outside, and enjoy visitors. They continued to nurse and nurture their newborn. Farm women, like slaves, had little choice but to return to work as quickly as possible. For slave and farm women, balancing the demands as mothers, productive laborers, and family caretakers must have been more than many could handle.

Some slave mothers had no choice but to carry their infant to the field, placing the baby in a shady spot, strapping it to their backs or hanging it in a pouch from a tree, and breastfeeding it every few hours. No one could constantly protect the baby from insects, snakes, heat, or inclement weather. Occasionally slave mothers had to leave young babies alone in their cabins without any care. They rushed back at prescribed times to nurse the infant. One bondwoman recounted sorrowfully that she believed her baby literally cried itself to death alone in the cabin. There was little she could do since her master insisted that she work unencumbered by a newborn. Larger plantations often offered a form of day care overseen by an older slave woman (a granny) or adolescent girls who watched and fed babies and younger children. Sometimes plantation mistresses would care for newborn slaves, notwithstanding responsibilities to their own families and households.

Slave women, like most mothers, adored their babies, but the realities of their existence—a demanding or insensitive owner, long work hours, exhaustion, or poor health—interfered with the attention and care they could provide. Slave mothers and yeomen farm women had little free time or energy to nurture their young. Additional burdens fell on those mothers who had to raise their children without a husband present. In such cases, overworked mothers must have welcomed the support of other family members, such as grandmothers or older children, and female friends. Few slave owners questioned the contradiction between the important role that the mother played during a child's early years and work demands, which interfered with maternal responsibilities.

Motherhood and Childrearing

Mothers were the principal caretakers of their children. White women received public encouragement for their responsibilities through maternal literature and public pronouncements acclaiming childrearing as women's sacred occupation. Typical of journalistic rhapsodizing was *The Magnolia,* a southern magazine for women that deemed motherhood the greatest profession on earth. "Who can estimate the power she exerts over the precious trust committed to her charge. How boundless her influence, how illimitable her sway; how irresistible the force of her instruction," noted one of its writers. Prescriptive literature celebrated mothers as the central figure in a child's upbringing. Few southern women ever questioned the accepted idea that they were the parent best fit to raise children. Fathers were busy with farm or plantation duties and some had little time or few nurturing skills to tend babies. Some men disdained the care of young children as an affront to their masculinity.

And yet it is important not to overlook southern fathers who were surprisingly attentive toward their children. They assisted with childrearing, prescribing and administering medicine, lancing gums (to help teeth emerge), calling for a physician, imparting discipline, and relieving their wife when a sick child required round-the-clock attention. When absent from the home, they often sent detailed advice to their wives concerning issues related to childrearing. Southern fathers seemed to play a major role in the education of their children, often determining which school their sons and daughters would attend and dictating their academic schedule. Children who were handicapped or suffered a disability such as deafness often fell under the care of their fathers who might select a special institution they could attend and write doctors for advice about their proper care. Their children's poor health prompted a few southern families to move from the miasmatic low country to an area more conducive to ensuring good health.

And while the antebellum South was rightly defined as a patriarchy, research indicates that, at least among the elite, parents treated their sons and daughters with a fair degree of equality when it came to dividing property. One might suspect that parents would give preference to their sons, but as both Jane Turner Censer and Orville Vernon Burton show in their respective studies of North and South Carolina, many parents tried to be equitable when dividing property among their offspring. The family home typically went to a son, but parents tried to equalize the distribution of their estate by dividing up slaves and other personal property among their offspring. When shares were strikingly inequitable, this was usually for good cause, such as a child needing extra property because of poor health, a disability, or because he or she had suffered financial reversals.

Whether their maternal role provided women with a heightened sense of self-worth and power is open to question. As mothers and principal caretakers of their homes, women may have embraced their responsibilities with greater dedication and found a high level of satisfaction. Some historians feel that the emphasis on domesticity encouraged women to believe in their roles as conservators and promoters of morality, roles that some would translate into an involvement in national reform movements. This appreciation may have enhanced their sense of self-worth. On the other hand, other scholars feel that such praise actually retarded women's desire to move into the public arena. By extolling domestic duties, men perhaps intended to keep women from competing in the male world.

Historians who study the family have debated the degree of child-centeredness and affection in southern families versus the hierarchical authoritarian power of the patriarchy. Jane Turner Censer and Daniel Blake Smith have argued that elite southern parents demonstrated a good deal of affection toward their children. They instilled lessons and class values by example rather than through discipline. However, these same characteristics seem to be evident in many elite northern families as well. Probably it was easier to be a loving parent when one enjoyed the benefits of wealth and had slaves to carry out the less desirable tasks associated with childrearing and household labor. Probably the amount of affection in families and the number of indulgent parents were as varied as they are in families today.

In farm families, a mother often delegated childrearing responsibilities to older children so as to free herself for household chores or working in the fields alongside her husband. This experience also helped to train female adolescents in practical nurturing skills. In plantation families, slave children or maids tended to assume many of the daily chores associated with childrearing, and as a consequence, some privileged white girls had little understanding of the complexities and demands of caring for a baby.

Not all decisions about childrearing were left to parents, especially among destitute families or mothers who were deemed unfit. As Victoria Bynum shows in her book *Unruly Women,* courts or state or local governments could step in as a patriarchal authority and claim that certain mothers were unable to raise their children properly. Here, class, race, and marital status were critical issues, and poor women who failed to adhere to an accepted code of moral behavior were the most likely to fall under a court's jurisdiction concerning mothering. County and state courts might punish single women, especially those who had borne a child out of wedlock, by denying them custody of their children. They could remove youngsters from their home, setting them up under an apprenticeship system where they were bound to work for another adult until reaching a particular age. Judges tended to see unwed mothers as deviant and lascivious, and thus, incapable of raising a child properly. In a sense, this upheld the perception that mothers had no legal rights of guardianship over their children; fathers were natural guardians of their children. Race was often a factor in these decisions, for court records show that free black women were more likely to lose custody of their children than were white women. Single mothers with children struggled to make a living and care for their children, and they, too, often fell upon the mercy of a local charity or the government. The Poor House in Edgefield District (South Carolina) cared for the helpless and handicapped, as well as its poor, the latter who were invariably single women with children.

Yet the majority of southern women had charge of childrearing. One of their most important tasks was to breastfeed their babies, contrary to mythical images that portrayed white babies suckling at the breasts of devoted black mammies. White women regarded breastfeeding as the most practical and healthiest means to feed a newborn. A mother also nursed her baby as an expression of maternal devotion and concern for its healthy future. Prescriptive literature supported her action. According to medical and maternal guidebooks, one of a mother's essential duties was to feed her own baby, and such substitutes as wet nurses were regarded with a wary eye. Slave women generally fed their babies until they were one or two years old, perhaps a slightly later weaning period than white children. (Many blacks have a lactose intolerance, ruling out cow's milk as an acceptable substitute.) Supplemental baby food consisted of a mixture of bread, water, and molasses or sugar. As the infant aged, it might consume porridge or food chewed first by its mother.

Although few white women in the Old South willingly gave up suckling infants to black mammies, a sharing of maternal milk was not unusual. And feeding crossed racial lines. Childbirth often left women prostrate and in poor health, and some were too debilitated to nurse their babies. Some mothers had an inadequate milk supply or painful abscesses on their breasts. Mothers might die in childbirth, leaving a newborn without maternal sustenance. In such cases, a substitute feeder was essential for infants. On large plantations, finding a wet nurse to share milk was not too difficult because several slave women had probably given birth to babies recently and presumably were still nursing. In cities and towns, the situation was more problematic. White families often advertised for a wet nurse through the local newspaper, and some women earned money by sharing their milk. In rural areas, a farm wife might feed both her own and a neighbor's newborn; a sister might feed her infant nephew; and in rare but verified cases, a grandmother who had just delivered a baby might feed her new grandchild. Sometimes strangers fed babies. One Tennessee woman, Virginia Shelton, who was traveling on a riverboat, noticed a motherless baby crying for sustenance, and she gave it milk from her breasts. It was also not unusual to have white women feeding black babies for the same reasons that black women sometimes nursed white babies. The most important consideration was to keep the infant alive during the most precarious time of life, giving whatever sustenance was required. Race was not an issue when a baby's life was at stake.

Bottle feeding was the least desirable means of feeding an infant, for bottles were not necessarily sanitary and fresh milk could be hard to find. Without refrigeration, bacteria proliferated in the bottles and caused diarrhea or other illnesses. In a few cases, an indulged woman who was determined to regain her shapely figure or avoid the demands of a newborn altogether might find a mammy to suckle her newborn or resort to bottle feeding, but this was the exception. Nursing was one of the most important duties associated with rearing children.

Raising children involved years of commitment and endless energy. Bearing so many offspring prolonged the duties for southern women, and they often spent three decades or longer—from first pregnancy to the lingering problems of their children's adolescence—raising a family. Elite southern women gained a reputation as devoted and affectionate mothers, and perhaps they earned such accolades, thanks in part to the assistance of their domestic servants and their commitment to family. Wealthy southern mothers had more time to devote to their children than farm or slave women. Domestic servants allowed them more free time to read, write, and socialize and relieved them from the stresses of ceaseless maternal and domestic duties. Mrs. Tarry of North Carolina thanked her mother for lending her a slave woman, thereby preserving her energy and health. "I could ride out and never feel the least uneasiness about the children, for I knew she would take care of them," she wrote. Obviously the servant allowed her time to write letters as well. Privileged mothers could pick and choose the more enjoyable duties associated with childrearing. Slaves often performed the more tedious or less pleasurable tasks associated with babies, such as changing dirty diapers or entertaining a cranky infant, while mothers selected the more personally rewarding duties of breastfeeding and holding the baby when it was clean and happy.

The greatest worry facing both black and white mothers was the endless string of health problems associated with young children and the constant threat of an infant's death. The South deserved its reputation as an unhealthy place for all its residents, but infants suffered more than adults. Despite the immunities that newborns acquire naturally from their mothers, personal writings and medical statistics indicate that antebellum southern mothers had to be vigilant from the moment of each baby's birth. Census statistics in 1850 show that 17 percent of all deaths among whites occurred among children one year of age or younger and 38 percent to those five and under. Including black babies, these figures in 1860 were nearly 21 and 43 percent respectively. Such statistics alarmed physicians and mothers, but they had few proven means to combat high infant mortality other than attentive nursing. Elizabeth Green of Georgia bore fifteen children, and only three survived to adulthood. Her only daughter who achieved adulthood died from complications in childbirth just before she turned nineteen. Considering the limitations of antebellum medicine and the usual failure of babies to respond positively to heroic treatment, it usually fell to parents to nurse and treat their youngsters. Mothers spent anxious years when their children were young, often sacrificing their own health and well-being to ensure the lives of their offspring. Healthy babies were deemed cause for celebration, for the norm was to be ill. One Louisiana mother wrote that her children were well, despite the fact that one had an ear that was oozing, another had a sore throat, and a third was suffering from a fever. Apparently things could have been much worse.

Slave women had no choice but to tend to their own babies and sometimes relied on a conjurer or skilled older woman in the slave community for advice if an infant was sick. In desperate cases, a slave owner would call a physician to help an ill black baby. Slave mothers had more cause for worry, for according to the 1850 census, twice as many slave newborns died as white babies. Kenneth Kiple and Virginia Himmelsteib King in their medical study of blacks, *Another Dimension to the Black Diaspora,* suggest reasons for this frighteningly high mortality among slave babies, attributing many deaths to the poor health and diet of slave mothers and newborns. They suggest that a majority of slave infants were born with nutritional deficiencies. As noted earlier, slaves ate a monotonous and nutritionally deficient diet, heavy in carbohydrates and fats and low in calcium and iron. Babies inherited the deficiencies of their mothers. (Many poor white farm women ate no better, so these comments would apply to their children as well.) The quality of a mother's milk depended on her nutritional intake and gradually worsened during her childbearing years as each infant depleted her of stored nutrients. Since many blacks suffered from lactose intolerance, babies had to be weaned from breast milk to food and other liquids besides cow milk. Many slave children subsequently suffered from mild malnutrition, the usual symptoms of which were slight edema and pot bellies. The pudgy black youngsters seen on slave plantations were not necessarily well-fed ones, according to Kiple and King, but victims of poor nutrition. Malnutrition and low birth weight were medical problems not easily detectable or resolved by nineteenth-century medical knowledge. Most physicians lacked an awareness of preventive medicine. In addition, malnutrition made all slaves more susceptible to other diseases. Finally, not until later in the century did physicians learn the importance of incubating newborns and keeping babies dry and warm. Slave mothers must have found it difficult to keep their infants warm when they had to be placed on the floor of damp cabins or on beds without adequate coverings.

Slave babies also suffered from diseases that typically affected all newborns—measles, scarlet fever, cholera infantum, colic, whooping cough, and chicken pox. Slaves had natural immunities to some forms of malaria and to yellow fever, but they were more susceptible to pulmonary diseases like tuberculosis and pneumonia. Conditions in slave cabins were particularly dirty and damp. Not until the late antebellum period did agricultural reformers and some physicians initiate a campaign to improve living conditions for the South's slave population. Such reformers correctly understood the connection between good health and a clean living environment. Unfortunately, the campaign occurred at the same time that southerners were caught up in the cotton boom, and plantation profits often superseded concerns for better care of slaves.

Conditions in the slave quarters exacerbated ill health. Cabins, made from local materials such as logs, bricks, or stone, were simple structures, measuring from sixteen to twenty feet square, with a fireplace and door but often no window. The floor might be elevated, but just as likely was dirt. Keeping slave quarters clean and dry was impossible. Roofs leaked, animals wandered in, and lice, flies, and mosquitoes were ever-present. Beds might be raised on frames, but many slaves slept on a mattress on the floor, with only a single blanket to cover them. And while slave communities fostered friendship and mutual support, close living exacerbated ill health. Contagious diseases like tuberculosis spread quickly among a large population living in confined, damp quarters. That any slave, much less a newborn, remained healthy was a miracle.

Such conditions made it almost impossible for slave babies to escape illness. One of the most frightening of all newborn diseases was neonatal tetanus, reported to be far more common among slaves than whites. This form of tetanus occurred within the first two weeks of life, caused by bacteria infecting the umbilical cord. The affected infant displayed alarming symptoms including clenched fists, a rigid body and smile, and an inability to suckle, leading to death within a day or two. There was no effective treatment once symptoms occurred. According to Michael Johnson, sudden infant death syndrome (SIDS) was also more common among slave infants than white babies, with an estimated 82 percent of all cases affecting black babies. No one understood what caused an infant to die in its sleep, though owners sometimes accused the black mother of ignoring her child or rolling over and smothering it. Even today, doctors are still unsure what causes SIDS, and thus the cause of these infants' death remains unanswered.

For slightly older black and white children, worms were a perpetual problem. Among slaves and poor whites, shoes were worn usually only in winter, and hookworms could easily enter through the soles of the feet, especially when barefoot children walked in fields and gardens fertilized with human and animal fecal matter. Tapeworms were found in undercooked food or were spread by flies. For the malnourished child, worms could be fatal. Diarrhea was probably the most common health problem for all antebellum children. Water was frequently polluted, unlined latrines seeped into wells or streams, and unrefrigerated food could be tainted with bacteria. Rearing slave children was difficult for their mothers, for they were helpless against the ravages of disease, malnutrition, and ill health, especially considering the limited time they could give to each child.

Literate white mothers often turned to maternal guidebooks for assistance in childrearing. Herb gardens provided necessary plants for homemade medicines, and a plantation medicine box usually stocked quinine, blue mass, calomel, laudanum, and perhaps arsenic for cleansing the system. Women nursing ill children relied on a combination of home cures, drugs, intuition, vigilance, and the assistance of a doctor. But physicians were not as valued in treating children as they were for attending deliveries. Many southern parents remained skeptical of doctors' abilities to cure their children and believed that death crossed the threshold when a physician entered the room. Doctors' often failed to adjust their cures for young children, and their heroic cures seemed unduly harsh for small constitutions. Much of what they tried was experimental or ineffective, and their medical responses to illnesses were guided by a child's visible reaction to certain cures. Misidentifying and mistreating diseases were common. Maternal intuition and parental care often served children better than antebellum medical training.

Southern mothers certainly had plenty of experience to guide them in caring for their sickly children, considering the frequency of illness among the many children they bore. They often made decisions about treating infants on their own, for their husbands might be absent or preoccupied and a doctor unavailable or unwanted. Mothers' diaries and letters reveal that many spent sleepless nights nursing sick children, perhaps aided by a kindly neighbor, domestic slave, or sympathetic husband. But when a child was ill, mothers assumed full responsibility and did not delegate nursing a sick youngster to a substitute.

White babies contracted most of the diseases that afflicted slave infants, though children born into elite families were less likely to suffer from diseases associated with filth, such as neonatal tetanus. Their houses were drier, brighter, and probably cleaner. Given the number of diseases that affected each child, southerners, except those living far from others, had acquired several immunities by the time they reached adulthood. The one disease that could be treated effectively during the antebellum period was smallpox. Inoculations and vaccinations proved successful if administered properly, and southern mothers did not hesitate to have their infants treated against the dreaded disease.

Strangely, the medical experts of the day considered "teething" to be a grave childhood illness. Cultural or societal attitudes often affect perceptions of what a disease is, even when it has little to do with genuine pathology. Such was the case with teething, considered the most serious disease in a young child's life and one that could occur anytime between four months to two years of age, the approximate time during which a child's teeth emerged. Because babies experienced diarrhea, high fevers, irritability, vomiting, and almost constant health problems, parents and doctors attributed all these illnesses to the most obvious change in the child's life—its emerging teeth. The "disease" demanded vigilance and action, and many young babies received quantities of calomel to cleanse their systems and relieve pressure, a periodic lancing of gums, and a variety of herbal remedies. Once teething passed, mothers breathed a sigh of relief that their child had survived the experience.

Few doctors understood the nature of contagious disease. Yet southern mothers displayed common sense in avoiding sickness, and they wisely kept a child at home if diseases like scarlet fever, whooping cough, or cholera were rumored to be in the vicinity. When yellow fever periodically hit such cities as Mobile or New Orleans, whites who could afford to leave fled the cities, leaving the poor behind. The same sort of exodus occurred during cholera epidemics in 1832, 1849, and 1853. Southerners also believed that miasmas pervasive in coastal and swampy areas carried diseases that affected human constitutions. The poor health of children was often a reason that southern families chose to migrate westward—and sometimes back home, if they found conditions to be worse than what they had left. Some privileged southern families spent the hot summer months in the foothills of the Blue Ridge Mountains, at the seashore, or vacationing in northern spas or ocean communities like Newport, Rhode Island.

Babies were often sick throughout infancy or suffered prolonged and serious diseases that demanded enormous maternal sacrifices. An illness like whooping cough could last as long as six months. Rebecca Hall admitted that she scarcely slept at night when she nursed her three girls by herself, admitting, "I am almost worn out in the cause." One child's illness could spread to every family member. Endless caretaking wore down the strongest of women.

With so many hardships to confront in ensuring their infants' well-being, it becomes apparent that mothers could not always save their children. Many had to face the death of an infant. Grieving and learning to accept the death of a beloved child were difficult but common experiences for southern women. Some mothers spent later years recalling the birthdays of each child who succumbed. We know of their sorrow through the personal accounts of elite southern women who often put their grieving into words, and undoubtedly the sentiments must have been similar for all mothers. Each departed child left an indelible mark. The death of a child is said to be the greatest loss that any parent can experience, and southern mothers became all too accustomed to grieving. The abundance of children in southern families did little to compensate for the suffering, nor did the frequency of infant mortality harden mothers to accept the inevitability of death. In fact, such bleak odds probably provided incentive for mothers to work even longer hours to maintain the health of each child.

As personal correspondence and other sources indicate, infant illnesses and deaths were everyday occurrences in the antebellum South. Two cemeteries on Edisto Island, South Carolina, show a line of tiny gravestones belonging to two families that experienced eight and nine infant deaths, respectively. Caroline Mordecai Plunkett of North Carolina became an expert at nursing and grieving. She lost two children within three days; her husband died eight months later; she bore a baby three months after that, but the child lived only nine months. It is little wonder that Caroline spent her final years in an insane asylum. Another North Carolina family reported losing five infants to the same disease in a string of woeful years. Some women felt like giving up, like Sarah Screven, who mourned after her baby died, "I am a child of sorrow and never do I expect happiness on earth." On the other hand, Lucy Shaw of Galveston uttered a more typical reaction. She had lost two children and witnessed a friend bury four but nevertheless observed stoically, "It is strange how much we can bear and still live on and still feel an interest in things about us."

Wealth and prestige were no protection against child mortality and tragedy. Lucretia Hart Clay, wife of Henry Clay, bore eleven children. All six of their daughters died young. One son was placed in an asylum for a year, another was briefly imprisoned, and one was killed while serving in the Mexican War. Margaretta Mason Brown, wife of a wealthy senator from Kentucky, lost a son when he was eleven months and another when he was two years old; their daughter died at seven, probably from an overdose of calomel. The traumatic and sudden death of Anna Page King's oldest son, Butler, when he was a grown man threw her into such despair and depression that she died less than eight months later. First ladies Varina Howell Davis and Mary Todd Lincoln each lost a young son during the Civil War.

Southern mothers had no choice but to deal with their grief, which they did by expressing their feelings openly, writing about their sorrow, and sometimes by donning mourning clothes and anticipating that any childhood illness might prove fatal. Mothers relied on divine support and strength and eventually concluded that in God's ultimate wisdom, heaven would prove a kinder place for their child than a life of suffering on earth. Some believed that they would reunite with loved ones in heaven. Antebellum society permitted women to grieve openly, and many mothers did not hesitate to express their sorrow. They found strength in the support of their husbands, relatives, and friends, and especially from many other women who also had experienced the death of a child.

Some privileged mothers depended on narcotics or addictive substances to drown their grief, and there was a close correlation between drug use among southern women and the sorrow associated with the death of a child. Many southern men drank alcohol; some southern women used drugs. Initially morphine or laudanum might have been taken innocently or only occasionally to get through a bad day, but this practice could turn into a destructive addiction. Obtaining opiates from a physician or apothecary was not difficult, and many plantation medicine boxes contained narcotics. Anne Cameron of North Carolina became addicted to morphine, opium, and laudanum as a result of her sorrow over the death of a young son, the ill health of another child, and her frequent bouts with malaria and headaches. She became so incapacitated that she was unable to perform her maternal duties, forcing her husband to deal with demanding family responsibilities and his wife's condition. Laura Wirt dealt with her deteriorating health, unhappiness, and loneliness by becoming dependent on opium or laudanum. Less harmful was an addiction to tobacco. For instance, Mary Chaplin, like several women, had a snuff habit which helped her endure her state of invalidism; it also affected her behavior and appearance. Whether slave women also had access to narcotics is unknown, but expense alone must have put them beyond reach. Some farm women smoked a pipe or chewed tobacco out of habit and pleasure, and a few elite women smoked small Cuban cigars. It is doubtful, however, that slave or white women enjoyed alcohol to the same degree that southern men did.

The complex combinations of children, stepchildren, and stepparents complicated motherhood for many women in the Old South. The death of a spouse, rather than divorce, was the most common reason a white marriage ended. Men might lose two or three wives in childbirth; women who married older men might outlive a husband by two or three decades and remarry or remain single, depending on their economic circumstances and perspective on marriage. A family might include children, stepsiblings, half-brothers and sisters, and cousins. Children sometimes considered stepparents and stepsiblings interlopers, regarding them with resentment. If a woman married a man with younger children, she might suffer ridicule and tension when she tried to nurture his children as her own. Such a situation was not an easy one, and women had to weigh the pros and cons before committing to such marriages.

Slave mothers had other considerations, for many were single parents. As we have seen, slave women were often the primary parent due to premarital pregnancy, rape, an "abroad" marriage, or because a partner had been sold or had died. One slave woman overcame enormous odds to create a strong family, and she managed to live a remarkably independent life despite her single status. Loren Schweninger relates the story of Sally, born around 1790 on the plantation of Charles Thomas, a wealthy Virginian. She was a field laborer, and at eighteen, suffered the sexual advances of a white man, probably Thomas's son. She bore a mulatto son in 1808 and another one a few years later. Her sons were automatically chattels despite the status and color of their father. When Thomas died in 1818, the slaves moved to Nashville with a new master. Sally received permission to hire out as a cleaning lady and to retain a portion of her earnings. She eventually rented her own home, converting the front room to a laundry. She built up a thriving business, and her sons found jobs as well. Sally saved her earnings, hoping to purchase freedom for her children. In 1827, she bore another mulatto son, this one fathered by a judge on the Tennessee Supreme Court. Two years later, Sally's oldest son was emancipated. Her second son escaped to the North, and shortly thereafter, Sally bought her third son's freedom. All three young men eventually prospered and became important members of their respective communities. The fact that Sally was not married, that her sons had white fathers, and that all three moved to other states did not diminish the importance of her family to Sally. Her foremost duty was as mother to her children. Her sons remained devoted to their mother, writing and visiting her frequently.

Being a mother affected how a bondwoman functioned as a slave. Simply stated, when they were able, they put their children

first. Thus, it is easy to understand why gender is such an important consideration when examining slave runaways. Far fewer
slave women than men ran away permanently and far fewer participated in rebellions. Slave mothers could not abandon their children to seek freedom. Nor could they take young children with
them, for trying to feed, clothe, care for, and protect youngsters
was a nearly impossible task. Even older children could tire
quickly or move too slowly to stay ahead of a slave patrol.

But mothers as runaways did exist, as related in Steven
Weinberger's *Modern Medea* (and fictionalized in Toni Morris-
on's novel *Beloved*). The Weinberger book was based on a startling and sad case that occurred in 1856. Margaret Garner, a Kentucky slave, and her four children escaped their master and made
their way across the Ohio River to freedom. Unfortunately,
Garner's owner, Archibald Gaines, discovered his missing slaves.
Under the nation's fugitive slave law, Gaines had the right to re-
claim his property, even though his slaves were now in a free state,
and he followed them to a small cabin where they were seeking
shelter. Garner, seeing no hope for her children's future as slaves,
killed her two-year old daughter by slitting her throat.

The most famous female slave runaway was Harriet Tubman,
the Maryland fugitive slave who rescued between sixty and 300
slaves (and at one point commanded a reward of $40,000 for her
capture). She probably would not have forayed bravely into the
South so frequently had she been the mother of any children. The
majority of slave women found other means to protest their oppression besides running away permanently, for their children
commanded their untiring devotion.

For all southern mothers, black or white, childbearing and
rearing were overwhelming responsibilities. When they remained
in good health and when their children behaved and made them
proud, no duty on earth could surpass the satisfaction and pride
that southern women derived from motherhood. Yet like all mothers throughout time, the results of ceaseless care and vigilant efforts could disappoint southern women. Eliza Otey was in despair
over a grandson who was lazy and dissipated, hung around the
house, and acted in an abusive manner toward his mother and sis-

ters. Apparently his mother bore his disgraceful behavior in silence. Sue Petigru King seemed to be engaged in ongoing battles with her mother. She disgraced her family by flirting outrageously with a variety of young men and by wearing flamboyant, revealing attire to various social events. Southern children, like offspring at any age, could be defiant, disobedient, unruly, or fail to live up to parental expectations. In such cases, it was necessary to make the best of the situation. Southern mothers carried on, hoping an ill-behaved child would mature, reform, or move away where he or she would not besmirch the family name. Fortunately, at a time and in a region of the country where family and household were the center of women's lives, these children proved to be the exception. For the majority of southern mothers, childbearing and rearing truly were a woman's "sacred occupation."

CHAPTER THREE

Social Concerns: Education and Religion

Education

While most southern women received no formal education during the antebellum period, the founding of female academies in the South during that era opened up new possibilities. Increasing numbers of white girls and some free blacks took advantage of the change, suggesting that the South would not tolerate an unschooled female population. During the colonial period, the Northeast had surpassed the South in educating young men and women. Early settlement patterns and a strong religious ethos that encouraged reading the Bible hastened the establishment of schools in the North. The South's rural settlement created a different situation. Young women who became farm wives seemed to have little need to learn to read and write. True, a few privileged southern girls during the colonial period were educated by a tutor or governess or, like Eliza Lucas Pinckney of South Carolina, were sent abroad to study. Girls might take several academic courses as well as ornamental subjects like music, dance, and embroidery to enhance their social graces and elite status. For wealthy planter families, educated daughters reflected positively on their social status.

Attitudes towards female education changed significantly, even in the South, after the American Revolution. Christie Farnham's study, *The Education of the Southern Belle,* argues that southern female academies in the antebellum period began to offer courses on a par with men's schools, undermining a long-standing assumption that only young men needed a rigorous academic education. The ideal of "republican motherhood" hit a responsive chord nationwide and encouraged a more political role for women. Important, too, were principles of the Enlightenment, which suggested that children were not born in sin; they were innocent creatures, ready to be molded into virtuous and intelligent beings. As mothers of the new republic and nurturers of the nation's young, so the thinking went, women could create a future citizenry worthy of the ideals of the new country. As principal caretakers, mothers needed an education of some substance to fulfill this important role properly. Females should be literate and gain an exposure to the larger world to serve as examples to their children. They also would make more pleasing companions to their husbands; schooling was seen as a positive attribute for a wife. For instance, in defending the many virtues she brought to her marriage, Virginian Lucy Watts stated that she had not only the wealth and high standing of her father but "all the advantages which are derived from education."

An educated southern woman reflected well on her family name and social class. She was to become not only well educated but refined and genteel. Of course, southern spokesmen felt that this idea of a well-schooled female should not be carried too far lest women become overeducated or desire to seek a role beyond the home. Thus, southern female education typically emphasized academic learning and good manners and offered an exposure to a smattering of the fine arts to reflect women's class position. This ideology appealed inherently to elite white women. Schooling for less privileged girls generally entailed learning to read and write and gaining some exposure to domestic skills in order to prepare them for a life of hard work. However, before the Civil War, only limited efforts went into creating public schools in the South to benefit the masses. Much of the general populace had to fend for itself.

The Second Great Awakening, the religious movement that galvanized the nation in the early nineteenth century, and an outpouring of evangelicalism generated further interest in educating the region's youth. An energetic Christian laity encouraged churches to assume greater responsibility for the behavior and education of young members. Beginning in the 1820s and until the Civil War, all denominations, but most notably the Methodists, Baptists, and Presbyterians, participated in founding female academies throughout the South. In part, the proliferation of academies reflected denominational competition as churches sought to establish schools and influence the young.

In the South and the nation at large, the antebellum period witnessed an unprecedented interest in, and commitment to, the education of women. A southern ladies' magazine, *The Magnolia,* reflected regional sentiment in declaring that "intellectual female society is the surest, most efficient instrumentality for the literary elevation of the state." Mothers had an enormous responsibility to raise their children properly. Southern spokesmen apparently felt that only educated mothers could counter the pernicious effects that slaves allegedly had on young children. They noted that because black and white youngsters often played together, white children developed bad habits and learned to speak improperly. Schooling, as well as a mother's influence, could temper these negative influences. By the 1830s, others expressed fear that northern abolitionist rhetoric and that region's reform movements might contaminate the minds of young southerners who attended northern academies; they promoted "home education" (schooling in regional academies) in order to instruct youngsters in supporting the South's institutions.

A significant number of southern female schools were founded in the antebellum period, especially between 1830 and 1860. They varied in size and offerings. Many were small, single-proprietorship institutions; others were more substantial. Towns such as Due West, South Carolina, and Holly Springs, Mississippi, established a female academy for local daughters of the elite. These local efforts reflected the heightening interest in female education and parents' desire not to send their daughters far afield for schooling. A plantation owner like Colonel John Bratton of upcountry South Carolina created a school on his property for his daughters and other girls living in the area. Margaret Wheat started a school for her offspring when the local academy refused to accept young children. Soon, neighbors began to send their sons and daughters to her, and her husband built a schoolroom on the side of their home to accommodate everyone. A few ambitious women like Catherine Ladd of Richmond, Virginia, founded and ran a number of female academies. Her Winnsboro (South Carolina) Female Academy eventually boasted eight instructors. Well-known female institutions like Salem Academy in Salem, North Carolina, and St. Mary's in Raleigh boasted more than 100 pupils and a score of teachers. Occasionally the state assisted these educational efforts. The Greenville (South Carolina) Female Academy, which opened its doors to women in 1823, successfully petitioned the state legislature for funding.

As noted earlier, some fathers played a substantial, even primary, role in seeing that their daughters received a sound education. Virginian William Wirt verged on being an overly directive parent when it came to selecting his daughter Laura's schooling. He was determined that his eldest daughter would achieve the finest education available to women. Unlike some fathers, Wirt encouraged her learning Greek and Latin and exposing herself to subjects that seemed more fitting to a man's education at the time. Yet when he decided that it was in her best interest to begin the courtship process and find a husband, Wirt abruptly ended her schooling, despite Laura's desire for more education. David Jamison of Orangeburg, South Carolina, apparently took great interest in tutoring some or all of his thirteen children. Fluent in French and Latin, Jamison taught these languages to both his sons and daughters. His oldest daughter Caroline recalled the attention he gave to her education, noting that she spent most of her girlhood ensconced in his extensive library with its 1,200 volumes.

The professed purpose of antebellum female education was to prepare women for their future role as mothers, expand their minds, and improve their manners and feminine character; personal fulfillment and loftier, more self-directed goals were not the issues. A southern girl was to be a lady—obedient, purposeful, and pious. In 1858, planter Richard Brumby wrote to his daughter who was attending school in Alabama: "The great object of female education should be the development of a girl into a lady, healthy in person, refined in feeling, pure in mold, and humble in religion." Similarly, the well-known southern magazine *DeBow's Review* extolled the numerous benefits of women's education. "The effect has been to improve their minds and manners without robbing them of the extreme delicacy and refinement for which they have always been distinguished," it stated. Ornamental graces such as dancing, music, and velvet painting were not to be ignored. In fact, a distinguishing feature of southern female academies was that most of them placed more emphasis on the domestic arts, manners, and deportment than did northern female academies. Salem Academy had a reputation for its outstanding classes in painting and embroidery. However, feminine skills may have been less significant by midcentury as the concept of educated mothers grew more important.

Despite the professed desire of some academies to offer a female education on a par with men, many schools offered only a smattering of courses and no real sense of progression through the institution. The knowledge and skill of the teachers who were hired to instruct young women both determined and limited the curriculum in these small female academies. A single individual might teach a range of courses that included philosophy, chemistry, piano, and French. Some proprietors still believed that women needed a less demanding curriculum than that offered young men, for women's private world held fewer intellectual challenges. To protect creatures often described as "delicate," academic work was kept basic to avoid taxing the female mind. There was always the nagging fear that schooling could be carried too far. Some southern writers actually warned that women who were too bright automatically discouraged potential suitors. As one Tennessee newspaper cautioned, "There is an unaccountable antipathy to clever women." The goal was clear: to achieve that balance between the need to create competent, eduated mothers, thereby ensuring the moral elevation of the region, and to preserve women's delicacy, submissiveness, and simplicity of spirit.

Federal censuses show that by the eve of the Civil War, the South had made significant advances in women's education. Though the region still lagged behind the North in overall literacy rates, increasing numbers of southern women attended school between 1830 and 1860, rising at a faster rate than the growth in population. The South educated men and women at roughly the same rate as the nation at large during this period. For instance, in 1850, 16 percent of all white females and 17 percent of all white males in Mississippi attended school; by 1860, the figure had risen to 19 percent for both young men and women in that state. Massachusetts had 22 percent of its females and 23 percent of males in school in 1850; the figures dropped a decade later to 19 and 21 percent respectively, probably reflecting an increasing population of immigrants in the state who were not attending school. Other southern states improved the percentage of women attending school, and both Tennessee and Kentucky matched Mississippi's statistics by 1860. However, the overall illiteracy rate among all whites was four times greater in the South than in the North. And only 10 percent of all southern blacks in 1860 could read, reflecting the fact that in several states, blacks were forbidden by law from acquiring an education.

The School Experience

Privileged antebellum southern women typically attended an academy for two to four years, usually entering when twelve to fourteen years of age. Some girls enjoyed no more than a few months at school. On the other hand, a woman like Mary Jones of Georgia benefited from seven years of schooling, and her correspondence displays her superior education. Mary Boykin Chesnut learned to read at her South Carolina home, enrolled at a nearby Camden academy as a young girl, and at twelve, began attending Madame Talvande's French School for Young Ladies in Charleston, one of the region's finest girls' schools. The Grimké sisters of Charleston obtained a "polite" education through private tutors, who taught them French, mathematics, drawing, writing, and various sewing skills. The oldest sister, Sarah, also studied with her brother Thomas, although her father forbade her to learn Latin.

Female academies generated widespread enthusiasm, though some southern observers balked at the idea of creating actual colleges for women. (This word had a different meaning in the antebellum period than it does today. In general, a "college" education was far less substantial, and pupils as young as twelve or thirteen might attend one.) More substantial academies offered courses in languages, history, reading, geography, botany, and rhetoric, as well as ornamental subjects such as singing, music, and painting. The South Carolina Female Institute in Barnhamville offered classical and modern languages, science, mathematics, reading, and writing. Generally, school principals agreed with Sarah Grimké's father that Latin was inappropriate for young women and that Greek likewise was a male preserve. Smaller schools, especially those run by a single proprietor, could offer only what that individual knew and could teach, and the curriculum in such institutions was limited.

The academic year usually comprised two terms, each one from four to five months in length, though the Greenville Female Academy divided its academic year into four terms. A girl could enter at any time during the year and remain as long as she and her parents wished. Southern academies often held commencement exercises twice a year, providing opportunities to laud the advantages of female education and to hear young women make rare public appearances as they read prize-winning essays to the gathered crowds. The cost of education varied from $80 to $200 per year, keeping private education well beyond the reach of the region's poor.

Public education, which was becoming available during this period in several northeastern states, was the exception in the Old South. North Carolina had a form of free education through some common schools that promised an education to both boys and girls. An 1839 state law gave North Carolina counties the right to apply for state funds to help support a school, but the actual building of a school house depended on private or community funding. The system had limited success and was hardly analogous to today's public school systems. A few southern cities set up publicly funded free schools, and a principal and teacher like Catherine Ladd was paid to instruct a handful of South Carolina's indigent children. Some churches established free Sunday schools to teach poor white children how to read and write, but these were few in number and classes small in size. Meeting only once a week also limited their impact. Mobile, Alabama, had a public school in the 1850s, with separate male and female departments. Charleston's town fathers, worried about the condition of the city's working poor, desired their children to be more in harmony with the privileged white community. In the mid-1850s, civic leaders there established primary schools for white children and a normal (teachers') school for adolescent girls. By 1860, more than 4,000 Charleston youngsters attended that city's public schools. Mississippi's Natchez Academy was a unique and successful experiment in public education, drawing several hundred boys and girls from the community each year for free schooling. The city fathers managed to create a respectable institution—and an unusual one in that it was coeducational—and taxed the town residents to fund it. Apparently, some wealthy planters balked and refused to support the Academy since they sent their own children to private schools. North Carolina Quakers promoted coeducational academies with separate living quarters for boys and girls. The majority of southern schools, however, were for the privileged and either designed for a particular sex or maintained separate departments for boys and girls.

Various denominations established a number of fine southern female academies. Catholics were active in this educational movement in certain areas of the South. One of the earliest girls' schools founded in the South was the Ursuline Academy in New Orleans, established in 1727. Catholics also founded Nazareth Academy and Loretta Academy in Kentucky, a state which had become a center for spreading Catholicism to the West. One of the most famous southern institutions was Salem Academy, founded by the Moravians in Winston-Salem, North Carolina. It began as a little girls' day school in 1772, but in 1802, the school opened its doors as a boarding academy to Moravians as well as nonchurch members. The school eventually gained a national reputation, drawing pupils from as far away as Texas and California by the

1850s. By that time, more than 200 young women attended the school. The South Carolina Collegiate Female Institute, founded by a Methodist educator, opened in 1828 and typified other southern female academies. Its advertising claimed that it was "admirably qualified to train up the future mothers of our state" and to that end, it offered courses in Spanish, Italian, French, chemistry, logic, Christianity, the poetry and essays of Milton, bookkeeping, and other subjects deemed appropriate for future mothers.

One women's school that gained widespread attention was the Georgia Female College, established in 1839 in Macon, Georgia. The Methodists provided the inspiration and much of the funding, but the city fathers of Macon contributed the land. This establishment, considered to be the first women's college chartered by a state to award degrees, saw its mission as a higher one than that of other women's schools. Its goal was to offer females a substantial education beyond the basics, though it also established a primary department for young women when it became apparent that some girls were not fully prepared for the school's rigorous courses. Dominating its hilltop site was a four-story building complete with classrooms, a chapel, the president's residence, sleeping quarters for the young women, and a dining hall. Open fields on four acres of land allowed women to exercise beyond the public's gaze. Girls were encouraged to dress simply, study hard, and take their education seriously.

To attract pupils and ensure the survival of these schools, many academies advertised energetically in southern newspapers and journals. This also reflected a spirit of competition between various institutions and their supporters and certainly demonstrated the region's interest in women's education. These advertisements touted the principal's credentials, variety of courses, physical facilities, and the institution's salubrious and safe environment. One such notice promised a school that would "cultivate the hearts and minds of young ladies," held in the proprietress's private residence and boasting of its "healthy, retired and pleasant" location. Reputation, support of a particular church or community, and word of mouth were important considerations in a parent's choosing to send a daughter to a particular institution.

However, most schools saw no need to advertise, for they drew pupils from the immediate vicinity.

Manners, behavior, piety, and cleanliness were critical aspects of female education, preparing at least elite young women for their future role in society. Most schools kept a tight rein on their pupils and maintained a rigorous daily schedule. Rising between five and six A.M., the girls had a full day: exercise, meals, classes, recitations, and an early bedtime. Though most academies were situated in small villages or rural areas, teachers always chaperoned girls when they left the school grounds. Slaves performed daily chores such as the cleaning and cooking. Some schools required each pupil to write home regularly and to keep a journal for self-scrutiny and self-improvement. Grades were given in all academic subjects as well as in deportment.

Southern girls generally thrived in their educational environment. In fact, many admitted later that their time in boarding school was the happiest period of their lives. Parting from the family caused temporary homesickness, but soon new school friends, interesting academic pursuits, and frivolous gossip and social activities became a part of daily life. Attending boarding school opened up a new world to those who had spent their childhood isolated on farms, plantations, or in small towns. Some of the teachers and tutors in southern schools were northern women, and exposure to a northern instructor must have had some influence on young southern women. Socializing was an important part of the school experience. Female academies held May Day festivals which might include a parade with a queen, court attendants, a band, and numerous spectators. Graduation exercises gave each of the girls an opportunity to deliver a speech before proud family members, with a "picknick of dainties" following the ceremony. Females forged close friendships with other girls of similar class and background, and such relationships often lasted a lifetime. Historian Carroll Smith-Rosenberg has argued that in such settings, young women often established relationships that were extremely affectionate and intimate. Personal letters reveal the depth of these friendships and the sharing of kisses, hugs, and secrets. M. Hooper wrote her former schoolmate Julia Pickens in

1832, recalling her "throbbing heart," their loving friendship, and their embraces and "eyes of love." Female relationships could be extremely close, but such intimacies were acceptable behavior during the antebellum period.

Southern academies seemed to do a good job in preparing girls to accept their future domestic role and secondary position in society. Education gave girls a mark of gentility and refinement; its intent was not to challenge the region's dominant ideology and belief that a woman's proper place was secondary to that of men. Prescriptive ideals for women's education celebrated the importance of motherhood, domestic responsibilities, and women's dependence on men. Yet it is also true that the actual schooling and rigors of academics could undermine the stated ideal by opening women's eyes and encouraging unconscious challenges that could lead women to question, explore, and see beyond the limits of their circumscribed world. For a few women, the transition from school to home and marriage created tension and momentary unhappiness. Some girls surely pondered the meaning of their future. But only a few southern women embraced such challenges enough to alter their behavior or expectations. The musings of young women who questioned the system must not have been too prolonged or deep, for southern girls were well trained to obey and anticipate a life similar to that of their mothers. Few contemplated nontraditional gender roles seriously, as a few northern women were doing. Most never thought to question slavery, male patriarchy, or a female's secondary role in the South. Once married, a woman had scant opportunities to join with other women to share such ideas. Perhaps they acquiesced, recognizing that the southern patriarchy was too strong to challenge. Perhaps they perceived the advantages of their privileged, prescribed and dependent role in the home. Few women had time to ponder or question their situation since maternal and domestic responsibilities sapped their energy and free time.

Educated southern women did not embrace the feminist spirit that was growing among a small group of middle-class women in the Northeast. The fact that feminist ideas were associated with abolition made them doubly threatening to the region. Several reformers, including Lucretia Mott, Elizabeth Cady Stanton, and

Planting sweet potatoes on
James Hopkins' plantation,
Edisto Island, South Carolina,
1862. *New Hampshire
Historical Society.*

Above: Farm
women take a
moment from
their sewing at
Cedar Mount-
ain, Virgina.
*Library of
Congress.
LC-B8171-
0502 DLC*

Right: Wooden
sewing box and
accessories,
c. 1845. © *NC
Museum of
History, neg. #
88.271.112*

Above: Students at the Salem
Academy, North Carolina,
waiting for the stagecoach to
convey them home, c.1857–58.
*Collection of Old Salem,
Winston Salem, North
Carolina.*

Right: Inset of two girls
wearing hoop skirts.

The Civil War diarist and
southern aristocrat Mary
Boykin Chesnut. *Courtesy of
The Museum of the Confed-
eracy, Richmond, Virginia;
Katharine Wetzel Photogra-
phy, neg. #3341.*

Portrait of a Nurse and Young
Child, daguerrotype by an
unknown maker, c. 1850.
*The J. Paul Getty Museum,
Los Angeles.*

Above: Tintype of "Sylvia," a
free black woman who worked as
a seamstress during the Civil War.
New Bern, South Carolina, 1863.
*Photograph courtesy of the Tryon
Palace Historic Site & Gardens.*

Right: Varina Howell Davis, wife
of the Confederate President
Jefferson Davis, ca. 1860.
Photograph by Matthew Brady.
*Courtesy of the Museum of the
Confederacy, Richmond, Virginia,
neg. # 5894.*

Above: Tenant family in front of a cabin typical of slaves' log cabins. *Courtesy, NC Division of Archives & History.*

Right: Abandoned slave cabin quarters in Louisiana. *Courtesy Louisiana State Library.*

Plantation during Federal
occupation, 1860s, Beaufort,
South Carolina. *Massachusetts
Commandery Military Order of
the Loyal Legion and the U.S.
Army Military History Institute.*

The Gideonite sisters and their
slaves, photographed around
1860. *The Westen Reserve
Historical Society, Cleveland,
Ohio.*

former Charlestonians Sarah and Angelina Grimké, saw both women and slaves as subordinate. Their cries for female equality and an end to slavery had little appeal to southerners. Within the privacy of their diaries, some southern women expressed dissatisfaction with the double standard, the prevalence of miscegenation, domestic misery, loneliness, and the patriarchal structure of antebellum society. Catherine Clinton, in her study of antebellum women, *The Plantation Mistress,* argues that privileged women actually felt that slaves were a burden on them. If so, this remained a private sentiment, uttered in diaries and an occasional letter. Dissatisfaction rarely translated into protest or public expressions of discontent. The Seneca Falls Declaration of 1848, drafted by Stanton, demanded major changes in women's position in American society and blamed men for women's subordination. That document and subsequent feminist conventions held in the North generally drew scorn and derision from the South. Southern writers mocked bloomerism (wearing loose-fitting pants as a reaction against women's fashionable but restrictive clothing), "Stanton-ism," and public displays by northern women that southerners regarded as masculine behavior. To southerners, the North had allowed females too much license; women and abolitionists were allegedly taking charge. Southern essayists, probably reflecting more than just a hint of desperation and fear, flooded magazines with writings deploring such activities and celebrating the ideal, delicate southern woman who knew her place.

Education for the Less Privileged

Education for slaves, free blacks, and yeomen farm girls, most of whom were excluded from formal schooling by skin color or poverty, was more practical in nature but also more limited. Girls learned valuable work skills from their mothers, fathers, or older siblings—how to churn, milk cows, hoe, weed, tend gardens and orchards, pick cotton, cook, sew, spin, and care for infants. Some farm girls learned to read and write from their mothers or briefly attended a local dame school usually maintained and taught by a single proprietress. By the 1850s, some agricultural reformers decried fashionable education and celebrated farm women who were "ignorant of all that boarding schools can teach." They preferred women who could "wash and iron, make bread and butter, and cheese, cook a good farmer's dinner, and set the daintiest of little stitches." Notwithstanding these compliments, most farm girls probably would have enjoyed an academy experience, but few had that choice.

Some free blacks acquired an education for their children despite the challenges and the state and local laws that worked against them. The District of Columbia and urban areas in the upper South had several dozen schools for free black children. Most of these schools were coed. An education was perceived as a means to elevate black women into the category of "lady" as well as prepare them to become teachers in black schools. They offered basics in reading, writing, arithmetic, sewing, morals, and religion; a few had a more advanced curriculum similar to that in white schools. Catholics were active in educating free blacks. Sisters in the teaching order of the Oblates of Providence played a major role in educating a number of antebellum black women. Ann Battles Johnson, a free black woman of Natchez, Mississippi, was determined that her children would acquire a sound education. She first had them tutored at home and then sent several of them to New Orleans, which had a handful of schools for free blacks. Savannah's free blacks operated their own schools, though they often had to do so in a clandestine manner. Jane Devereux conducted a school for Savannah's free blacks that operated for more than thirty years. A group of North Carolina Quakers established a school for free black children that met two days a week.

Slave girls' education came from their learning essential skills as young children. Only in rare instances and with great determination or luck did they learn to read, and if so, it was usually under the tutelage of a kind mistress. Harriet Jacobs's mistress taught her to read and write. Before they moved to the North, the Grimké sisters had tutored their black maids. Black and white children played together while they were young, and sometimes slave children overheard bits of lessons or copied letters drawn in the dirt or sand. By the 1830s, though, nearly all southern states had passed laws prohibiting whites from teaching slaves to read and write; a violator would be fined or even jailed. Most southern whites believed that slaves were better off in an ignorant and docile condition. Certainly an education would not help them become more productive workers. Worse yet, whites felt that teaching slaves to read and write might fill their heads with the wrong ideas. If slaves knew how to read, they could gain insight into the larger world or pay heed to abolitionist voices from the North. Some whites were so fearful of slaves learning too much that they spelled out words or sentences to one another when domestic servants were present.

Probably the single most important lesson that slave girls learned was survival. This included passivity, accommodation, and subtle forms of resistance, but rarely overt rebellion. One elderly slave woman recalled a useful lesson she learned: "If your head is in the lion's mouth, it's best to pat him a little." Slave parents at times exhibited what seemed to be unduly harsh or insensitive reactions towards their own children. They realized that youngsters needed to learn what difficulties lay ahead. While slave children often led a relatively carefree existence and were usually safe from punishment, parents tried to prepare them for adulthood by hardening them to life's realities. Children's lives changed significantly once they matured and became productive members of the labor force.

While slave women rarely had access to formal learning, this does not imply that they did not value an education. Its importance became evident at the end of the Civil War, when an overwhelming response of former slaves was demonstrating their desire to learn to read and write. Thousands of blacks of all ages flocked to schools opened by northern missionaries and the Freedmen's Bureau and staffed by northern schoolmarms. Having been previously denied the opportunity, former slaves regarded education as a means to elevate themselves and gain access to a world long closed to them.

White Women and Religion

One of the most meaningful activities for all southern women beyond their families was participating in religious activities and
church services. In spite of, or perhaps because of, the South's rural environment, religion was a central force that guided most
southern women's lives. Next to the family, the church was probably the region's most important institution. Gender was a factor
in southern religion. Far more southern women than men participated as communicants and members, indicating the importance
of religion to southern women. Donald Mathews's study of southern religion shows that women constituted more than 65 percent
of the region's churchgoing population. The ratio of women to
men in two of Charleston's leading churches, St. Michaels and St.
Phillips, was a surprising ten to one. The Congregational Church
there had a ratio of five female members to every male. The
church provided an acceptable (and often the only) social outlet
for women outside the home and was an important source of community. Benevolent activities associated with churches attracted
female participants. They gave women a meaningful role outside
the home and had an unquestioned legitimacy about them; they
promoted virtue and piety, traits highly prized in white women.

Nevertheless, church played an interesting role in women's
lives, reinforcing their subordinate role but offering them a place
where they found some protection for their person and a sense of
equality and strength in the eyes of God. While churches held out
the promise of spiritual equality, ministers articulated a commitment to the prevailing social order. Historian Stephanie McCurry
asserts that yeomen farmwives flocked to church where they
could hear that earthly distinctions held no meaning to God. They
listened to messages of hope, self-respect, and love, even as society urged them to do their Christian duty and follow the natural
order by being submissive and passive.

During the colonial period, the Church of England (Episcopal) became the established church in several southern colonies,
meaning that all citizens paid taxes to support it, whether they
were members or not. The mid-eighteenth century saw the spread
of evangelical denominations throughout the region, fostering the

religious pluralism that would define the antebellum South. By the post–Revolutionary period, Baptists, Methodists, and Presbyterians had well-established footholds throughout the South. Maryland had long been a haven for dissenters and Catholics. Louisiana and Florida, with their Spanish and French settlements, also attracted many Catholics. Thomas Jefferson's famous "Statute for Religious Freedom," passed by the Virginia state legislature in 1786, set an example that most states followed, formally ending the union of church and state, outlawing taxation for the support of any religious institution, and diminishing the power of the Church of England. The large migration of Scotch-Irish to the Piedmont areas of the South further diminished the influence of the Church of England in that area. North Carolina was home to a number of Quakers who settled the Piedmont area as early as the late seventeenth century. Their stance opposing war and slavery put them at odds with many other white southerners, and eventually many of them would migrate westward. Moravians living in the same area adhered to the idea of church-owned property and a centralized economy. Moravian women's behavior was strictly monitored, and young women lived in separate housing until they married.

The Second Great Awakening had its initial rumblings on school campuses in the Northeast during the 1790s, but its most visible expression occurred on the southern frontier in the first decade of the nineteenth century. The Awakening elicited an enthusiastic response from rural settlers who felt dispossessed and removed from religious fellowship. The Awakening was deeply personal for many converts. The camp meeting was the centerpiece of this evangelical movement, and for a few years, was ubiquitous throughout the South. The first major camp gathering in the region occurred in 1801 at Cane Ridge, Kentucky, a tiny community with no more than a few thousand people within a day's ride. The meeting drew an estimated 10–20,000 people who met for several days of preaching, praying, and renewal. For the next few years, camp meetings occurred weekly across the South but tapered off by the second decade of the century. These meetings would become more protracted and sedate, often held in permanent camp-like settings.

Camp meetings attracted a surprisingly interdenominational crowd and drew in all classes of whites as well as black participants. Evangelical preachers representing several different churches sermonized, prayed, exhorted, and won new converts. Crowd behavior sometimes bordered on the extreme as the spirit moved individuals to shake, dance, jerk, bark, and howl. Entire families brought tents, bedding, food, clothing, children, and servants to these religious events. Participants prepared for weeks in advance, regarding them not only as religious renewals but as opportunities for socializing. Women found these camp meetings an opportunity to escape the routine of their demanding lives and leave behind domestic responsibilities for a few days. Here they could engage in the same kind of behavior as men did and give physical expression to their faith. M. S. Rucker of Washington County, Texas, was thrilled with several excellent revivals held in the county, noting that they were "attended by the most desirable consequences." Southern women enjoyed the emotional, physical, and romantic ecstasy of communing directly with God.

It was not only camp meetings but also the tireless work of itinerant ministers, missionaries, and Christian women that helped to establish evangelical denominations throughout the South. As people gravitated to the frontier, churches followed. Women in isolated areas felt bereft without a church, and ministers and religious leaders expressed deep concern that people living on the fringe might escape the influence of God. Frontier churches were often makeshift, and ministers might preach in private homes, barns, or in open fields. In 1825 residents of Greenville, South Carolina, met in the town hall until an interdenominational structure was completed. Denominations made a concerted effort to spread their message throughout the South, and some competition between various churches emerged. For many women, however, denominational competition was immaterial, and they often attended whatever church was nearby or wherever a minister happened to be preaching. In Madison, Georgia, Dolly Lunt Burge wrote that because the minister of her Presbyterian church could not preach, she happily attended the Baptist service instead.

Church membership often reflected class structure. The Episcopal Church remained strong among elite planter families in coastal areas like the Sea Islands of Georgia and South Carolina, the Chesapeake region, and cities such as Charleston and Richmond. Baptists and Methodists were most successful in frontier areas. Episcopalians and Presbyterians had greater difficulty reaching the masses, in part because they insisted on a seminary-trained clergy. Also, the formal liturgy of the Episcopal Church and its historical ties with the elite made that denomination distasteful to many poor farm families.

However open the Second Great Awakening seemed in spirit, its participating churches permitted only white males to preach and interpret God's word. Despite their overwhelming numbers within various congregations and their involvement in Christian benevolence, women had no sustained power within the church; they were excluded from positions of influence. It was a rare southern woman who challenged this concept. In 1839, "Sister Roberts" of Beaufort's Primitive Baptist Church suddenly grabbed the pulpit in order to preach. She was physically dragged away and then excommunicated for her bold and totally inappropriate action. Women in the church had to know their place. They could serve in a secondary capacity: leading prayers, observing meetings, teaching Sunday school, and participating in Bible groups and charity associations.

But women were natural church members. Held up as pious and virtuous in the ideal, white women were seen as the domestic embodiments of Christian fortitude and morality, setting an example to family members and spreading God's teaching in the home. They were to convince reluctant husbands and children to come into the fold. Mary Boykin Chesnut spent several frustrating years beseeching her husband to join the church, but like many southern men, he was not interested. Mary Jones's greatest cross to bear seemed to be her beloved second son's refusal to convert, despite the family's strong commitment to Presbyterianism. In nearly every letter, she urged him to repent but without success.

Plantation mistresses assumed the additional task of bringing the word of God to their slaves. Ida Henry of Texas reported that on Sundays, her mistress "would call us together, read de Bible and show us pictures of de Devil in de Bible and tell us dat if we was not good and if we would steal and tell lies dat old Satan would git us." A few plantation women established Sunday schools for slave children, reading them Bible stories and teaching them the importance of obedience and good manners.

Religious devotion involved more than church attendance and family proselytizing. For many southerners, in fact, it was often a difficult task merely to get to church, and alternative outlets and activities were essential. In rural areas, the nearest church might be many miles from home and accessible only in good weather. Family responsibilities, poor health, a child's illness, or an uncomfortable pregnancy interfered with female church attendance. If a church was too distant, several women might gather weekly and hold prayer meetings or Bible readings in a home or diligently read their Bible and say prayers on their own.

White women found satisfying means to practice their faith. Many read and reread their Bible and turned to it for comfort. Women read collections of sermons, religious tracts, and inspirational novels. Some kept journals, not only to record their activities and create memories for their children, but also to scrutinize their faith and correct their faults. Lucilla McCorkle, daughter of a minister and married to another, used her journal to instill self-discipline, record achievements or failures in her spiritual growth, and remind herself of her vows for self-improvement. An exceptional Martha Hancock of Bedford County, Virginia felt that her belief in God liberated her from feminine confines. She defied social conventions by acting in the name of a higher authority, leading prayers at church meetings and organizing and teaching Sunday school. How members of her congregation responded to this is unknown. Like McCorkle, she kept a diary to monitor herbehavior and the condition of her soul in order to guard against backsliding and chart her course to heaven. Apparently Hancock found the time to spend several hours in prayer, meditation, and scripture reading every day. "I enjoy a sweet peace which cannot be described," she wrote one day after reading the Bible. Slaveowning women interpreted their benevolent and paternalistic actions toward their slaves as efforts to act out the teachings of Jesus. They regarded their patient efforts to teach slaves better work habits and manners and to improve their living conditions as exemplary Christian duties.

Mothers took seriously their religious responsibilities toward their children. Catherine Carson, a particularly concerned mother, dedicated herself to her youngsters' religious education. To this end, she had her children memorize two verses of Scripture and a verse of Presbyterian catechism every day. On Sundays, the youngsters had to recite all the verses they learned during the week. Her children could not play outside on the Sabbath, and the only books allowed to be read that day were the Bible and religious tracts.

Churches sometimes disciplined their members, serving as another institutional curb on bad behavior. Periodically, evangelical churches assembled a tribunal to pass judgment on a member's misdeeds. When an individual sinned in the eyes of the church, a committee of male church members listened to testimony of accusers and witnesses, and the defendant would have an opportunity to explain his or her actions. Women were often spectators at these hearings, though they could not serve on the tribunal or vote on the outcome; such public activity was an affront to their femininity. But they did bring cases against those who had wronged them. Church accounts show that women were also among the accused. The widespread belief in southern women's pious and pure nature notwithstanding, females misbehaved. They were held accountable for bad behavior, especially when their transgressions challenged family stability. Whether women actually committed as many sins as did men is unknown, but certainly their misdeeds were more visible to the community because of the high standards to which the southern social order held women.

These confessionals reveal the disparate treatment that churches meted out to men and women. More men were disciplined, but women's transgressions were viewed as more serious. Jean Friedman's study of southern women and religion, *The En-*

closed Garden, shows that only 6 percent of men compared to 44 percent of women who testified were accused of sexual transgressions. It is unlikely that more women than men engaged in sexual indiscretions; in fact, the reverse probably held true. But it was harder for women to hide incriminating evidence (most likely a pregnancy). More important, southern society was more willing to forgive men for sexual indiscretions: the double standard prevailed. If an unmarried woman came before a tribunal because she was pregnant, she, not the father of the child, was censured, even if the father's identity was known. In one instance, Martha Cole was reprimanded because her child was born only six months following her marriage. Interestingly, the committee then cited Martha's mother for failing to properly counsel and raise her daughter. No action was brought against her husband, yet Martha admitted her own guilt and repented. Churches sometimes expelled a woman who bore an illegitimate child or who engaged in dissipated behavior. Women were supposed to be pious and virtuous, even if men were not, and churches assumed responsibility for women's public conduct. In fact, an underlying assumption among church members was that women needed to uphold the morals of the region. Men had difficulty controlling their sexuality, their drinking, and occasionally their violent behavior. Virtuous women, according to church views, could dissuade southern males from wanton acts.

The church held an ambivalent position in southern women's lives. As Stephanie McCurry suggests, in extreme situations, women sometimes used the church to challenge their dependent, secondary position, believing that in God's eyes, they were equal to men. They turned to the church for protection, especially when they were the victims of male abuse. Here they could seek redress when wronged; women were more likely to gain protection from a church court than from a secular one. While women may not have challenged men's right to wield power, they challenged men's right to abuse that power. They also found that the experience of conversion gave them a sense of self-definition and worth. Yet while the church held out the idea of spiritual equality, it did not preach worldly equality. Women had to know their place, a place made clear by Biblical dictates. The church, led by men, preached messages it believed important, including a commitment to a proper gender and racial order.

Women's Benevolence

Urban southern women were fortunate to have additional outlets for their Christian spirit and desire to serve God. They formed charitable organizations, maternal societies, and prayer meetings and taught Sunday school. Their energetic involvement in benevolence and reform was part of a larger, nationwide movement to improve the republic. Plantation women were less likely to engage in reform or benevolent activities than were urban women because of their isolated circumstances. They did not reach out to poor white women, other than relatives, and rarely ventured into a world beyond the confines of home. The exception to this was plantation women's charitable gestures toward their slaves. Many women believed that investing in the lives of those they owned and, in a few cases, toward whom they developed some affection, was a noteworthy activity. Southern women could extend their benevolence to improve the lives of their slaves, as long as they did not challenge the system or try to reform it. For instance, Annie Clay of Savannah established a school for slave children on the family plantation, a school she conducted for sixteen years.

In the North, many women (and men) embraced a broad range of causes that included temperance, abolition, health reform, missionary outreach, and women's rights. Southern women had scant choices and fewer concerns, but not because the South was any closer to perfection. A limited number of urban centers in the South hindered the development of organizations whereby many people could participate in such activities. Some white southerners felt uneasy about reform activities. As we have seen, by the 1830s, a number of southerners began to feel threatened by northern women's activism and the nature of their grievances. Reform implied a need to change, to cleanse the nation of bad elements, and to create a better world. White southerners, for the most part, did not welcome such change; most were convinced that their own world was quite acceptable and did not demand overhauling. A simple reflection on southern society would have exposed slavery as its most inhumane system, but this was a taboo subject for most southerners. Despite strong proslavery arguments fashioned to reinforce southerners' views that their labor system was ordained by God and served whites and blacks well, it would not have taken much questioning to provoke the uneasy consciences of southern whites. It was better not to even raise the issue. Slavery was an increasingly important social and political issue in the North, and southerners like Sarah and Angelina Grimké who publicly criticized the "sacred institution" left home.

For women, especially those living in towns and cities, reform activities that took them out of the home were acceptable when undertaken in the name of the church and Christian benevolence and did not challenge the social system or upset the patriarchy. Performing charitable works was often necessary, since public authorities did little to assist the indigent. Religious impulses frequently motivated women to engage in charity work, deeds that won the approval of southern society. Members of the Female Bible Society of Lexington, Kentucky, raised money to purchase Bibles and distribute them door to door. The Ladies German Benevolent Society of Savannah, established in 1853, served as the primary Jewish group to aid immigrant women and children. It helped poor women by providing health care and medicine and paying burial costs. Charleston's elite formed the Ladies' Benevolent Society. Its members ministered to lepers, located nurses to assist those who were ill, and interceded on behalf of poor women who needed financial assistance. But members encouraged destitute women to become self-sufficient rather than dependent on charity, sensing the importance of women's financial independence and not burdening the larger community with their needs. Protestant churches in many communities organized a women's missionary society that raised funds to help Christianize Native Americans and foreigners. In Natchez, the wife of a Mississippi state senator founded a temperance society that attracted several of the town's bachelors. It lasted only a short while, perhaps because a critic exposed the fact that some male members had failed to uphold their pledge of abstinence. (The raucous frontier life of a Mississippi town was not the best setting for a temperance organization, however much it might have been needed.) Presbyterian women in Petersburg, Virginia, organized a variety of female associations, including a Young Ladies' Missionary Society, a Married Ladies' Society, a Tract Distribution Society, and an Education Society to raise money for poor young men training for the ministry. Female Mite Societies raised money for church projects and missionary work, and to purchase Bibles and Sunday school books. Women sold handmade goods and farm produce, supporting a good cause with the money they raised.

Comments sprinkled throughout women's diaries describe their benevolent activities: attending prayer meetings, establishing orphanages and asylums for the poor, teaching Sunday school, and working at church fairs. These ladies' fairs were a successful means of raising money; women sewed, embroidered, made bonnets, and baked cakes and pies (or ordered their slaves to do this work) to raise money for a worthy cause. In 1831, Charleston held its first Ladies' Fair. Miriam and Henrietta Cohen organized a community fair in 1843 for women in Savannah's Jewish congregation who produced and sold $1,500-worth of baked goods. Though usually successful in raising money for particular causes, this type of fundraising effort never became as popular in the South as it was in the more urban Northeast. Nevertheless, for southern women whose lives revolved around family and home, charitable programs were an important outlet and a welcome public activity in their otherwise confined lives. Here they found their own space, discovered female companionship, and gained a sense of self-worth by running an organization or working for a meaningful cause.

Catholic nuns also devoted their lives to charitable work. Though Catholic immigrants never flooded the South the way they did the Northeast, there were pockets of Catholic influence in the South. Nuns living in convents in Louisiana and Kentucky established hospitals, orphanages, and female academies. Catherine Spalding was one of the most active Sisters in the antebellum South. She became mother superior of the Sisters of Nazareth in Kentucky, and her order worked to improve the lives of the unfortunate. They founded and ran schools, orphanages, and infirmaries and nursed the ill. During the Civil War, many nuns devoted their energies to nursing wounded and ill soldiers.

Black Women and Religion

Religion was important to slave and free black women alike. Judging how many slaves actually belonged to a church is impossible to determine, though recent studies suggest that a majority of slaves probably never joined a church. Like whites in the antebellum South, more probably attended than actually converted. Some relied on remnants of their African faith and turned to conjurers and magicians to drive away evil spirits and provide answers to life's hardships. Others turned with increasing frequency to Christian churches, finding in the teachings of Jesus and the promise of a better life in heaven beliefs that paralleled their own understanding of suffering and redemption. Many slave women initially were attracted to the Methodist faith as it spread throughout the South because of the church's early stance opposing slavery and the values of that denomination in promoting simplicity, humanity, sobriety, and charity—a sharp contrast to the values of some slave owners. (Methodists altered their abolitionist position when they discovered that many wealthy slaveholders refused to join the church.) Many slaves also enjoyed the Baptist faith because of its belief in total immersion for baptism, which resembled African rituals.

Of all antebellum southern institutions, churches were the most interracial. While blacks usually had to sit in the balcony or in the back of the church, on Sundays blacks and whites often listened to the same Christian message and sang the same hymns. For some slaves, attending church was appealing, giving them a change of pace and the chance to socialize with slaves from other plantations. As one slave woman stated, church was "the onliest place off the farm we ever get." Slave women found camp meetings pleasing, not only for the religious activities they offered but for the social life as well. Here they could meet others and flirt with attractive men. Church-going gave women a welcome opportunity to dress up, shed their burlap, homespun, or sack cloth, donning their single dress-up outfit and covering their head in a bright bandana or scarf.

Slaves also enjoyed the emotional and physical aspects of conversion in evangelical denominations. Slaves' participation in church tended to be extremely physical and emotional, with demonstrations of singing, yelling, praying, and leaping. Frederick Law Olmsted attended a black service in New Orleans and commented that "shouts, groans, terrific shrieks, and indescribable expressions of ecstasy—of pleasure, or agony—and even stamping, jumping, and clapping of hands" defined the congregation's reactions. He noted that when one planter built a chapel for his slaves, he had to remove the benches because the furniture impeded slaves' freedom of movement.

During the colonial period, few masters had bothered to ponder the spiritual education of their slaves. Some whites feared that Christianizing their slaves could give them a sense of equality with whites. But there were obvious benefits in exposing slaves to Christianity. Many antebellum owners began to recognize that a Christian message could encourage submissive behavior and act as a positive influence on slaves. Religious leaders like Charles Colcock Jones of Georgia argued that the plantation could actually serve a missionary purpose, bringing slaves under the proper influence of the church and encouraging them to convert and presumably become more responsible, moral, and devout. Sometimes when a white family became members of a church, their slaves also had to join. Some masters encouraged their slaves to be baptized, married, and buried according to Christian ritual, and even provided a minister for these occasions.

In some churches, black women were able to find respect as well as protection when they shared their grievances. As historian Betty Wood shows, slaves brought a surprising number of charges of bad behavior before church tribunals for arbitration. Punishable acts included adultery, fornication, drunkenness, lewd behavior, rape, and sometimes even dancing. In 1812, two slave women were able to bring charges against a white minister for unacceptable sexual advances toward them. The church committee took their petition seriously and actually dismissed the minister. Here was a place where slaves could testify against whites, for they were not allowed to do so in most courts of law. In a few instances, slaves played a role in shaping the character, morality, and behavior of the religious communities they cohabited with whites. Churches tried to correct white members' behavior by reprimanding them, by demanding a public apology, or even by excommunicating them when the offense was serious.

Slave men and women and free blacks attended white churches in greater numbers as the antebellum period progressed, but urban free blacks also established their own churches, as they did in Charleston and Savannah. Black ministers often preached at these churches. They had their own benevolent and temperance societies, Sunday schools, and church choirs. But church activities were not always a matter of choice, at least for slaves who usually had to comply with their masters' wishes. James Henry Hammond built his slaves their own chapel, not out of goodwill, but because he feared his slaves' attending the black churches of nearby Augusta and mingling with that town's free blacks. Many masters preferred that slaves attend white churches where they could be watched and hear what whites defined as an appropriate sermon that instilled obedience and a strong work ethic. A former bondwoman, Lucretia Alexander, reported her church experiences:

The preacher came and . . . he'd just say, "Serve your masters. Don't steal your master's chickens. Don't steal your master's hawgs. Don't steal your master's meat. Do whatsomeever your master tells you to do." Same old thing all the time. My father would have church in dwelling houses and they had to whisper. . . . Sometimes they would have church at his house. That would be when they would want a real meetin' with some real preachin'. . . .

As Lucretia related, slaves often had their own ideas about religion. They discovered a religious life outside the church and away from their masters. They often held their own prayer meetings and all-night singings. When the master forbade slaves from gathering independently, they held secret services in the dark of night or deep in the woods, hidden from watchful white eyes. Through their African religious traditions, slaves found both cultural autonomy and a sense of community beyond the reach of their owners. Thus, religion became another means by which slaves subtly tried to assert independence from their masters' authority. Their spirituals, which were hybrids of African and American music, often expressed religious themes and slaves' sense of hope and redemption. Christianity professes far more than a spirit of acceptance and docility. It has an empowering message, and many slaves truly believed that in the end, they would triumph. There was no doubt that their masters were going to hell. The River Jordan promised peace and a good life for blacks, not whites. The outcome of the Civil War would merely confirm what they had known all the while about the inhumanity of the slave system they had endured for so long. Slaves saw heaven as their answer to the travails of life on earth—and if both whites and blacks appeared in heaven (which many slaves doubted), there would be a reversal of authority.

Religion was a powerful force in the lives of most southern women. It provided black women a means to deal with oppression and their difficult existence. For white women, it was an opportunity to discover fulfilling outlets and to seek guidance for proper living. For all women, faith provided the strength to withstand the burdens of their lives. They turned to God in moments of grief and loss and often found the strength necessary just to get through another day.

CHAPTER FOUR

Women and Work

The Meaning of Southern Women's Work

A persistent myth about life in the Old South is the vision of a serene and easy routine for privileged white women, made possible by slaves who happily sang as they labored in the fields. Some people's view of the Old South still includes images of magnolia-scented gardens, columned porches, and beautifully dressed women lounging in leisured splendor. Even before the Civil War, as regional tensions grew over the slavery issue, proslavery advocates defended their way of life, trying to convince both southerners and northern critics that a civilization based on slavery was a superior form of existence for all concerned. They pointed to the dismal working conditions, inadequate housing, and meager wages of northern laborers. As the argument went, slaves were better off under the attentive care of paternalistic masters. Slaves learned proper work skills and became productive laborers. Southern whites convinced themselves that they lived in a superior society where the less skilled performed field work. Myths that depicted idle white women and happy slaves intensified in the decades after the Civil War, when Confederate defeat and northern occupation created in many white southerners a romantic longing for a time when life must have been better. Novels, memoirs, and movies recast the region's history and ignored harsher realities of the Old South.

The truth, as should be apparent by now, was far different. For most southern women, life was a stream of hardships sprinkled with a few moments of joy. Even privileged slave-owning mistresses did not always feel that their labor system eased their existence. Domestic slaves demanded training, managing, and constant watching. Mistresses expressed annoyance when tasks remained uncompleted or took too long to accomplish, when slave children ignored their young white charges, or when domestic servants stole food from the larder or slowed down their work pace. Elite women lived in close proximity to their domestic servants, often having responsibility for clothing them, doling out weekly food supplies, and tending health needs. Sarah Williams, a New York woman who married a southern plantation owner, realistically observed her adopted land. After moving from North Carolina to an Alabama plantation and bearing several children, Sarah confessed to her parents, "People may talk of the freedom from care of southern life, but to me it seems full of care." Many plantation women shared Sarah's sentiments at various times in their lives.

There are also misconceptions about women's work and what it implied. The fact that most southern women did not receive wages or credit for their labor does not suggest that they didn't work. Women, then as now, spent their lives working hard, but during the antebellum period, most southern women toiled in agricultural and domestic labor, without compensation or recognition of their productivity. As Stephanie McCurry shows, less privileged women were a vital part of the household, working beside their husband in the fields, helping to produce goods for market, and taking charge of domestic chores. For most antebellum southern women, work differed from the experience of those New England farm girls who flocked to textile mills or into teaching. The fact that so few southern women worked in the public sphere, received pay, or were included in factory statistics has somehow lessened the attention paid to their labor, at least in history books. Southern farm and slave women rarely received credit for their significant contributions to the region's economy.

In addition, the evolution of "separate spheres," where men fashioned careers in the public world while women remained in their private world, was beginning to define the daily lives of some men and women in the Northeast. As we have seen, even though the concept of separate spheres had less meaning in the agrarian South, southern spokesmen upheld this idea and spent an inordinate amount of time and ink extolling the virtues of submissive, maternal women who devoted themselves to their domestic duties. Whether such pronouncements were uttered out of fear or wishful thinking is not totally clear, but certainly southern men heralded those white women who knew that their place was in the home. It is unlikely that southern women would have strayed far from such duties with or without such pronouncements, for domestic and agricultural responsibilities consumed most of their daily existence. And unlike some northeastern women who discovered that paid work experiences broadened their horizons, southern females usually discovered just the opposite. The labor that confined them to the family farm or plantation was so demanding and time-consuming that they had little time to explore or even ponder a larger world.

Slave Labor

Though all women labored, work demands and conditions differed depending on their race, class, and region. Female slaves, unless they were young children or old women, had no choice but to work. It is important to bear in mind that slavery was a labor system, and planters tried to maximize profits by extracting the maximum amount of work from their slaves. Gender often determined the type of job that a slave performed and the conditions under which one labored. But both male and female slaves usually worked from sunup to sundown, and in summertime, the work day could last twelve to fourteen hours. At peak times, such as cotton picking during the fall, field workers might work seven days a week as well.

Slave women performed triple duty as plantation workers, wives, and mothers, as Jacqueline Jones describes in *Labor of Love, Labor of Sorrow*. They rose at dawn, prepared a hurried meal for the family, and reported to the fields. On smaller plantations, where labor was less likely to be differentiated by gender or task, some bondwomen completed housekeeping chores for the white family before going to the fields, or left early in the afternoon to tend to domestic jobs. A noontime break was brief, and work continued until dinnertime. Women then had to prepare supper for their family (except on some large plantations where a central kitchen prepared food for all the slaves) and tend to their children's needs. A former slave, Betty Powers, recalled her mother's work:

Mammy and Pappy and us twelve chillen lives in one cabin so mammy has to cook for fourteen people 'sides her field work. She am up way befo' daylight fixin' breakfast and supper after dark, with de pine knot torch to make de light. She cook on de fireplace in winter and in de yard in summer. All de rations measure out Sunday mornin' and it have to do for de week. . . . Pappy makes de shoes and mammy weaves, and you could hear de bump, bump of dat loom at night, when she done work in de field all day.

As mothers and laborers, slave women knew the meaning of "no rest for the weary."

Gender could affect field work. On large plantations, women might be separated into female gangs, laboring alongside other females and benefiting from female companionship. Some planters or overseers expected less work from women, categorizing them in their plantation records as "one-half" or "three-quarters" of a hand (anyone less productive than a full-grown male worker was designated by fractions). This formula especially applied to young girls, older women, and pregnant females. Economic historians have estimated that slave women typically picked 80 percent as much cotton as a man each day and less if they were pregnant or nursing. But slave women were valued as productive workers, and in the antebellum South, they performed similar roles to those they had carried out in African tribal societies where they had done most of the field labor.

Historian Leslie Schwalm explores female slavery on rice plantations in the antebellum South Carolina lowcountry in her book, *A Hard Fight for We.* Schwalm claims that for five generations, slave women were critical to the economic success of that area. She asserts that "on antebellum rice plantations, field work was slave women's work." This was the type of work many women had undertaken in West Africa where they had been the primary cultivators of rice. Female slaves cleared trees and brush from the fields, hoed, built and maintained tidal plantations along coastal waterways, and cultivated the rice crop. The work was unremitting and extremely unhealthy. Unlike what one might suspect, Schwalm shows that some lowcountry rice plantations would not have profited without slave women, who often comprised the majority of prime field hands.

Bondwomen proved themselves every bit as hardworking and sometimes as strong as men. In some situations such as those Schwalm explores, gender distinction had little meaning. Both female and male slaves worked as field laborers. Slave women performed nearly every plantation chore, including picking, hoeing, plowing, mending fences, burning fields, weeding, raking manure, burning brush, planting, and harvesting. The number of slave women undertaking such demanding work struck northern visitor Frederick Law Olmsted when he traveled to the South in the 1850s. In one instance, he observed that "the ploughs at work, both with single and double mule teams, were generally held by women, and very well held, too. I watched with some interest for any indication that their sex unfitted them for the occupation. Twenty of them were ploughing together, with double teams and heavy ploughs."

And of course, female slaves were domestic servants, with certain household jobs reserved for them. The degree of specialization of household chores depended on the size of the plantation labor force and particular needs. Slave women served as child nurses, cooks, laundresses, seamstresses, spinners, and maids. On small farms with only a couple of slaves, a woman might work beside her mistress and perform whatever job was demanded of her as well as labor in the fields. Yeomen farm families who scrimped and saved to purchase their first slave often preferred a female over a male. A woman cost less, could help with all the demanding household chores, free older white children from childcare and domestic labor to allow them to work in the fields, and offer the promise of expanding the family's labor force through any children she might bear.

The percentage of slave women who worked as domestic laborers is unclear, but with the increasing sophistication and growth of the plantation system, the number of domestic servants rose significantly during the antebellum period. Paul Escott recounted in *Slavery Remembered* that from the hundreds of Federal Writer's Project oral interviews he examined, a surprising number of former bondwomen claimed to have been domestic servants. Several factors may explain the large percentage of female household slaves. Female slaves had to be versatile, and they often worked both in the fields and the master's home, depending on seasonal demands, their age, and health. The large number may also reflect the fact that those interviewed in the 1930s were mere children before the Civil War, and, as youngsters, they likely performed simple domestic chores. Though too young to sow or harvest, slave girls as young as six years old learned simple household tasks. Also, whites liked to think that work in the "great house" carried status, and some blacks may have agreed with that assessment and boasted a bit. Owners selected female domestics whom they could train easily and who performed properly and obediently. Some whites apparently preferred light-skinned slaves as domestics, believing that a mulatto slave had more status. Yet others selected dark-skinned servants to ensure that slaves knew their place.

Young slave girls received training as household workers at an early age. Finding seven- and eight-year-old girls working in a slave owner's home was not unusual. Children could dust, empty chamber pots, sweep floors, fill wood buckets, swat flies, fetch water, set and clear the table, gather eggs, make beds, pick up trash, and watch babies. One white mistress wrote that her husband had just purchased a six-year-old slave girl to mind their infant. Cicely Cawthon, a former slave, recalled her early years as her mistress's helper. "I stayed around and waited on her, handed her water, fanned her, kept the flies off her, pulled up her pillow, and done anything she's tell me to do," she stated. Lighter duties, once the drudgery was completed, might include brushing and arranging hair, straightening hoop skirts, and tightening corsets for the white mistress.

Plantation production had significant bearing on the type of labor that slave women performed. A plantation's level of self-sufficiency depended on the number of laborers, availability of purchased goods, and prices for its staple crops. In flush times, it made sense for masters to put their resources into crop production; but when cotton demand slackened and prices fell, planters might opt for greater self-sufficiency. Slaves could be shifted from home to field and vice versa as the need arose. Large plantation enterprises often had their own carpenters, blacksmiths, coopers, and tanners—jobs that demanded special skills and were peformed almost exclusively by men. The remaining farm work fell to both men and women. On large plantations, women performed the bulk of productive domestic work, making candles and soap, slaughtering animals for meat, tending egg and dairy production, spinning, weaving, sewing, cooking, and baking. Throughout the antebellum period, as food products became more readily available and prices fell (especially in rural areas), it became more economical to purchase items at local markets than to waste valuable labor on home production. And frequently during slack times, owners hired out their slaves to friends and neighbors who needed extra hands.

In the mind of a slave woman, field and household labor had both advantages and disadvantages, though rarely was her preference taken into account when determining her work. Age, work habits, and behavior influenced a job assignment. If the master viewed a domestic servant as obstreperous, slow-witted, or incompetent, she might be sent from the main house to the fields, to be disciplined by an overseer or slave driver. If she proved uncooperative in the fields, the bondwoman might be punished or transferred to a work house to labor on public projects. However, if a slave woman pushed too far, she might be "sold to Mississippi," a fate feared by all slaves who believed the worst conditions existed in the Deep South.

The principal advantage of field work was the opportunity to work beside others. Gangs of slaves enjoyed companionship, sometimes talking quietly, passing messages, singing, and sharing their dreams and woes. Some slave women worked in all-female gangs and benefited from a sense of sisterhood—or, on occasion, indulged in jealous outbursts. On the other hand, the heat, back-breaking labor, pesky insects, and long hours made outdoor work difficult and left slaves little time to call their own.

Household labor had its downside when performed under the constant scrutiny of a demanding white woman. Job satisfaction in this situation depended on the personal relationship between slave and mistress. Work conditions could be rigid, the hours were long, and in some cases, slaves could not return to their own quarters at night but had to sleep outside their mistress's door or at the foot of her bed. One slave woman who worked as a domestic stated that she married at thirteen so that she could escape her white mistress and return to the slave community at night to be with her husband. Advantages of domestic work included the occasional gift of dis-carded clothing or plate of leftover food provided at the end of the day, being privy to household secrets, which could be shared with the black community, and perhaps opportunities to snatch food from the larder. Some bondwomen enjoyed close relationships with kind mistresses, others faked intimacy with them, and still others found a harsh or overbearing white mistress too much to en-dure. Some slaves who felt that domestic work carried a higher status may have kept such sentiments to themselves to avoid fos-tering resentment within the black community.

Black women and children sometimes worked in heavy indus-tries such as lumber, sugar refining, or rice milling. Slave women apparently made up half of the labor force that built South Carolina's Santee Canal. They assisted in building Louisiana's levees. A few even worked in iron mines. Their owners might hire them out, or a factory owner might purchase several slaves or hire free blacks. Some industry owners preferred slaves to white labor-ers because they were easier to control. Mill owners often preferred women and children, for they were less expensive to rent or buy. But just as important were their skills, nimble fingers, and ability to perform some tasks better than men.

In their spare time, some slave women found ways to earn money by selling woven cloth or farm produce from their own gardens and serving as midwives. Women on plantations where the task system was used had greater autonomy and more free time to engage in such activities than did slaves working on gangs. Once they completed their assigned chores, the remaining hours of the day were theirs, and some fashioned hand-made goods and carried on a lively trade in local markets. Slave women living in towns and villages might earn extra money by cleaning hotels and boarding houses, doing laundry, or selling their sexual services in prostitution. Slave owners often permitted bondwomen to retain their earnings, seeing this as a positive incentive and allowing them to purchase an article of clothing or extra food. Some slave women carefully saved their meager earnings, hoping one day to accumulate whatever it might take to free themselves and their children.

Slave Protest

Though records of antebellum female slaves' involvement in overt rebellions or escape attempts are rare, slave women were success-ful in lessening their work load, protesting their situation, or de-ceiving an overseer or owner. As women, they had natural excuses to avoid work, begging time off by complaining about a difficult pregnancy or uncomfortable menstrual period. In some cases, these excuses were feigned; in others, they were real. Studies show that slave women earned an average of four to eight days off each month for menstrual problems and several days off during the last trimester of their pregnancies. No overseer or slave owner could distinguish accurately between those excuses that were le-gitimate and those that were pretense, and who wanted to take the chance and put a woman's fertility or fetus at risk? Probably the most common form of protest among slave women was truancy, where a woman would run away from a plantation for anywhere from a few hours up to a few weeks, hiding out in the woods, a cave or another slave cabin. This could be risky behavior since truants needed food, water, and shelter. Plantation owners might track the runaway slave with dogs or a slave patrol. Running off typically occurred after the slave had endured a whipping, sexual assault, or onerous work load, in an effort to heal body and soul, find privacy, or gain some control over her life. Sometimes, however, slave women ran away to visit a man living on another plantation or to have fun, perhaps attending a dance or religious meeting nearby. Slave women often helped one another hide by providing food and shelter and helping care for their children.

Slave owners had to tread a fine line in running an efficient plantation, allowing women time off to treat health problems while at the same time not wanting to appear too lenient. Owners always had an underlying fear that slaves might retaliate if pushed beyond their endurance. Canny slave women learned to judge the tolerance of their masters or overseers, pushing as far as they dared in order to improve their own situation. Many learned when to ask and when to keep quiet. Occasionally an overseer called a bondwoman up short if she complained once too often, punished her, and sent her back to the fields. Masters had to judge how far to prod their slaves without causing them to protest, run away, or retaliate.

How concerned masters were about the health of their female slaves varied by individual as well as by plantation needs. A glance at the high black fertility rates throughout the antebellum period suggests that owners were generally sensitive to slaves' needs, or at least concerned enough to protect their own economic interests by doing what was needed to ensure a successful pregnancy. On the other hand, a higher number of miscarriages and infant deaths in the 1850s seems to belie this suggestion of empathy and kindness. As cotton prices rose and competition increased during this decade, owners may have driven their slaves harder, consequently threatening the women's fertility and contributing to higher infant mortality.

Slaves learned to act cautiously as well. The threat of punishment or sale and the breakup of the family always loomed large and gave white males enormous power over their slaves. Since higher levels of productivity brought slaves no personal rewards, they saw no reason to work hard, only hard enough to avoid punishment. Travelers to the South and even residents of the region observed how sluggishly slaves labored, commenting on their shuffling feet, slow speech, and measured motions; and they concluded that slavery was unproductive. A former Virginian, in a letter to the New York *Daily Times,* wrote that even the best slaves perform "one-fourth of a white man's daily task" and require constant watching "to get even this small modicum of labour." Yet these observers failed to understand that work slowdowns were an effective and subtle form of slave resistance. Owners used various means to encourage more work. During peak labor demands, such as during cotton-picking season, owners and overseers might pressure or encourage their slaves by using the whip more often, or by promising them extra days off or gifts if certain goals were met.

White Women and Work

White farm wives and plantation mistresses were a critical part of the region's labor force as well. Most farm women worked beside their husbands and sons in the fields, performing strenuous jobs typically performed by slave women and men. Field work eroded the social distinction between free women and slaves. Although poor farm women tried to disassociate themselves from doing "slave work," a few living hand-to-mouth sometimes hired themselves out to a wealthy plantation owner to pick cotton or corn during harvest season. Farm wives also were responsible for domestic chores, including child care, cleaning (what little they had time for or cared about), cooking, sewing and mending, and washing. It is little wonder that many farm women were exhausted and run down by a lifetime of endless labor. Like slave women, they seldom received compensation or public recognition for their economic contributions.

In farm households that had no slaves, field work was men's and women's work. For farm families to maintain a degree of self-sufficiency, usually everyone in the family above a certain age had to work in the fields. Here, white women's field labor was typical rather than exceptional. James Sloan, who kept a journal detailing the work of each family member, noted that his teenage son and two daughters worked alongside him in the fields. They chopped and picked cotton and hoed, attending school only in August when work demands lightened. His wife also worked in the fields. Her only reprieve came when she suffered a miscarriage and again when she gave birth to a baby the following year. Sloan was more fortunate than some, for he hired a slave girl to help him plow, hoe, and harvest the crop when his wife was indisposed. A farmer gained status if he could hire or own slave laborers to keep his wife and daughters out of the fields.

What set apart elite white women from the majority of poor white women like those in Sloan's family was that they did not have to work in the fields, thus saving themselves from the debasing influences of field work. Yet even if they didn't work in the fields, plantation wives were rarely women of leisure, despite myths to the contrary. As Anne Firor Scott notes in her study of elite white women, *The Southern Lady,* most worked extremely hard. Only a handful of privileged women lived a life of glamorous ease. Sally Hampton, who wed Frank Hampton and married into one of South Carolina's wealthiest families, was one such woman. She led a seemingly privileged life. As newlyweds, Sally and Frank lived with his parents in an enormous mansion. Living on the Hampton plantation with its 300 slaves gave Sally a taste of wealth that few southerners ever realized. Sally spent her mornings visiting and writing letters, her afternoons napping, and her evenings attending dinner parties or balls, dressed in elegant silk gowns. Though she breastfed her infants, a servant woman dressed, washed, and tended the babies. Eventually, though, Sally assumed management of her own home, a task she tackled but felt ill prepared to handle. Still, even such indulged lives like Sally's were not as carefree as they seemed. Women like Sally were often in ill health and unable to fully participate in the running of a household. Some wives who seemed pampered were actually plagued by illness and had to lead a quiet life or even remain in bed. As noted earlier, many women experienced difficult pregnancies or lengthy postpartum recoveries. Annual bouts with malaria caused debilitation. Some mothers suffered from a prolapsed or fallen uterus (the falling of the uterus, sometimes through the vaginal opening) causing them intense pain, difficulty in walking, and incontinence. Surgery, still performed in a primitive fashion and without an understanding of the importance of cleanliness, could lead to infections and lifelong suffering.

In addition, drug habits led to a certain level of insensibility. Women addicted to laudanum were languorous and incapable of working. Calomel was the nineteenth century cure-all for most maladies. This mercury-based medicine, taken to cleanse the system and to cure various illnesses, led to bleeding gums and caused many antebellum women to suffer dental problems or to lose their teeth altogether while still young. Ann Raney Coleman, who took calomel for numerous fevers, described her reaction to the medicine. "I was so badly salivated that for several weeks I held my head in a position for the saliva to run out. . . . Pieces of flesh half as long as my finger would fall off the inside of my mouth." Mary Chaplin was another unfortunate invalid, spending almost seven years in bed until she died at the age of twenty-nine. The only visible contribution that Mary made to the household and family was to continue to bear children, despite her condition, and she delivered three babies while bedridden.

Plantation women in decent health, however, worked hard though they, too, received no public recognition. Eliza Robertson, who lived on a coastal Lousiana plantation, labored endlessly. She slaughtered hogs, made sausage, salted and prepared pork, chopped meat, made preserves and syrup, cleaned house, cut out curtains and clothing, mended, gardened, pruned, darned, killed rats, washed dishes, prepared mosquito netting, made diapers, and heard her children's school lessons. Lucy Shaw carried on many traditional domestic duties and assisted her husband in running their hotel in the frontier village of Galveston, Texas. In addition, she operated a small school for her own and the neighbors' children. Elite women handled grubby and exhausting tasks. One especially unpleasant but essential job that fell to women was overseeing each winter's hog butchering, a chore that privileged females like North Carolinian Anne Cameron and Matilda Fulton, wife of Arkansas's territorial governor, experienced. Though slaves performed much of the actual labor, white women participated, emerging bloody and exhausted after several weeks' work in the middle of winter. In addition, women also gardened, weeded, managed the dairy, knitted, sewed and mended endlessly, nursed sick children and slaves, and occasionally cooked. Plantation mistresses had to manage their domestic slaves, which proved a trying task for many. Though delicacy was touted as an ideal feminine characteristic, it had little to do with the reality of women's lives. The household needed strong women to take charge of demanding tasks. Jobs required skill or strength or both, and successfully completing certain duties must have provided women a degree of satisfaction. Women could not, and did not, expect to measure their productive worth by income or praise but rather by completing their tasks and ensuring the survival of their families.

Weaving, sewing, and mending clothes were nonstop duties. In their letters, women described cutting out shirts, shifts, and trousers from cloth, and mending torn clothing. Outfitting an entire plantation was an enormous responsibility and could involve cutting hundreds of yards of material and sewing dozens of individual items of clothing for both slave and white families. Some fortunate mistresses supervised a small staff of seamstresses after they had taken charge of cutting the cloth.

Young plantation wives, often unfamiliar with household management, typically experienced frustration during their early married years. In contrast to slave and farm women, privileged females with an academy education lacked appropriate training for their role as domestic managers and household laborers. Most learned on the job through trial and error. Women often complained about their inability to complete specific duties and their unfamiliarity with household demands and this new level of responsibility. Lucilla McCorkle, an especially self-critical North Carolina woman, complained that she "was not trained for householders" as she struggled with daily chores and young children. It was difficult to train servants if one could not set an example or establish standards.

As youngsters, privileged girls had been part of households where slaves performed the most tedious chores and mothers oversaw household management. Girls might be away at school during the period when they otherwise might have benefited from observing or participating in household chores. Plantation parents who indulged their children probably did their daughters a disservice. Fredrika Bremer, who visited Charleston, noted that "parents, from mistakes of kindness, seem not to wish their daughters to do anything except amuse themselves and enjoy liberty and life as much as possible. I believe that they would be happier if they made themselves more useful." Certainly her assessment proved true when those women ultimately married. Academies failed to teach practical lessons. Velvet painting and French lessons didn't prepare one to run a household. Those southern women who married as teenagers found their responsibilities all the more difficult. Adding to the problems a young wife faced was the progression of family demands. Relative newlyweds sometimes had to contend with limited resources, few or no slaves, demanding young children, and for the woman, difficulties in childbirth.

Work on the Frontier

Southern women who migrated to the frontier faced even greater challenges than those who stayed put. During the antebellum period, however, cheap land, economic incentives, and the cotton boom beckoned tens of thousands of southerners to the Southwest. "Alabama Fever" drew waves of southerners to Texas, Louisiana, Mississippi, Alabama, and Tennessee, especially following the War of 1812 and again following the economic crisis of the late 1830s. Native Americans, whom whites regarded as a nuisance and a barrier to the expansion of "civilization," were pushed further westward by the 1820s and 1830s. Poorer whites migrated to the piney woods, sand hills, and Piedmont areas, settling on inexpensive or free land that often resembled what they had left behind. Wealthier whites descended on lowland areas where cotton and sugar cane could thrive.

The cotton fever that bit men rarely affected southern women; most remained reluctant participants in the westward trek. As Joan Cashin argues, gender was an important issue in responding to westward migration. Many women balked at leaving home, kin and friends, and most found their new surroundings dismal and lonely. The journey itself could prove difficult, especially when traveling through land without roads or ferries. Attacks by Indians, bad weather, flooded streams and rivers, and wild animals added danger to any westward trek. Upon arrival, land needed clearing and trees felling before a home could be built. Sarah Fountain, who moved to Alabama in the 1830s, wrote of the isolation that typically afflicted southern women. Sarah found herself "in this strange country without house or home so far departed from my dear friends, and as yet I see nothing enticing in the place." It would take years to recreate the community that Sarah left behind. But wives had no choice; it was axiomatic that the dutiful wife followed her husband. One South Carolina woman tried to divorce her husband on grounds of desertion when he took the children and moved away to Louisiana. She refused to follow, claiming that he had promised before their wedding that she could always live near her mother. The legislature that heard her petition had no trouble determining that desertion was her problem, not his, and insisted that as a wife, she had a responsibility to follow him.

In migrating, southern white women gave up most of what they treasured: family, neighbors, familiar surroundings, churches, schools for their children, and often treasured possessions. Loneliness was a common complaint in moving to an uninhabited frontier area. M. L. Brown of Howard County, Missouri, wrote that almost all the visitors they entertained were men. "No person," she lamented, "my dear Sister[,] can realize the trouble and deprivation a person has to undergo who moves out here, but those who try it." She longed for the comforts and familiarity of her former home. Moving meant confronting new health problems and adjusting to unfamiliar surroundings and greater demands. Jane Woodruff and her husband left their comfortable Charleston home (and the graves of their four infants) in 1826 to live on his Florida land. They arrived to discover only a tiny log cabin and endless hardship. Their personal belongings had been lost at sea, and Jane had to beg the local Indians for food. Distemper killed dozens of their farm animals, and disease was rampant among many of their slaves. Jane, who was pregnant, had to work in the fields beside her husband. Their food deteriorated, and they found themselves eating maggot-infested meat and hominy. After Jane lost her baby in childbirth, life seemed to have little meaning.

Southern women like Jane Woodruff left a familiar, often comfortable existence and had to learn new skills for tackling demanding jobs. As James Oakes notes in his study of the southern planter class, *The Ruling Race,* luxurious dwellings were not possible for even privileged families on the move. Like the Woodruffs, most settled in one-room log cabins or simple frame structures that could be erected hurriedly. Women initially undertook the type of work their grandmothers had performed, such as cooking over an open fire and hauling water. Kitchens were large fireplaces at the end of the room, and chinked walls and roofs with a "great many air holes" let in more of nature than women desired. Bugs, mice, and snakes infested these structures. Women had to plant, harvest, and preserve food and maintain the family's self-sufficiency. Babies required constant watching, for new dangers abounded, including those from wild animals, open fires, polluted water, unfriendly Indians, and unfamiliar diseases. In most cases, frontier living remained primitive for years, and families struggled to recreate the lives they had left behind. Men eagerly invested their life savings into land and slaves, not into decent housing or amenities. Women were expected to cope. Though women were essential to survival on the frontier, moving westward did not necessarily foster their greater equality with men.

Yet for the fortunate, healthy, and hard-working settlers on the frontier, family wealth gradually accumulated and life improved. Building a larger home of brick or wood reflected a family's elevated status, though this could be a long time coming. Frontier towns grew, and women played a critical role in recreating the institutions and sense of community they had left behind. Yet elite frontier wives often had no choice but to play a major role in the household. Rebecca Boone, wife of Daniel, was often left alone in charge of their home, their ten children, and an assortment of kin and motherless children. Lucretia Hart Clay, wife of Henry Clay, bore and raised their eleven children, ran Ashland plantation, marketed produce, and made a significant amount of money. Henry spent his time politicking in Washington, D.C., and gambling away the plantation profits. Margaretta Mason Brown, wife of Senator John

Brown of Kentucky, demonstrated her capability by taking charge of their frontier home and making many decisions on her own. These may not have been roles that frontier women desired, but they apparently undertook them with a degree of determination and energy.

Migrating could be extremely hard on slave women. Slave-owners who moved westward sometimes took only a portion of their slaves with them. The long journey for slaves was a difficult one, for they never had the privilege of riding in a carriage or wagon. Even pregnant slave women walked the entire distance. Work demands intensified in the new location, for slaves had to clear land and build a home for the planter family and cabins for themselves. Living conditions were primitive during the initial months of settlement. A new climate, virulent and unfamiliar diseases, and strange foods took their toll on black as well as white women. White behavior toward blacks may have worsened on the frontier without the social and legal constraints that existed in more settled areas.

Paid Employment

A few southern women held paid jobs, though options were limited in a region that had made no major commitment to industrialize and in which a woman's place was in the home, not the workplace. However, some southern women had no choice but to work outside the home, especially free black and poor white women living in towns and cities. During his journeys through the South in the 1850s, Frederick Law Olmsted described poor white women in Columbus, Georgia, earning $8 to $12 per month working in textile mills. This translated into a few cents per day when working a typical six-day work week. From Alabama he described "scantily clad women and children shoveling iron ore and working as hard as any man." Factory jobs for women were rare, although some free black women worked as stemmers in tobacco factories. White teenage girls and widows and their children moved to the smattering of textile mill towns, though this industry was only in its nascent stage of development in the region by 1860. Textile mill work was poorly paid and could be demanding due to bad conditions and long hours. Free urban black women and immigrant and poor white women earned money by running laundries, serving as midwives, hiring out as seamstresses, running small businesses, taverns, and boarding houses, or earning wages as cooks, maids, or prostitutes. But they remained a minor part of the wage economy. In Petersburg, Virginia, according to Suzanne Lebsock, antebellum women never owned as much as 10 percent of all legitimate enterprises, though they often operated businesses without official sanction because they failed to purchase a license.

If they could work at home, women could successfully run a business while raising a family, though this was unusual and often implied a state of poverty. Urban white women dominated millinery and mantua-making jobs (by this period, mantua-making meant dressmaking). Milliners apparently occupied an elevated position among female laborers, earning a decent income using their knowledge of the latest European fashions to find the right silks, ribbons, and straw for their wealthy clients' stylish hats. Upon being widowed, a woman sometimes took over a family business such as a grocery store, tavern, or shop. White women who needed to stay home often opened their homes as boarding houses and managed to scrape by, feeding and housing transients as well as family members and acquaintances who came to visit. Jewish women in Savannah rarely worked outside the home but several contributed to the family income by taking in lodgers.

A number of southern white women taught school, and the percentage of females teaching in southern schools increased over time. Of all paid employment open to women, teaching commanded the greatest respect. Some mothers set up a school for their own children and engaged in what we today call home-schooling. More typical were young women who taught for a year or two between the end of their own schooling and marriage. Spinsters and widows might teach or serve as governesses throughout most of their lives. It took no additional education beyond an academy schooling to join the profession, merely the ability to stay ahead of one's pupils. The actual number of southern women who taught is unclear but was higher than any census indicated. Personal correspondence reveals a surprising number of women who moved in and out of the teaching profession. Although males and northern women formed a significant portion of southern teaching staffs, demand grew as many new academies opened during the antebellum period.

Women were desired as teachers because they were cheaper to hire than men and because educating the young was a natural extension of a female's maternal nature. Eliza Clitherall, a North Carolina plantation mistress, taught school when her husband died. Frances Bumpas, married to a minister and slave owner, resumed her teaching two months after bearing a child. She seriously pondered opening an academy as a "means of future support to myself and family." Due to her husband's inability to support the family with his medical practice, Dolly Lunt Burge had to teach school. When her husband died, she became a full-time teacher at a school in Madison, Georgia, until she remarried. The same was true of Catherine Ladd who served as both principal and teacher in several South Carolina schools. Her husband's floundering career as a portrait artist made Catherine's work essential to family survival. Jacob Mordecai ran a girls' school in Warrenton, North Carolina, between 1809 and 1818 and saved himself major expenses by employing his daughters as teachers.

Plantation women supplemented the family income by their involvement in market trade, producing and raising crops and garden produce for sale. This was not just an activity reserved for slaves and poor whites. Mississippian Minerva Hynes Cook and her husband owned eighty-seven slaves and a large plantation, but wealth did not detract from Cook's profitable endeavors. With the assistance of slaves, she created a lively trade selling surplus farm products, including turkeys, geese, eggs, sausage, melons, milk, and butter at the nearby Vicksburg market. Other women wove hats and baskets, and made clothing, candy, and baked goods which they peddled or sold in markets throughout the South.

A number of single women and widows owned and managed their farm or plantation, work that was critical to their own and their family's survival. As Anya Jabour reveals in her study of Elizabeth Wirt, women were capable of participating in the traditional male world of business. Wirt, who was fifty years old when her husband William died and already known as a keen businesswoman, now operated as a *feme sole* and made decisions on her own. She took over the family's struggling enterprises, facing some $20,000 in debts and an unproductive plantation. Wirt eventually negotiated back payments for her late husband's legal services, sold his law library, and administered his estate as his sole executrix. She dealt with banks and lawyers to maintain ownership of their home and plantation and to stave off bankruptcy. She even moved to Florida to oversee the property that William had purchased. Affected by the economic panic of 1837, she was forced to sell several personal articles. But the family and the Wirt property survived. Not until her later years did she turn over most of the family business to her brother.

A few southern women took up their pens and joined the "scribbling women" of the nineteenth century who produced romantic novels, essays, and poems. The antebellum South's literary endeavors never rivaled the North's, and the region failed to produce the kind of writers who emerged in the New England Renaissance. This was due in part to the fact that the region lacked large urban centers usually associated with the intellectual environment conducive to producing, publishing, and distributing books and journals. The South had yet to develop a female literary culture like the one that supported northern women writers. The few southerners who wrote for the public almost invariably resided in Charleston or a comparable urban center. Most of the South's literary energy, according to Drew Gilpin Faust, went into proslavery rhetoric. Few southern females ever achieved the renown of northern authors like Catharine Beecher or Lydia Maria Child, though some tried. Southern women certainly had the education to write professionally, but few made the effort. Most literate women poured their writing talents into letters and diaries, typically focusing on family events and addressing a familiar audience.

Probably the most famous southern women who gained both literary and political attention were Sarah and Angelina Grimké. These sisters found slavery so distasteful that they renounced their wealthy Charleston upbringing and moved to Pennsylvania, becoming actively involved in abolitionist and female reform. Among their works were Angelina's "An Appeal to the Christian Women of the South," published in 1836, and Sarah's "Epistle to the Clergy of the Southern States," written in 1837, both reviled in the South since they criticized slavery. Another wealthy Charlestonian, at the other end of the political spectrum, was Louisa Cheves McCord who embraced her upbringing as a southern woman and slave owner. She inherited her own plantation when only twenty and married a decade later. Her writings defended the white southern viewpoint on both slavery and women, upholding marriage as the most desirable goal for all females. McCord criticized as misguided those women who sought personal fame, and she ridiculed northern reformers. Her 1852 proslavery tract, "Enfranchisement of Women" challenged the women's suffrage movement, declaring it "but a piece with negro emancipation." She insisted that the South embraced God-given distinctions of sex and race and criticized the North as unnatural. Esther Cheesborough, also from South Carolina, became a writer of local renown, producing poems, short stories, and essays. She was somewhat of a rebel: she rejected her upbringing, became a teacher, and never married. Her writings portrayed women as strong, able to overcome adversity, cope with weak husbands, and survive disappointment. Caroline Gilman was a New Yorker who settled in Charleston with her husband. In the 1830s, she began a journal for children, eventually changing its focus to appeal to young women. The *Southern Rose-Bud*, later called *The Rose,* included poetry, essays, readers' letters, and Gilman's own writings. Catherine Ladd, under the alias of "Morna," wrote poems that were published in the antebellum South's most important periodical, *The Southern Literary Messenger.* Between 1830 and 1860, the South produced a dozen periodicals specifically for women—some short-lived—that provided female readers with moral instruction, poetry, and fiction and gave southern female authors an audience for their writings.

Another group of southern women writers who gained a brief moment of prominence were those who produced "Anti-Tom" novels, written in reaction to Harriet Beecher Stowe's *Uncle Tom's Cabin,* which appeared in 1852. These books defended the South and presented an appealing glimpse of the gentility of southern society and the inevitable comparisons between miserable northern laborers and happy southern slaves. Some of these women writers, like Gilman, Caroline Lee Hentz, and Mary Schoolcraft, were originally from the North but embraced the South's political and economic preferences.

Generally, though, occupational opportunities for southern women were limited. There was a stigma attached to the woman who worked in the public sphere, for it usually implied economic need or a family crisis. Women were supposed to marry and devote themselves to the home. Southern honor dictated that white men should support their wives and children. Few girls ever made plans that included a future beyond marriage and motherhood. Once married, the demands of children, household, and farm labor precluded thoughts of anything else, as did the cycle of pregnancies, confinements, nursing, and nurturing. A handful of radical northern women at Seneca Falls, New York, in 1848 may have demanded women's rights and access to a variety of occupations normally reserved for men; but for all but a few southern women, the task at hand was to make it through another day.

Nontraditional Roles

Some southern women ventured beyond the boundaries prescribed for them, while others made important contributions to the region, and still others proved women's independent capabilities. Single women, free black women, and widows, from choice or the inability to find a husband, usually had to work. Nearly all free black women who were single lived in towns or cities, where it was relatively easy to find a job. As noted earlier, finding a husband when eligible men were so scarce was another matter; other women preferred to remain single. Many of these black women were also heads of households and responsible for their children's survival. They lived and died in poverty, working for low wages that barely allowed them to scrape out an existence. They were the South's poorest of the poor and faced discrimination as both women and blacks.

Yet a handful of single black women did more than survive and actually accumulated or inherited some property and, in a few instances, even wealth. In fact, a larger percentage of free black women than free black men living in a city like Vicksburg, Mississippi, were property owners. (Whether this was typical or not will demand research on other antebellum communities.) Like some free black men, these women became landholders and, as single women, retained their own property and income. A few free black women were even slave owners. The wealthiest free black woman in Vicksburg owned eleven slaves in 1856, and her net worth in the 1860 census was listed as $2,100. Natchez had a solid class of free blacks, and some single women achieved a fair degree of status within the black community. As we have seen, Ann Battles Johnson, the widow of barber and land owner William Johnson, inherited considerable wealth when he died, including land, houses, and eight slaves valued in 1860 at $16,000. New Orleans had the largest population of free black women. They worked in a variety of occupations, and some held considerable property that they purchased or received as the result of a relationship with a white man. Apparently after 1830, owning property became increasingly difficult for free blacks throughout the South because of rising prices, more immigrants creating competition for jobs, and a more hostile racial climate.

Most single women, especially those who never married, faced difficulties carving out an acceptable role in the South, beyond serving as objects of charity. Family members often took them into their home where they assisted with childrearing, attended confinements, sewed, and performed household tasks. But some had to live alone, struggling to survive. Widows were in a better position than spinsters, for people were sympathetic to their condition.

Some southern widows like Elizabeth Wirt were amazingly plucky, probably discovering inner resources that they had never recognized while living under the care and control of a man. Older plantation women were in the unusual situation of having slaves to help them run their property. Slave-owning gave single elite southern women significant power as they aged, for they assumed control of a plantation rather than sinking into a state of dependency, the usual course for elderly women at the time. In 1854, Martha Gaffney's husband died just as the family was to migrate from South Carolina to the Red River area of Texas. She and her five children moved anyway. Gaffney sold the family property, packed and shipped all of their possessions, established credit with local Texas merchants, and took over management of the new plantation. With the aid of fifty-five slaves, she produced 115 bales of cotton her first year, and by 1861, her net worth was $45,000. She also maintained a fine lifestyle, shopping in New Orleans for crystal, fine furniture, and fancy silk dresses.

As a single woman running a plantation, Martha Gaffney was not as exceptional as one might think. No historian yet has undertaken a study of women like Gaffney, but when accomplished, it will surely reveal some interesting variations on the existence of southern women. A survey of 440 South Carolina plantations with more than 100 slaves each showed that women were the owners in fifty cases. A surprising number of free black and white women in Louisiana were listed as plantation owners in the federal censuses of 1850 and 1860. Recall Frances Bumpas and her successful editing of the Methodist newspaper *Weekly Message* for twenty years after her husband died. Natalie de Delage Sumter ran her plantation single-handedly, without an overseer, an enormous undertaking (and also an illegal one in some states, for single women were supposed to hire an overseer). Rachel O'Connor of Louisiana married when she was fifteen, bore one child, and was widowed at eighteen. She made an unfortunate choice the second time, marrying an alcoholic who eventually drank himself to death but left Rachel a fairly wealthy widow at forty-eight. She hired an overseer, dealt with unscrupulous creditors, and worked hard producing cotton. Rachel also was acquisitive and aggressive, purchasing whatever adjacent property she could get her hands on. Apparently she was an exceptionally kind mistress, personally ensuring the health and well-being of each of her slaves; none of them ever tried to run away. When she died in 1846, Rachel left an estate of $33,000. What Rachel and several other single women proved was that they could succeed in the southern male world, using their own skills, bright minds, and personal ambition; it was a lesson that far more southern women were to learn during the Civil War.

Another topic that has attracted recent scholarly attention is the role that antebellum southern women played in the traditional male world of southern politics. Of course, southern women did not have the prerogative to vote, serve on juries, or hold office, but they found other means to address and express their political views. Female involvement in politics seems to defy the ideal characteristics of a southern lady and challenge the view of them as sequestered quietly within the home. A few scholarly works, including Elizabeth Varon's study of Virginia, *We Mean to be Counted,* argue that southern women evidenced more political acumen and involvement than most historians have recognized. Women played an important role as spectators at militia rituals and parades, for their presence helped to validate these masculine enterprises. As symbols of virtue and morality, women participated in parades, perhaps dressed in white gowns and riding on a wagon bedecked with garlands. They made banners, flags, and uniforms to support and celebrate a local militia unit. Demonstrating a true public spirit, Ann Pamela Cunningham founded the Mount Vernon Association in 1853 to undertake a fundraising campaign to save George Washington's home, Mt. Vernon. The organization promoted its fundraising efforts in magazines like *Godey's Lady's Book* and the *Southern Literary Messenger.* Such advertising proved effective; Alabama women responded by sending $1,000, which one woman had collected in a single day.

Women's public and political activities changed throughout the antebellum period and moved beyond charitable activities and temperance efforts. In the 1830s, some women demonstrated an interest in the American Colonization Society, believing that it might put an end to slavery or at least rid the region of disruptive free blacks. In the 1840s, the Whig Party articulated a new concept of civic duty that sought to incorporate women, insisting that they could contribute to party politics and soften and elevate the traditional rough-and-tumble image of politics. Virginia women eagerly rallied behind the political efforts of Henry Clay. Whigs attracted a number of Virginia and Tennessee women who attended party rallies, marched in parades, sewed banners, wrote speeches and essays and inculcated family members with Whig values. A Whig parade in Kingsport, Tennessee, included 1,000 male and 1,000 female participants, and single women wore sashes demanding, "Whig husbands or none." An especially political woman was Sarah Polk, wife of James Polk, who served as his unofficial campaign manager by stumping Virginia on his behalf and organizing his political efforts there. (The fact that she was both competent and childless undoubtedly aided her efforts.) Yet this visible female activism in the South seemed to decline by the late 1840s as northern female reformers demanded abolition and women's rights, putting women's public roles in a light that seemed to threaten southern society. Nevertheless, southern women found new outlets. As southern nationalism grew, women became staunch defenders of their region, just as they would do with greater vehemence when the Civil War began.

Interracial and Class Relationships

The bonds that might have united black and white women were most tested in their work roles. But even then, relationships proved tentative at best. Paul Escott's study of slave testimony shows that neither black nor white women had a more favorable attitude toward the other. Yet as wives, mothers, and laborers, black and white women shared similar experiences. They bore, nursed, and raised children, worked extremely hard, embraced their religion, and suffered ill health. They both lived under the dominance of southern white men. And yet, an enormous chasm separated their worlds and kept them from developing a sense of sisterhood and mutual support. Distrust, jealousy, racism, and a tradition of oppression were ever-present. Black women felt more handicapped by racial than by sexual oppression and maintained their strongest ties to the black community. Until the Civil War, most white women accepted slavery; some defended it as well. Those who benefited by owning slaves recognized that their situation and class position depended on slavery.

Slave women's reactions to white women, and especially to their mistresses, varied significantly. WPA (Works Progress Administration) oral interviews and slave narratives provide clues about these relationships. Yet it is difficult to determine if these sources reflected the general sentiments of black women. Slave narratives, written or narrated by those who escaped, generally addressed a northern audience, trying to convince their readers of the horrors of slavery. Some accounts were highly dramatic and played up the vulnerability of slave women's sexuality and the difficulties black women had in fulfilling their maternal roles. Interviews with former slaves suffered from just the opposite problem; the passage of time had often filtered out former slaves' harsher memories. Moreover, since whites usually interviewed former slaves, those blacks who resided in the South in the 1930s might have been hesitant to openly express anger towards a former owner. Blacks had learned well to hide their feelings in order to protect themselves. Thus, for conflicting reasons, the principal sources for learning of slave women's reactions toward their owners must be read with care. Nevertheless, in general, black women did not identify with their mistresses. African Americans lived, worked, and socialized with other slaves. They all shared a common enemy. Few regarded their owners as paternalistic. When whites gave them a gift or otherwise acted in a benevolent manner, most slaves assumed that something bad was about to happen or that their owners wanted something more. To slaves, both white men and women represented oppression. Yet when they had a problem, slaves were more likely to turn to white women than white men, for they believed that mistresses were more sensitive and caring—albeit also less powerful than men.

As managers of domestic servants, mistresses came in closer contact with their slaves than did their husbands. Thus, planters' wives had more opportunity to react to and comment on slave women. They usually wrote about an individual rather than the slave community or system as a whole. Some white women were extremely affectionate toward black women and lovingly commented on them in their personal writings. Some mistresses acted in a paternalistic manner, believing that as caretakers, they were to uplift those whom they perceived as ignorant and childlike. Their feelings of racial superiority were often couched in benevolent language. Other mistresses expressed frustration, anger, and even jealousy toward female slaves. White mistresses might be ambivalent about slavery despite the benefits it brought to their lives. As Lucy Muse Welton Fletcher of Middleburg, Virginia, commented in 1856, "Sometimes I think that I shall probably be subject to the trial of having servants about me as long as I live. I feel a kind of desperation that is difficult to overcome." In a sense, she felt trapped by her responsibilities and frustrated at the burdens of supervising household servants. Because Fletcher assumed she was a kind mistress, she expressed surprise that her servants failed to express gratitude toward her benevolent behavior.

Of course, racism was not confined to white southerners, and conversely, a small number of southern women identified with abolitionist ideals. Northerners enacted discriminatory laws toward their free blacks, and outsiders who came to the South sometimes had difficulty hiding their intolerance. Fanny Kemble, the famous British actress and abolitionist, visited her husband's Georgia plantations and was horrified to discover that her husband was a slave owner. Unlike most observers, Kemble was sympathetic to the plight of female slaves, and she tried to improve their situation. Despite her sensitivity, however, her journal entries frequently included condescending remarks on slaves' filthy clothing and cabins, childlike behavior, and dependence on whites.

Historians have debated the issue of how kind mistresses were toward their slaves, especially when compared to men's behavior, but they have yet to reach a consensus. Many mistresses showed kindness and affection toward particular domestic servants, and they felt personally responsible for beloved slaves. Whenever Mary Jones was away from home, she sent letters with "howdys" to all the servants and inquired about their health and well-being. Rachel O'Connor's personal nursing of ill slaves was touching and sincere. Sometimes white women included slave women in their wills, leaving them money or items of clothing, occasionally even manumitting them or restricting the terms of their sale to prevent the breakup of a family. Some mistresses detested punishing slaves for bad behavior (but carried through nevertheless). Others mourned the death or sale of a particular slave or the frequency with which slave families were disrupted when a parent was sold. Like Fanny Kemble, some pleaded with their husbands to improve living conditions or provide additional time off from work for poor health. Though often visibly saddened that slave mothers had so little time to spend with their children, white mistresses did not translate these sentiments into lighter work or shorter hours for their bondwomen. Some white women like the Grimké sisters taught their maids to read, breaking state laws by doing so. And yet these sympathetic responses never produced greater challenges to slavery nor any individual protests that could have interfered with plantation profits. As Elizabeth Fox-Genovese argues in *Within the Plantation Household,* southern plantation women upheld the system because they benefited from it. Their wealth and privilege derived from the toil of slaves.

Southern women responded with ambivalence toward slaves and the slave system. Elizabeth F. Perry of Greenville, South Carolina, had eleven slaves but found the situation rife with tension. "No one could be kinder to their servants than we are," she wrote, "and yet they are an unhappy, ill-natured, discontent set; always wrangling among themselves and displeased with their owners. The fault is with us, that we give our servants too little to do and are not strict enough with them." Like some owners, the Perrys refused to use corporal punishment on their slaves, but Elizabeth concluded that this extent of kindness did not work well if one was to ensure obedience and guarantee hard work from slaves. Miriam Brannin Hilliard of Chicot County, Arkansas, whose husband owned 131 slaves, reached a similar conclusion but took steps to force obedience. "Idleness is the devil's workshop, and they have abundant time to hatch plenty of mischief," she complained. "I believe it to be my duty, so long as I own slaves, to keep them in proper subjection and well employed."

Yet a woman like Grace Brown Elmore of a distinguished, wealthy South Carolina family, was convinced that her affection for at least one slave was profound. Since childhood, she had her own slave woman, Mauma Binah, to care for her every need. When Binah died, Elmore depicted her as a noble servant. "I loved her dearly," she wrote in her journal, and she now wanted to erase "each feeling of coolness, every unkind thought or cold tone I ever had." Elmore regretted that she had not acted toward her slave in a more charitable, loving manner. How Binah felt about Elmore is unknown, but it is easy to imagine she did not share feelings of deep affection toward her mistress.

What is striking about most white mistresses who expressed affection for particular slaves is that they rarely pondered critical moral questions publicly or seriously considered trying to abolish the system altogether until the Civil War. Even those women who appeared to be outwardly benevolent usually accepted the oppression and lowly status of slaves. They were raised to believe in slavery and regard it as a normal condition. Most honestly believed that the system worked well for all concerned and provided the South with a superior form of civilization. Lessons inculcated from birth were hard to overthrow. Many southerners probably agreed with Thomas Roderick Dew, president of William and Mary College, who claimed that slavery actually elevated the southern white woman, for she was "no longer the slave but the equal and idol of man," able to lead a delicate, privileged life.

A mistress's benevolence toward slaves, when it existed, was easy to maintain when slaves behaved the way they were supposed to, but next to impossible when they behaved in an indolent or defiant manner. The kindest of mistresses could break into a rage toward a slothful servant or over a burned dinner. Close interaction between slaves and their mistress could foster tension and the unleashing of frustration over work that was poorly executed or never completed. These breakdowns became strikingly evident as slavery disintegrated toward the end of the Civil War. Mary Jones, one of the kindest slave owners, acted in a caring and loving manner toward her slaves, whom she considered almost part of her extended family. And yet, at the end of the war, slaves began to leave the Jones plantation, seeking their freedom. Jones, like so many other southern slave owners, was horrified to learn that her most devoted house servant had left, and she bitterly described the woman as ungrateful. The helpless slaves, whom Jones had supported for so long, in her eyes apparently had betrayed her. Slaves, she discovered, disliked their involuntary servitude, despite what she had been taught to believe and however kindly she had acted toward them. She was shocked to discover that her slaves could prove "false and rebellious against all authority or restraint." Given the chance to respond like free human beings, slaves did not react the way that southern whites desired. Most slave mistresses failed to perceive the overall inhumanity of their system. The challenges that came in 1865 were almost too much to endure.

White women were just as likely to disparage their slaves. Many mistresses described their frustrations in trying to manage slaves and criticized their work habits, clothing, body odor, and slovenly manners. White women expressed annoyance at having personally to instruct and oversee slaves who seemed to have little incentive to work hard. The situation that created the greatest friction was suspected miscegenation between a husband or son and a bondwoman. As noted earlier, mistresses took their frustration out on the victim, rarely choosing to confront their husbands.

Though white mistresses could be just as cruel as white men, it is doubtful that they were any more racist towards their servants, despite the ever-present possibility for antagonistic feelings and frayed tempers. Since white plantation mistresses were in closer contact with bondwomen than were white men, they had to deal with their feelings on a daily, even hourly, basis. White men were more detached in overseeing the entire plantation, and most slaves recognized male power and were less likely to challenge the master than they were the mistress. Southern white women had slaves in their homes, cleaning their furniture, watching their babies, cooking their food, and sometimes sleeping outside their bedchamber. This was intimate living, and many things could go wrong. Mistresses criticized slaves who stole, ignored their babies, failed to clean properly, and disobeyed orders. Women lashed out at slaves who worked too slowly, misunderstood directions, or acted in an insolent manner. Enraged women were known to attack their domestic slaves with knives, knitting needles, or even boiling water. White women were sometimes sadistic toward slaves, as were white masters. A Florida woman reported that her landlady was brutish toward her slaves. "Sometimes she whips them till her strength gives out, and then calls her sister to finish it for her," she observed sadly.

Though white women could be cruel, slave women knew that mistresses never wielded as much power as did white men. Masters often showed little interest in household management and left the monitoring of domestic work and slave behavior to their wives. Probably sensing this, a bondwoman was far more likely to challenge her mistress than the master. In confronting a white woman, a bondwoman questioned the system that oppressed her, something that a white woman was not willing or able to do. Perhaps having less to lose emboldened black women. Certainly desperation, frustration, and anger toward their oppressor prompted such actions. Undoubtedly their inner strength gave them courage. Some slave women took out their feelings on white women whom they momentarily could overpower.

Slave interviews reveal cases of black women exhibiting spirited aggressiveness. In one instance, mere words hit the mark. A slave mistress became increasingly angry with the family cook for failing to produce dinner on time. Entreaties to speed up preparation, followed by shouts and reprimands, did little good. The black woman finally responded "I works all I can." She then threw in the ultimate insult, telling the white woman that her former mistress, the master's first wife, had been far kinder. "We almighty sorry our Mis't is dead," the cook declared. The white woman could only retreat and weep. In another case, physical violence erupted. A mistress threatened a slave woman, Fannie, who was known for her volatile temper. Fannie fought back, and the two women wrestled in the kitchen and then in the yard. Fannie ripped the clothes off her mistress, leaving her virtually naked. Help came only when cries attracted attention. Another slave girl, after being reprimanded, turned on her mistress, threw her down, and beat her face repeatedly. A neighbor predicted that the girl would be hanged, though the actual outcome is unknown. In one unusual and extreme example, a slave woman's boldness actually won her freedom. The mistress of Silvia DuBois scolded her for her work. Silvia sassed her, the mistress hit her, and Silvia punched her with a closed fist, sending her flying. Silvia's master got involved, scolded the slave woman, but also assessed the situation realistically, knowing that selling a feisty slave woman like Silvia would be difficult. He told Silvia to take her child and leave as a free woman for New Jersey. These slave women, only a handful among many, had been pushed too far and reacted in the only way they knew how. Their frustration probably stemmed less from the precipitating incident than from an accumulation of injustices including overwork, inadequate food, exhaustion, and possibly the sale of a husband or child.

Finally, a topic that deserves more scholarly attention is an understanding of white women's relationships across class boundaries. Privileged southern women had no trouble making class distinctions when skin color was the defining factor. Limited sources and scattered comments suggest that elite southern white women had their limits in terms of whom they would befriend and whom they would interact with on familiar terms. Beyond the give and take of family dynamics and the benevolent gestures that some white women made to assist the downtrodden, elite southern women rarely reached out to befriend or interact with poor white women.

Research suggests, in fact, that privileged white women were more likely to express and uphold a sense of class superiority than were men. Many southern men interacted with a wide range of male acquaintances in their business transactions, depended on various men's skills as blacksmiths, overseers, and wagon wrights, and often encountered a broad variety of men in public spaces. A male plantation owner could not snub or ignore yeomen farmers and poor neighbors who might vote and had a stake in the South's political and economic future. Wealthy women, on the other hand, living in a more sheltered environment, seldom occupied the same space as their poor female counterparts. Poor white women rarely interacted with elite women, in part because they had little time to socialize other than attend church and probably would have felt uncomfortable doing so. Wealthy women probably had little desire to socialize with anyone far beneath them. They were less dependent upon the poor than were men; lacking political power, they had no need to court poor women's support. Elite women felt little compunction about touting class privilege—through the clothes they wore, the activities they engaged in, and the negative comments some wrote about lower-class women. A planter woman tried to maintain a social circle representing those of her elite station.

Those Who Questioned Slavery

How readily did outsiders who moved to the South accept its ways? White women who were most likely to examine slavery, question it, and write about it were those from the North who married southern slaveholders. Their feelings are instructive, though marrying into privilege certainly compromised some women's perspectives. Many nineteenth-century women had also been well trained to accept their husband's controlling influence.

Some northern women who moved South often came to accept and even defend slavery. For instance, Tryphena Blanche Holder Fox ventured to Mississippi to take a job as governess to a plantation owner's children. She later met and married the son of another well-to-do planter. Fox neither denounced slavery nor adopted an abolitionist stance but admitted to her mother in 1856 that "ranting abolitionists" might think she had become "a southern monster." She realized that slaveowning was a part of her life as an elite southern woman and gave her the status she craved. Like many southern women, Fox could easily become impatient when slaves were ill-behaved, lazy, or disobedient.

Some of these white women who moved to the South were dubious of the system's benefits. Sally Hampton, who gained all the advantages of a leisured life, noted that "the responsibilities of slave holding and the care and anxieties of a mistress particularly, seem almost an impossible burden." New Englander Rebecca Pilsbury, who settled in Texas, discovered that she and her husband had little success managing their slaves. In a telling comment, she concluded that slaves were far happier than their masters. Lucy Shaw rented several blacks to assist with their Galveston hotel, but she also hired an English couple to serve as family servants. She found slaves unmannerly, overly familiar, and "the laziest creatures you ever saw." But such sentiments did not prevent the Shaws from using slave labor. Mary B. Carter, wife of Hill Carter of Charles County, Virginia, had wedded into one of the state's most illustrious families. From their 4,000-acre Shirley Plantation, she quietly confessed her abolitionist tendencies. "O, I wonder how any one can approve of slavery, or not feel that in our enlightened age, it is a great sin, national and individual, when it can be avoided." Obviously these were views she could not share with her husband, nor with many white southerners for that matter.

Yet others embraced the sacred institution. When a group of British women, allegedly under the direction of the Duchess of

Sutherland, wrote an "Address to the Christian Women of America" criticizing slavery, Julia Tyler of Virginia responded with a ringing defense of the system. Her letter appeared in a Richmond newspaper, and Tyler became a southern heroine despite the fact that she was a former New Yorker. Sarah Williams, also a New York woman, was initially skeptical about the system, but she defended slavery during the Civil War. Many women who moved South expecting to confirm their disapproval of the system and to find slaves treated poorly, instead came to accept what they found, apparently not all that bothered by the oppression that surrounded them.

Some women born in the South exhibited a degree of ambivalence as well. A slave owner like Frances Bumpas was grieved by slavery, no doubt due to her deep Christian spirit as well as general frustration with her own slaves. Bumpas concluded that slaves were "a continuous source of trouble. They need constant driving, they are the source of more trouble to house-keepers than all others things, vexing them and causing much sin." Anna King of Georgia believed that her slaves had a negative influence on her children, causing them to be lazy and tyrannical. Virginian Anne Randolph Page opposed slavery on religious principles, and she freed her slaves upon becoming a widow in 1826. A few southern couples tried to manumit their slaves, but by the late antebellum period this was more difficult than one might imagine. Most states passed laws that forbade manumissions or insisted that freed slaves go elsewhere, or they refused to admit free blacks from other states. Southern women were unlikely to protest publicly such statutes, since such a political stance was unladylike and also increasingly unacceptable as a practical matter as the region became more defensive about slavery. And those women who might have been most likely to question or protest—southern farm wives who owned no slaves—were generally silent. They accepted slavery, believing that it had little impact on their lives; most desired eventually to become slave owners themselves.

The Civil War would make such feelings irrelevant. In 1861 a region that embraced the right to own slaves and defended a citizen's prerogative to move anywhere in the nation with human property would go to war to protect its sacred institution. War turned the South upside down, including the lives of its women.

CHAPTER FIVE

Southern Women and the Confederacy

By the time the Civil War began, southern women's hardiness had been well tested. Yet four long years of hardship and sacrifices lay ahead, followed by a dozen challenging years of Reconstruction. As historians know well, wars invariably affect those on the home front, forcing women to adopt new roles and undertake greater responsibilities in the absence of men. The Civil War was no exception. Because most of the war was fought on southern soil, it had a greater impact on all women there than it had on their northern counterparts.

For anyone interested in understanding the female experience during the Civil War, manuscript sources are rich and extensive. A number of scholars have made use of these sources and examined the war by looking at gender, studying females who carried on, raised their children, and produced the food, clothing, and supplies needed to support the war effort. Sensing their changing world and wanting to communicate with loved ones, a number of southern women (at least those with the ability, time, and resources) wrote extensively, leaving a rich profusion of diaries and letters. In addition, oral narratives from the twentieth century provide personal sources by former slaves who experienced the home front first hand.

The Civil War altered the South in nearly every respect. The female character of the region changed profoundly, as hundreds of thousands of men left to join the Confederate Army. Mobilization of white southern men was high, due in part to conscription laws and patriotic fervor. But it was also due to the region's slave labor force, which could perform much of the essential farm and factory labor, thus freeing more white men to take up arms. Nearly three-quarters of all eligible men served in the Confederate Army at some point during the four-year conflict.

Elite White Women

Once war broke out in April 1861, privileged women had to face decisions and responsibilities they had never before considered. Many were now left alone, without a husband or father to oversee agricultural production, manage slaves, and help meet family and household needs. These tasks became a woman's responsibility. Females now had to make important decisions related to planting and harvesting crops, as well as balance budgets, make essential purchases, oversee farm production, sell their produce, and take charge of children and slaves. Many had to learn basic but unfamiliar skills, such as how to cook, chop wood, and perhaps use a gun. More now worked in the fields to ensure family survival. While a man's patriotic duty to defend the Confederacy was clearcut, women entered unfamiliar, often unpleasant terrain, and they struggled to understand what they had to do and how to succeed at the myriad tasks before them.

The Civil War further politicized southern women. Though unable to vote, females evidenced little shyness in expressing strong opinions. Lincoln's election in 1860, the emotional debates over secession, and the meaning of the southern cause fostered intense political feelings among women. Southern men assumed that white women would uphold the Confederate cause, and few could have been disappointed with their initial responses. Many exhibited fervent feelings toward the events unfolding around them.

From the moment that secession and war threatened, southern women responded passionately to military and political events and became more visible and outspoken. During the 1860 Democratic Convention in Charleston, the Petigru women sat in Institute Hall and watched delegates from eight southern states, unable to agree on a suitable presidential candidate, march out of the meeting. The election of Abraham Lincoln in November 1860 elicited widespread fears throughout the region. Southern women were stunned by this and predicted that the nation was now headed for total ruin under the leadership of a Republican President. Georgian Mary Jones could scarcely contain her ire and even welcomed the idea of war, for "if it must come, [it] would be preferable to submission to Black Republicanism." South Carolina's vote to secede in December 1860 created a heady time in Columbia, the state capital. Women and men there took to the streets and celebrated their state's decision. Florida women decorated their hats with palmetto cockades to show support for South Carolina's stance on secession. At the secessionist convention in Tallahassee, Florida, women packed the galleries and cheered the outcome when delegates voted to join the Confederacy. The Confederate victory at Fort Sumter caused many southern women a moment of jubilation.

Yet other women expressed a different response as disunion threatened. Some questioned the wisdom of southern states severing ties with the nation and the Constitution. Anxiety surfaced as they envisioned widespread destruction and death that war could bring. Southern women, like men, were not of one mind about secession and war, and women feared the impact that war could have on their home and family. Some hoped that cooler heads would prevail and curb what seemed to be the South's hasty move toward disunion. Amanda McDowell of Tennessee felt that secession was wrong. "Oh God! That such things should be in a Christian land," she wrote, "that men should in their blindness rush so rashly on to ruin . . . but drag along with them so many thousands who will rush into the fury with blind enthusiasm, never stopping to question whether it be right or wrong. . . ."

Others worried that families might be split by members' loyalty to one side or the other. The Petigru family faced this dilemma, for the family patriarch, James Petigru, was loyal to the Union and, in fact, was probably South Carolina's most prominent and loyal Unionist. His daughter, Caroline Carson, shared her father's sentiments but prompted the rest of her family's disapproval when she moved to New York and took up with northern friends. The Robert Smith Todds of Lexington, Kentucky, was another family split in its loyalty. Mary Todd Lincoln supported the Union; eight of her fourteen siblings and step-siblings were loyal to the Confederacy. Yet whatever initial fears they harbored, most southern women, once their state had voted to secede, ultimately supported the Confederacy and its government.

Throughout the war, plantation mistresses continued to be political creatures and expressed strong opinions. Their letters and diaries are sprinkled with lively opinions and comments on political and military figures and major events that unfolded. Women second-guessed military campaigns, and they criticized or praised various military leaders for their actions and decisions in particular battles. They continued to denounce "black" Republicans and Yankee soldiers and reacted to perceived or real injustices inflicted by the North. In the eyes of many southern women, Yankees were vile people. Sparing no words, Grace Brown Elmore wrote, "My God! That such a race should blot the earth." As the South began to lose the war, she feared a future dictated by Yankee policies. Even at the bitter end, many women still remained loyal to the Confederate nation. With the fall of Columbia, South Carolina, in 1865, Emma LeConte noted the United States flag now flying over the state house. She reacted to it with disgust, calling it "That hateful symbol of despotism."

Unlike northern women, many southern women witnessed or confronted the actual horrors of war. For those in or near areas that became battlefields, the war took its toll. Families living near the Stone's River battlefield near Murfreesboro, Tennessee, found their homes transformed into Union and Confederate hospitals or scarred by cannon balls that left holes in exterior walls. Near Front Royal, Virginia, Lucy Buck witnessed war being waged first hand. Battles were fought in the front yard of Bel Air, the

Buck family plantation. Buck yearned for male protection, fearing bullets and cannon balls less than marauding Union and Confederate soldiers who frequently camped in her father's fields and demanded food and other provisions from her family.

Elite women demonstrated their patriotism by undertaking collective efforts to assist the Confederacy. With the firing on Fort Sumter, women across the South quickly organized soldiers' relief societies and sewing groups to produce essential items and raise money for the cause. Rural and urban women established hundreds of female wartime associations. The most popular activities reflected tasks that fell within women's domestic sphere—sewing clothing and knitting socks for soldiers and producing and preparing food for the battlefront. In July 1861, forty-two women gathered at a church in Chapel Hill, Louisiana, to form what became known as the Ladies' Volunteer Aid Society of the Pine Hills. The group wasted no time in electing officers, established a name for the group, set a membership fee of one dollar, and engaged in their patriotic endeavors. Mrs. Fleming Nobles urged fellow members to dedicate themselves to the tasks ahead. "Do not think that we cannot do anything" she insisted. "We can do much to assist our countrymen. We can knit socks and make all kinds of clothing . . . we can prepare pickles and fruit to send to them . . . and above all we can pray." Like tens of thousands of women across the South, Chapel Hill ladies recognized that their domestic skills and energy could be put to good use.

Like-minded women gathered to stitch uniforms, flags, and banners, roll bandages, knit socks, and prepare food. Mary Jones helped organize the women of Liberty County, Georgia, into an association to raise money to purchase cloth and sew uniforms. She also dried herbs from her garden and sent packets of them to Confederate physicians. Women sewed coverings for sandbags that were used to protect coastal areas. In Montgomery, Alabama, Jewish women formed the Hebrew Ladies' Sewing and Benevolent Society. By the end of 1862, these women had knitted 114 pairs of socks for Confederate soldiers. Females in Shreveport's Military Aid Society collected wool and cotton for soldiers' socks and blankets. The Florida legislature appropriated tens of thousands of dollars to purchase cloth, much of which they turned over to ladies' societies for making into uniforms. As the Confederate government gradually took over the responsibility of making and distributing military uniforms, female organizations turned their efforts to sewing for family members and men in local regiments.

Women also stepped out of their traditional female sphere by undertaking nontraditional tasks, such as gathering scrap iron for the construction of gunboats. The women of Savannah prepared cartridges for muskets and cannons. Females became experts at soliciting money and holding fundraising events. They organized fairs and donated their jewelry to raise money for the southern cause. The Women's Relief Society of Tennessee raised money by presenting a series of tableaux* and concerts in order to raise funds to purchase artificial limbs for disabled soldiers. Women in aid societies like the Greenville (S.C.) Ladies' Association set up a wayside home to care for convalescing soldiers.

Some of these volunteer associations lasted throughout the entire Civil War; others disbanded within a year or two. Reasons for their demise reflected the realities of war—Union soldiers occupying the area, demanding responsibilities that left women little free time, female services no longer being needed, or war disrupting travel and making it impossible for women to gather. While these female associations and the tasks they undertook reaffirmed traditional roles, their existence empowered women, defining their duties as separate and apart from men and demonstrating what women could achieve as they organized and ran their own organizations. In an all-female setting, women made new friends, shared gossip and advice, discussed the war, and undoubtedly sympathized with and worried about men on the battlefront. For the first time, many southern women found an outlet in which they could engage in activities with other women, fostering a common female identity. Women in the urbanized Northeast had long enjoyed such opportunities, but most privileged southern white women had lived in relatively isolated circumstances and focused on family, home, and church. Patriotic sentiments encour-

---

*An entertainment consisting of staged and costumed scenes, illustrating, for example, scenes from history or mythology.

aged Confederate women collectively to support the cause and, in the process, fostered female identity.

Women also aided the war in more public venues. They watched and participated in parades, cheered brave soldiers and sent them off with the banners and uniforms they had made, and prepared food which some of them delivered to troops camped nearby. Women apparently were effective at publicly shaming those men who refused to join the Confederate army. They also entered the public arena as canteen workers, dispensing food and beverages to wounded soldiers. Privileged females gave up their finery and proudly donned dresses of calico or homespun, cloth that slave and farm women traditionally wore. This fashion statement became a visible, patriotic gesture that gave evidence of one's loyalty. As Kate Stone commented, "Fashion is an obsolete word."

Some women took bolder action by trying to undermine federal efforts. With the Union occupation of New Orleans in 1862, women in the Crescent City mocked Union soldiers and spat in their faces, and one even poured the contents of her chamberpot on an officer. So bothersome were these females that Union General Benjamin Butler issued Order 28, stating that any local woman who persisted in this unbecoming behavior would be treated like "a woman of the town plying her avocation" and arrested. Federal officials arrested a brave sixteen-year-old Sara Jane Smith for cutting and destroying four miles of Union telegraph wire near Springfield, Missouri. They sentenced her to be hanged, but the punishment was commuted to life imprisonment. Apparently poor health led to her release five months later.

A few southern women, out of patriotism, a desire for adventure or to follow their husband into battle, changed their identity and joined the Confederate Army. It is estimated that some 400 women from the North and South did just this. Mary Ann Pitman of Chesnut Bluff, Tennessee, became Lieutenant Rawley and served with the infantrymen she recruited for Nathan Bedford Forrest. Mrs. Malinda Blalock enlisted in the 26th North Carolina Regiment as Sam Blalock. The identity of most of these women was not discovered until they became sick or were wounded. In at least one surprising case, a southern woman managed to fool everyone until she gave birth. Other brave women did not engage in cross-dressing, but they were determined to take up arms. Sallie Eola Renneau suggested to the Governor of Mississippi that she be allowed to organize the "Mississippi Nightingales" who would don uniforms and carry guns. Mrs. T. Brown Morgan and other women of La Grange, Georgia, took up arms to defend their town as Yankee soldiers approached, but they surrendered before a single shot was fired.

Southern women also served as spies, like the well-known Belle Boyd, who used her feminine wiles to make her way into enemy lines and gather Union secrets. She passed information about Union troop movements to Stonewall Jackson. When caught and imprisoned in Washington, D.C., she convinced the prison manager to buy her new clothes; apparently he even wished to marry her. She later seduced a Union captain as she was being transferred to a northern prison. In the summer of 1861, Union officials jailed Eugenia Levy Phillips of Savannah for three weeks, convinced that she was a Confederate spy. A year later, Phillips had a run in with General Butler in New Orleans who accused her of being "an uncommon, bad and dangerous woman" after she allegedly celebrated the funeral of a Union soldier. Butler banished her to Ship Island off the coast of Mississippi where she remained for some three months. Women proved especially effective at carrying supplies, letters, medicines, and clothes across enemy lines, usually hiding the goods under their petticoats and hoop skirts.

Another important public activity that attracted southern women was nursing. With the growing number of Confederate soldiers wounded or sick, women were needed to care for them. Nursing traditionally had been a male occupation, for society deemed such duties threatening to female delicacy and refinement. The demands of war altered that perception. However, as historian Drew Faust argues in *Mothers of Invention,* nursing during the Civil War was not an activity that many elite southern women relished. Many found such work distasteful, and the squeamish could not face the gore, filth, and nude bodies. In such grubby, bloody circumstances, it was often difficult for women to uphold their privileged class position. Some women evidenced no desire to nurse lower-class soldiers or to work beside poor white women, for both offended their elite sensitivities.

But with demand so great, some dedicated southern women were more concerned about helping suffering or dying soldiers than worrying about their own status and sensitivities. Lay nurses cleaned wards, wrote letters, fed soldiers and washed their wounds, and eased the burden of dying. Kate Cumming threw herself into nursing soldiers. She served in hospitals on the western war front and gave advice to other women who volunteered for this work. Sally Tomkins founded the Robertson Hospital in Richmond, and when the military took over its management, Jefferson Davis gave her a military rank as Captain. Phoebe Yates Pember oversaw nursing operations as matron of the South's largest hospital, Chimborozo in Richmond, taking charge of the daily medical needs of some 15,000 Confederate soldiers. Hospitals also hired free black women or leased slaves to tackle the dirtiest and most back-breaking chores, such as cleaning, cooking, and laundering. Nuns, well trained by years of service, received pay as hospital attendants and devoted themselves to nursing the Confederacy's ill and wounded. The situation nurses faced could be tense when male physicians and medical attendants resented their presence and were uncomfortable taking orders from a woman. Whatever resistance women may have encountered, patients welcomed female attendants because they offered warmth and attention. More important, female attendants made a difference; apparently where women took charge, the hospital mortality rate was cut in half due to their concern with proper diet, fresh air, and clean quarters.

The paucity of men on the home front meant that paid work became an option for more women, although working for a living usually implied poverty rather than desire for a meaningful job. Both the Confederate and state governments hired women to work as scribes and accountants. Jane North of South Carolina, apparently strapped for money, began to work as a clerk in the

Confederate treasury office in Columbia, South Carolina. Southern women constituted a growing proportion of the region's school teachers as male teachers left to join the military and governesses and female teachers from the North quit their jobs and went home. A writer for an Augusta, Georgia, newspaper recognized the shortage, noting that southern women "must of necessity be our teachers, or we shall have to dispense with any." Because the work seemed so well suited to women's maternal role as instructors of the young, few southerners objected to the feminization of this profession. The Civil War did force the closing of scores of female academies and disrupted the education of many southern girls. Nevertheless, institutions like Salem Academy remained open, in part because parents wanted their daughters in school where the felt they would be safer than at home.

The Civil War greatly affected most southern families, whether they desired to be involved or not. The shortages of goods were felt by nearly everyone; even the privileged had to make do with less or do without. Although the Confederate government tried to downplay the effectiveness of the Union's blockade of southern ports and federal control of southern rivers, goods once transported to the South by water became scarce. The war disrupted train service, also interfering with the transport of food and staples. Basic and luxury goods that southerners had taken for granted were now unavailable, in short supply, or sold at vastly inflated prices. Southerners did without coffee, salt, fabric, shoes, needles, and luxury items—or they found substitutes. Salt, a basic necessity in all southern households, became almost nonexistent; during the last months of war, women resorted to scraping the floor of their meat house to find lingering traces of salt. Okra seed apparently became the favorite substitute for coffee after southerners experimented with brewing drinks from roasted acorns and various grains. Without medicines, southern families now relied on herbal remedies.

Some wealthy women found the war especially difficult because they had been used to so much. With so many southern families suffering from hunger, it is difficult to sympathize with a handful of elite women who complained about the loss of what they deemed real necessities. In 1863, Amanda Worthington of Washington County, Mississippi, lamented that she had to sleep alone in her home for the first time in her life. But she was not alone; rather, a slave would no longer be sleeping in her bedroom. Gertrude Thomas complained that she could no longer purchase the books she had imported from England, and an aging Jane Amelia Petigru of Charleston could not longer procure the morphine she needed to alleviate her numerous ills and satisfy her thirty-year addiction. Some women in Union-occupied areas found a way around these problems by consorting with the enemy and trading their services or what they produced for desired items.

And yet it is surprising to find a few southern families who scarcely seemed affected by the war. Some families living in areas far from the fighting continued to produce and enjoy what they needed to survive. They socialized and visited family and friends on nearby plantations. While these women may have had to make do with a feather hat and frayed silk dress now hopelessly out of fashion, their children were fed, clothed, shod, and perhaps even attending school.

One example of how warfare scarcely seemed to alter life was the extravagant, well-orchestrated Charleston wedding of Della Allston to Arnoldus Vanderhorst in June 1863, a celebration that stood in marked contrast to its time and place. Though federal troops were camped just south of the city and food was in short supply, the Allstons provided Della with a dress of Brussels net and white silk that had been smuggled through the blockade. At the reception, the Allstons served French champagne that they somehow had procured. The array of food served to wedding guests perhaps made everyone forget, at least for a few hours, the reality of war. A few resourceful or fortunate families seemed to survive reasonably well throughout the war.

A seemingly bizarre response to the war was the sense of desperation that set in among a handful of elite residents of southern cities like Richmond and Charleston, behavior that belied the fact that the region was fighting a war. Despite food shortages, the privileged living in the Confederate capital continued to enjoy occasional dinner parties and balls. More extreme were a few wealthy couples who threw caution to the wind, sensing that with no possible happy outcome ahead, they might as well enjoy themselves. Near the war's end, some women gave extravagant parties and dances, serving delicacies and beverages and wearing once-fashionable silk gowns to dance the night away.

But this behavior was hardly typical. Most women had to find the means to survive endless, exhausting, and depressing days, weeks, and months as they faced the horrors of war. As they had during the antebellum period, Confederate women turned to their faith to deal with hardship, death, and sorrow. These four years certainly tested their religious faith. Most found strength by turning to God, believing that He would never desert them. Grace Brown Elmore believed, as did many women, that "Our country and our people are wonderfully favored by God." Having heard proslavery rhetoric for years that relied on the Bible to justify the institution of slavery, women turned to their Bible to affirm the rightness of the Confederate cause and find proof that God was on their side. This was an easy task as long as the South was winning the war or holding its own. But with more northern victories, a mounting death toll, and widespread deprivation, women understandably began to question and transform their faith, wondering why God would punish them this way. Some redefined their belief, seeing the war as God's test for the South. Women had to bear up under the burden of this chastening. Many women emerged at the end of the war with a faith that was less optimistic than the one they had formerly embraced, but one that continued to give meaning to their lives.

Many elite women now faced the enormous task of taking charge of agricultural production and managing an entire plantation. Some accepted these duties and rose to the occasion; others were overwhelmed and worn down by the ceaseless demands on their time and energy. Initially, concerned husbands wrote from the battlefront, sending home detailed instructions with specific orders about planting, harvesting, and maintaining slave discipline. A concerned Private Henry T. Morgan of Claiborne Parish, Louisiana, gently encouraged his wife Ellen, "I want you to do the best you can." No doubt Ellen Morgan did just that, but probably she was on her own. Gradually the realities of war distracted men from plantation concerns to worries about their own survival, and women had to cope and make decisions on their own. Some fortunate females depended on an overseer; others turned to an older male relative or neighbor for assistance, but many undertook the tasks singlehandedly and demanded more of their children.

Class and gender lines blurred as plantation women rolled up their sleeves and worked in the fields and personally directed their slaves. One particularly successful woman was Carey Petigru who took over the family plantation, Cherry Hill, near Abbeville, South Carolina, which had stood empty for two years. The skills she acquired in running the family's North Carolina plantation during her husband's frequent absences before the war had given her valuable training. Most women were not so lucky; running a plantation was tiring and especially challenging to the uninitiated. While today we might conclude that the new duties thrust upon southern women and the greater sense of authority they achieved might have given them a sense of empowerment, most southern women did not see it that way. They were too weary to appreciate their strength and independence or celebrate their accomplishments. Many yearned to return to a more tranquil, well-ordered time and relinquish these duties to men. Plantation and farm women rose to the challenge but only out of wartime necessity.

As the months of fighting dragged on, deprivation and malnourishment became more extreme and widespread. The shortage of available goods meant the need for greater self-sufficiency. Yet without men to aid with farming, agricultural productivity declined throughout the South. In addition, marauding soldiers and foraging parties existed on both sides, stealing corn, chickens, eggs, grains, and other staples. Confederate agents confiscated food to help feed the army. Meat became a luxury; some families learned to survive without it or to eat it only once a week. Facing severe shortages of food, one plantation woman decided to adopt a vegetarian diet and also serve less food at mealtime. When her husband arrived home on leave and saw the gaunt bodies of his children, he declared that meat would be served daily, whatever that would take.

Confederate women now felt less constrained by traditional social mores that had limited them during the antebellum period.

Again, the change resulted from the realities of war and the absence of men. Some women traveled long distances without an escort, going by train, wagon, or horseback to visit their son or husband or return home to see their parents. A growing number of women and children became refugees, and women had to make the difficult decision to abandon their home and head to safer ground. Families on plantations situated along the coast of North and South Carolina and Georgia were among the first refugees to flee; others in areas of Tennessee, Virginia, and Arkansas eventually fled home as well. Packing and moving all family members and slaves were overwhelming tasks. Even more difficult could be finding new living quarters in what might be an unfamiliar and hostile community. The fortunate moved in with family or friends, but many did not enjoy such luck. Refugee experiences were often stressful and difficult. The presence of so many strangers affected communities where refugees flocked, and local residents resented this invasion which put added pressure on housing and limited food supplies.

Perhaps one of the most unsettling, challenging situations that plantation women now faced was the altered, more assertive behavior of their slaves. Slaves now found more opportunities to talk back, disrupt work, and run away. They slowed down the pace of their work and became more defiant, something they rarely did a few years earlier. Many escaped to freedom, running away when Union soldiers were camped nearby; or they followed northern troops like Sherman's soldiers as they marched through Georgia and South Carolina. Without the presence of a white male to maintain order and discipline them, slaves felt more license to assert themselves and do what they wanted. The slaves' defiant behavior caused white women endless grief, and they felt a sense of helplessness about their situation. Watching household servants disappear or become less tractable was startling to many privileged women, for they had convinced themselves that slaves and whites alike benefited from the South's paternalistic labor system.

Mastery over slaves, typically accomplished by the threat or use of violence, was at the heart of the slave system. Without men around to discipline and punish slaves, managing them and forcing them to work became an onerous task. Certainly antebellum women had whipped or slapped a sassy or lazy household slave, but systematic, harsh punishment was needed to deal with an entire workforce. Punishing slaves traditionally had been a man's job; women were less comfortable with the use of systematic violence to uphold the labor system. Slaves understood this. With white men absent, they could get away with more and were less likely to suffer the consequences. White women began to complain bitterly about the behavior of their slaves, the slowdown in productivity, and their own inability to handle the situation. Some women began to question whether slavery made sense. To a growing minority, the system seemed to be more trouble than it was worth, especially with the shortage of goods and the expense of owning slaves. Women's frustration with slaves' growing assertiveness in the absence of men exposed them to a shortcoming of the South's labor system. One of the many ironies of the Confederate cause was that as white men fought and died to protect southern rights and the region's labor system, slavery could not survive in their absence. It required powerful men to command a labor force, and without their presence, slaves took advantage of this absence of authority.

Yet despite the frustrations, most privileged women could not imagine a life without slaves. One southern plantation woman was extremely upset after her cook ran away. But she was soon relieved when she found another slave to take her place. "Newport has taken the cooking," she wrote, "and we are all ladies again." Plantation women defined themselves in terms of what it meant to be a lady, and to the elite, this meant having domestic servants to perform the grubby, tedious domestic chores.

The most devastating effect of the Civil War was, of course, the death of so many southern men. Historians estimate that 40 to 50 percent of all those who served were either killed or wounded, meaning that many southern families lost at least one man in the war. Approximately 18 to 20 percent of Confederate men of military age were killed. Women became experts at grieving and mourning, donning black clothing if they owned any and carrying out the rituals associated with grieving. But as Drew Faust shows, mourning rituals were sacrificed to the exigencies of war. Coffins were in short supply, and as more Confederate soldiers died and destitution heightened, a proper burial became a thing of the past. Dead soldiers might be buried in ditches right beside a battlefield rather than being shipped home for internment in a family cemetery. Women turned to their religion and private grieving for strength, trying to resign themselves to the inevitable and to understand God's plan when death was so pervasive. With the burdens so great, some women scarcely found time to mourn for husbands, sons, or fathers.

The years of fighting and hunger and the growing number of fatalities began to affect the psyche of southern women. Some seemed to resign themselves to their situation; others expressed deep despair. Missing the men in their lives was a sentiment shared by most women. As Elizabeth Ann Russell of Louisiana wrote, "I feel more lonely and desolate than I have ever felt in all my life before." Women aged quickly, well beyond their years. Only a year into the war, Mississippian Louisa Henry wrote, "I feel ten years older than when the war commenced." Her hair had already begun to turn gray, and she yearned to sleep and not awaken until the war ended. With the fall of New Orleans in May 1862, Lucy Buck confessed to her diary that victory seemed an unachievable goal. "There seems to be such a vast fathomless gulf of misery through which we must wade to attain it," she wrote. Little did she realize that there were nearly three more years of despair, deprivation, and fighting ahead.

Certainly a woman like the first lady of the Confederacy Varina Howell Davis, who spent four years in the limelight, found her stability and well-being constantly challenged. Like most first ladies, Davis was the victim of endless public responses throughout the war, many of them highly critical of everything she did. Raised in Mississippi, Varina received a good education, having been privately tutored and then educated at a Philadelphia female academy. She met Davis, a man twice her age, at a party in Mississippi, and they married two years later. The couple spent the first years of their marriage often living apart while Davis served in Congress and then in the military during the Mexican War.

When President Franklin Pierce appointed him Secretary of War, Varina accompanied her husband to Washington. Here in the Capitol's social circle, this delightful conversationalist and charming hostess was in her element.

The Civil War brought unanticipated difficulties. Jefferson Davis's election as President of the Confederacy in 1861 threw the couple into the center of the war. Living in Richmond proved difficult, and Varina never found her niche in that city's well-entrenched social circle. The Davises lost a young son in 1864 when he fell from the porch of the Confederate White House and died. Varina's husband was often moody, in poor health, and over-whelmed by the demands of his job. The fact that she could be sarcastic, high strung, and temperamental undoubtedly fostered family tension. In some people's eyes, neither Varina nor Jefferson could do right. People criticized her for extravagant en-tertaining when so many went to bed hungry. They condemned her fancy clothes and northern education, and she became a scapegoat of politicians who wanted to get back at her husband. At the war's end, Varina apparently threw a cloak around her hus-band to protect him as Union soldiers pursued the fleeing presi-dent, and this gesture seemed to emasculate Davis in the public eye. Northern critics and cartoonists had a field day mocking this moment.

One can understand how the Civil War gradually exacted an emotional toll on women. Many women who had expressed in-tense patriotism and excitement in 1861 began to sound bitter and weary as the war ground on. In July 1861, as Georgia sol-diers departed for the battlefront, Gertrude Thomas had written, "I am proud to see them exhibit the noble, manly spirit which prompts them to go." Less than four years later, her pride had transformed into exhaustion. "I am tired, so tired of this war. I want to breathe free," she confessed. Confederate women had proudly watched loved ones depart for the battlefront and had sent their men off in a blaze of glory. But the tragedies of war overwhelmed women. Some of them endured more sorrow than one can imagine. For instance, within a fourteen-month period, Elizabeth Whitfield Croom Bellamy lost both her children, and her husband died of typhoid fever while serving as a doctor for the Confederate Army. By 1865, exhaustion and relief colored the emotions of women who finally welcomed their soldiers home.

At the very end of the war, a number of southern women faced real fear. Sherman's march through Georgia and South Carolina terrorized hundreds of elite southern families. General Sherman believed that "total war," which meant the destruction of homes, crops, and domestic animals, was necessary to break the will of the Confederacy. His troops pillaged and burned homes. Frightened women tried to protect their homes, most of them doing so without the assistance and protection of a man. Mary Jones, a Georgia widow, described her terror in facing Sherman's soldiers as they surrounded her plantation while her daughter went through a difficult labor. "We are prisoners in our own home; we dare not open windows or doors," wrote a distraught Jones three days after the infant's birth. Grace Elmore and her mother exhibited bravery by remaining in Columbia, South Carolina, to try to save the family home from Sherman's soldiers. Most men had long since left the city, and the majority of women and children had fled to safer ground. Elmore and her mother stayed on, exhibiting coolness in the face of the enemy and managing to save their home. Elmore had no use for Yankees, and she even began to question southern men. Her disappointment in men's failing to defend the South or protect their families became a theme in her journal. "I do not think they come up to the mark," she admitted tersely.

But more commonly, plantation mistresses now had difficulty making sense of the war. They became increasingly disenchanted with the Confederate cause and the endless sacrifices they had made. Some actually felt betrayed by their husbands' and sons' absence, becoming increasingly angry and resentful that they were left to carry on alone. They had never anticipated that managing a plantation, family, and slaves would be thrust upon them. The enormous responsibilities and unending sacrifices became undesirable burdens. Many prayed for the war to end and cared little about its outcome. As the months and years passed, some transferred their anger from Yankees and blamed Davis, Confederate military officers, and government officials for the South's and their own dismal situation. They expressed frustration with the army's loss of spirit, probably not realizing that they, too, had lost any enthusiasm for war.

Slave and Free Black Women

The Civil War offered slaves a far different and more hopeful end than what whites imagined: they anticipated freedom. Slaves were savvy and most had enough information to understand that this war could abolish slavery forever, especially with Lincoln's Emancipation Proclamation in January 1863. Even though this statement only freed slaves residing in Confederate territory (over which the Union had no jurisdiction), it gave slaves real hope for freedom and became a significant Union war aim. Not surprisingly, slave owners dismissed the Proclamation as a decree by the enemy, and they denounced Lincoln's arrogance and misguided stance. It would take a Union victory and the passage of the Thirteenth Amendment in 1865 to free slaves. But for four years, slaves yearned for a Union victory. Ultimately, the abolition of slavery would be one of the most significant changes emerging from the long and bitter conflict.

Nevertheless, the four years of fighting and twelve subsequent years of Reconstruction also brought slaves challenges and hardships. With the scarcity of food during the war, slaves were the first to experience hunger or eat a more monotonous, less nutritious diet as owners cut the amount of food they distributed to slave quarters. Cloth and leather were scarce, if available at all, which meant that tattered clothes could not be replaced. Slave shoes, or brogans, produced in factories in the Northeast, were now unavailable. Slaves often lost what few possessions they owned, for they, too, were vulnerable to marauding Confederate and Union soldiers. Those living near battlefields watched soldiers invade their cabins and take their food, clothing, and blankets. Soldiers stole pigs, chickens, and garden produce. Slave women feared sexual exploitation or rape. While no evidence shows the frequency of rape, a few comments, military court cases, and slave testimony reveal that both Union and Confederate soldiers sometimes raped slave women.

The instititution of slavery had begun to deteriorate long before the actual fighting ceased. The number of slaves who escaped increased as the war progressed. Those living in border states or near Union-occupied territory found it easiest to seek freedom. Some sneaked out at night, still fearful of being caught, but the brazen set off in full daylight, sensing that there was little whites could or would do to stop them. The declining number of slave patrols and the presence of Union soldiers and refugee camps now encouraged entire slave families to escape. Whereas female slaves had rarely run away before the Civil War, by 1863, more women and children responded to the tug of freedom. Some slaves cleverly planned their escape. In a dramatic instance, a seventy-year-old Georgia bondwoman gathered her twenty-two children and grandchildren on a flatboat and drifted down the Savannah River to freedom.

Yet reaching the Union side could prove a mixed blessing. Life there might be more difficult and unhealthy than they had anticipated. Slaves found that available land abandoned by southern owners was rarely available to them; northern soldiers claimed the property as the spoils of war. Federal soldiers often could not care properly for so many slave women and children who sought freedom; numbers overwhelmed their resources. The thousands of slaves who followed General Sherman to the coast encouraged him to issue a field order that set aside for them a swath of rich coastal land, running south of Charleston to the Florida border. (President Andrew Johnson later rescinded this order.) Northern soldiers also expected slaves to earn their keep, and some could scarcely hide their racist sentiments. Some northern white soldiers exhibited as much contempt toward blacks as had some southern whites. Slave women had to cook and wash clothes for Union soldiers, tasks they had formerly performed for southern whites. But at least now they were free and no longer threatened by the lash. A few freed people were able to carve out a life by finding a plot of land, planting a garden, and selling produce and homemade goods in area markets. But demeaning comments, bad treatment, and rape, or at least the threat of rape, were realities for former slave women.

In some instances, especially on abandoned coastal plantations, slaves took out their long-brewing frustration on white homes. After its white owners fled, slaves at Chicora Wood near Georgetown, South Carolina, destroyed the furniture, mantles, and banisters and smashed the windows of this elegant plantation home. Elsewhere they ruined furniture, rugs, and draperies, tore apart wood paneling, and burned barns to remove any reminders of white privilege and black oppression. Long symbolizing injustice, inequality, and sorrow, these plantation homes fell victim to slaves who vandalized and destroyed scores of them.

A few slaves and their children who made it to Union-occupied territory began to enjoy a rudimentary exposure to education, something that had been denied them under slavery. During the War, scores of northern men and women, imbued with missionary fervor and a desire to assist the downtrodden, came South to areas like the Sea Islands to establish schools and teach freed people how to read. Historian Willie Lee Rose examined the situation of slaves on the Sea Islands of Georgia after Union troops occupied this valuable cotton land. Her study, *Rehearsal for Reconstruction,* shows the interplay of freed slaves and northern white men and women. Missionaries sought to uplift the freedpeople, expose them to religion and an education, make them economically productive, and instill Yankee values. The schools established for former slaves would be duplicated in the postbellum period, providing African Americans with an education and dreams of full acceptance and equality in a white world.

Always vulnerable, slave families experienced major upheaval during the war. The large number of slave men impressed into Confederate service to dig trenches, construct forts, and repair railroad track or hired out by their owners meant that additional burdens fell on slave women. Men's absence disrupted slave family life; women now had total charge of childrearing duties and more back-breaking farm chores. The shortages of basic goods and the need for greater self-sufficiency meant that slave women had to spend more time spinning, weaving, and making candles and soap from scratch. The blockade affected slaves as it did whites, and they had to make do without basic necessities such as needles, fish hooks, salt, and other essentials. They experienced shortages of goods they had come to expect from their master such as shoes, cloth, blankets, and meat. The customary distribution of goods that planters dispersed dwindled or disappeared as the war dragged on.

With fewer black men around to protect them, slave women may have become more vulnerable to physical abuse and rape. This is a topic lacking extensive research, though slave women certainly faced threats of sexual exploitation during the war. Leslie Schwalm describes a "chaotic maelstrom of violence" enveloping South Carolina slave women at the end of the war. Union and Confederate soldiers, guerrilla troops, and disgruntled civilians probably took advantage of slave women. Catherine Clinton in her book on Confederate women, *Tara Revisited,* claims that the military punishment for rape was execution and that this must have mediated against soldiers raping white women during the war. Skin color protected most of them from physical attack by soldiers. It is less likely that slave women enjoyed such protection and more likely that men took advantage of them. But most evidence is lost to the past since black women would have been unlikely to swear out a complaint against a white man.

Yet despite instances of slave defiance, runaways, work slowdowns, and destruction of white property, what is perhaps surprising in the midst of wartime chaos was that most slaves stayed put until the war's end. They carried on with their work, even if it was now performed on their terms. Several reasons help explain why this occurred. Many slaves were cautious about the future, unsure what the war implied and what it might bring. A minority of slaves never even knew that freedom was a possibility until after the war ended. Perhaps they were so resigned to enslavement that it was difficult for them to envision a future without masters. Their presence may also reflect slaves' deep attachment to the land and to ancestors who were buried there. As historians Margaret Creel and Leslie Schwalm explain, slaves, at least on lowcountry South Carolina plantations, felt a tie between the living and the dead and held dear to their physical surroundings. They were reluctant to leave a critical link to their home and land, even if it was associated with slavery. The land held important, sacred meaning to many African Americans. Also, slaves who had the good fortune to have a relatively kind owner probably decided that they were better off staying put rather than venturing into the unknown. Union soldiers who took control of the Sea Islands of Georgia were struck by the number of slaves who spoke fondly of their masters, even though they decried the institution of slavery itself. Dangers beyond the plantation still existed. Southern soldiers captured slave runaways; Union soldiers forced others into the army. Slaves also were cautious about Yankees. After all, most were white, and blacks were unsure that they were any kinder than the southern variety. They had seen northern anger at work. Union soldiers set about systematically to burn fields, ransack homes, and steal domestic animals, heirlooms, and food. Slaves watched northerners invade their cabins and take anything they could find. Occasionally soldiers tortured slaves in order to learn secrets, especially the location of hidden food supplies and valuable heirlooms. One bondwoman recalled that Union soldiers dragged away her mother and raped her. Many Yankee soldiers were out for themselves, frustrated and exhausted by protracted war, and some took out their anger on blacks.

At the war's end, however, slaves were jubilant. They danced, sang, shouted, and prayed. "Freedom! Rejoice, freedom has come!" was a typical response. Blacks believed that God had finally answered their prayers. Within a few months, the Thirteenth Amendment was in effect, ending slavery in this country forever. The future seemed to hold enormous promise. African Americans were dazed by the events rapidly unfurling before them, many not even sure exactly what freedom meant.

Yeoman and Poor Farmwives

But despite the hardships that elite white and slave women experienced, the burden of the Civil War fell most directly on 6 million nonslave-owning southerners: yeomen and poor white farmers. Men from this class made up the largest portion of the Confederate Army. Because conscription laws forced so many poor white men into military service, the war has often been called "a rich man's war, a poor man's fight." Like privileged women, farm women were left alone, to manage agricultural production and raise their children. Yet unlike elite women, they had no slaves to help them. Most had only the elderly and young to assist them. Overburdened before the war, farm women found their responsibilities overwhelming without grown men present. They struggled to plant and harvest crops and tend to their domestic and maternal duties. Understandably, agricultural output fell, and families had less to eat. Being overworked and underfed fostered a cycle of ill health and poverty among the South's farm population.

In some instances, yeomen and poor women took advantage of paid work opportunities that expanded during the war. Urban residents were most likely to find such jobs. Some women and young girls worked in factories, sewing uniforms and producing munitions. But paid work usually represented desperation. Wages amounted to little more than a dollar a day, and inflation ate into that. A number of poor women, especially in southern cities, turned to prostitution, which proved to be one of the more lucrative ways they could make a living. Several dozen brothels operated in the Confederate capital to serve government officials and workers and soldiers. Apparently Richmond's law officers took a fairly lenient view of these women, arresting them to show they were upholding the law but releasing them a day or two later. Records show that some prostitutes were in and out of Richmond's jails with some regularity, apparently making enough from their trade to pay their fines and get back to their profession.

War also brought unexpected results to a few women. For instance, in a documented case, war propelled a farm woman and her family into the slave-owning class. An Appalachian woman, Mary Bell, purchased the family's first slave in 1864. With her husband in the army, Bell used investments and collected payments owed her husband in order to purchase slaves and upgrade the family status. Prices for slaves were now attractive in the southern mountains, for owners had moved a number of slaves there to remove them from harm's way. Even in 1864, apparently Mary envisioned a bright future for the Confederacy. Despite her husband's contrary advice to buy land, she purchased a man, his wife, and their three-year-old child, moving the Bells into 10 percent of all mountain people who owned slaves. Mary's action, however, proved unfortunate. Owning slaves did not give her the respect she craved or ease her life. She discovered the challenges of slave ownership, including tending to their many ills, constantly watching their work, and providing them adequate shelter, clothing, and food. Most disappointing was Mary discovering that the woman she bought was actually free, as was her child, meaning she really only owned one slave. Mary would have been wiser to pay heed to her husband.

While more research is needed to understand the Civil War experiences of poor women, historians George Rable and Victoria Bynum offer us some insight. Certainly poor women suffered greater deprivation than they had during the antebellum period. Everyone on southern farms appeared more threadbare and malnourished. Without a grown man present, families were susceptible to hunger, deprivation, and hardship. Wartime scarcities brought many families to the brink of poverty and fostered social chaos. Thefts, larcenies, and riots increased during the war, and desperate women initiated much of this crime. Some women traded with the enemy, turned to prostitution, as mentioned, and sold or used goods they stole from neighbors.

As the war dragged on and the situation worsened, farm women, who generally had been silent during the antebellum period, began to speak out and protest publicly. They, too, became political creatures. Women watched infirm husbands, elderly fathers, and young sons scarcely old enough to carry a rifle recruited into the Confederate Army. Some petitioned their state or the Davis government, pleading with officials to release their husband from military service so he could come home and run the farm. In most cases, their pleas fell on deaf ears, the letters often filed away and ignored. Poor women demanded public assistance to help them feed and clothe their hungry children. Antebellum

laws had always seemed to favor slave owners, but Civil War statutes gave even more privileges to the elite. Poor women railed
against the injustices of Confederate laws that benefited the rich
at the expense of the poor. Men with twenty or more slaves were
exempted from serving in the military, and men who could afford
to do so purchased a substitute to serve in their stead. Soldiers
who provided their own horse, rifle, and uniform sometimes
served a shorter duty. Laws gave the government the right to seize
a family's mules or wagons. This was especially hard on poor
farm families who might have only one mule, making it almost
impossible to till their fields or get their produce to market. Some
women publicly denounced these laws; others broke into grain
depots and mills; and many protested the actions of suppliers who
hoarded food and speculators who charged inflated prices.

Farm women despaired as they watched their children become thin and languid. The Davis government seemed insensitive
to their needs. In early April 1863, hundreds, perhaps thousands,
of Richmond's poor engaged in what became known as the Richmond Bread Riot. Protestors marched on the Governor's Mansion, broke into stores, smashed windows, looted, and engaged in
a free-for-all to protest the government's inability to feed them.
While most of the rioters never received the food they demanded,
their message was clear. The government worried about such
threats, especially when orchestrated by women who were supposed to be supporting the Confederacy, and it tried to suppress
news of this unfortunate incident. Yet similar protests broke out in
other cities, including Raleigh and Salisbury, North Carolina, and
Mobile, Alabama. The Confederate government did not relish in-
ternal chaos while trying to fight a war.

Some states responded to widespread destitution and took
steps to alleviate suffering by establishing limited forms of public
assistance, distributing surplus food or providing cash payments
to the needy. Approximately a third of all Alabama families received a dole from the state between 1863 and the end of the war.
Unfortunately, most efforts were too little, too late, or poorly administered. Inflation ate into what little assistance was provided,
and the needs of soldiers always came first. Poor women became

increasingly disenchanted with a government that was supposed to protect them.

It is little wonder that many women also wrote directly to their soldier husbands, describing the family's financial woes, endless work, and hunger. Wives urged their men to come home to protect and help the family rather than defend a dying nation. To women, loyalty to family superceded loyalty to the state or nation. As the war wound on, it is evident that poor women were hardly united behind the cause of the Confederacy or the defense of slavery. And any hint of paternalism seemed to have died now that there was so little to share. Wealthy landowners who might have aided a poor neighbor or relative held on to what they had. Class tension heightened.

Yeomen farm wives lost faith in the South. They mourned for loved ones who had died for what seemed to be a meaningless cause. The government intruded into their daily lives in unprecedented ways. Before the war, state governments demanded little and provided little, leaving southern families a degree of independence that they had treasured. Now, wartime taxes imposed severe hardships. The government dictated what crops could be planted. In order to drive up the price of cotton, fields were burned. Government agents took what they needed to assist the war.

Whether women's actions fostered widespread disillusionment with the war is debatable, but historian George Rable suggests that women may have contributed to a loss of will in the Confederacy. By 1863, soldiers began to desert by the thousands, and wrenching news from home was often the cause. Eventually, more than 100,000 soldiers abandoned the battlefront. Protecting their family was more important than defending the Confederacy.

Coping Skills and Union Supporters

Confederate women of all classes who lived in areas threatened or occupied by Union soldiers faced difficult situations. Women and children in Vicksburg, Mississippi, probably faced the most desperate situation of the entire war. They had no choice but to stay put when federal troops surrounded their city in the summer of 1863. For weeks, residents survived constant shelling by living in caves during the long siege. Totally cut off from everything, people ran out of food, and some were so hungry that they ate dogs and rats. With the Union occupying Memphis by June 1862, women there found means of supporting the Confederacy now closed off to them. One attractive southern belle who worked as a spy became the victim of unfair criticism by her family and friends. They failed to realize that she was purposely flirting with Union soldiers in order to gather information for Confederate officers. Yet several families in that city were forced to find new living quarters when northern military officials confiscated their homes, transforming the houses into Union hospitals, military headquarters, or boarding houses.

Finally, a group of southern white women about whom we know little but who also represented various social classes were those females who remained loyal to the Union. Pockets of the South, such as the Appalachian mountain area, northwest Arkansas, and areas in several border states were home to a number of female Unionists. Historical sources provide only a glimpse of these women living in an area where, because they supported the North, they now became the enemy. Though eleven states declared their loyalty to the Confederacy, not all southerners in those states supported the new nation. A number of southerners remained Unionists throughout the entire war. Other southerners became increasingly disenchanted with the Confederacy and began to pray for a Union victory.

Southern women who supported the North, especially those left alone while their husbands fought for the Union, encountered significant problems. Gender had little meaning in affecting the treatment that Confederates meted out to known Unionists. Southerners assaulted a woman living in Walton County, Florida, for not revealing the location of her Union husband. When she refused to talk, they unleashed their dogs on her and killed her two children. In 1862, Confederates opened fire on families trying to flee to the safety of Federal gunboats anchored off the Florida coast.

The archives of the Southern Claims Commission (which operated from 1870 to 1881 to investigate and reimburse southerners who had supported the Union) provide a few insights into these women's experiences. In North Carolina, some families who opposed the Confederacy joined the Society of Friends (Quakers), since its pacifist stance gave them an excuse not to fight for the South. An underground resistance group, the Heroes of America, aided deserters and draft dodgers who wanted to avoid Confederate military service. Women played a role in undermining the southern cause. They watched for Confederate conscription officers and warned their men if one was in sight. A few women turned their farms over to Union authorities in order to hide southern deserters. Sarah Bailey concealed deserters on her farm and dressed up her stepson as a woman so he wouldn't be drafted. North Carolinian Louisa Stiles, whose husband, two sons, and two brothers fought and died for the Union, used her home to aid the Union cause, even though neighbors threatened to kill her and destroy her house and property. At one point, they put ropes around the necks of her children and threatened to lynch them if she did not stop her traitorous activities.

On the other hand, Union supporters had an advantage if they lived in an area that came under federal control. Suddenly they gained a sense of security, and new opportunities opened up to them. Women happily swore an oath of allegiance to the Union and thus had access to supplies of foods and staples. An attractive Union widow living in Augusta, Florida, took full advantage of the situation and was delighted with the number of northern men now residing in her community. She opened her home to federal officers and welcomed them with food and entertainment.

End of War

Much to the relief of millions of southerners, the war finally ended with Lee's surrender at Appomatox on April 12, 1865. Women responded with sorrow or with joy—but certainly with relief. Grace Brown Elmore wrote only a couple of weeks after that event, "There is a stillness over the whole land, a peace that is no peace reigns, our Confederacy, our pride, our glory is departed, we as a people are no more." Despite the relief felt by many southern women that the fighting and killing were over, some feared the worst. A Georgia girl declared that Lee's surrender marked "the darkest page in the book of time." But she assumed that God's will would be done and that He would deliver the South from ruin. A few elite women had trouble understanding why slaves eagerly fled the plantation and predicted that slaves, who in their eyes had always been so childlike, would be unable to cope with freedom. A privileged Virginia woman seemed to have no idea what enslavement meant. To her thinking, slavery had "so largely contributed to the happiness both of master and servant." Enslaved women hardly saw it that way. They responded to Confederate defeat with jubilation, knowing that freedom was at hand. At least for a brief while, they dreamed that they would soon achieve equality and acquire the opportunities long available to whites in this country.

Of course, for southern whites, the South did not die. Nor did southern blacks suddenly find their dreams fulfilled. Southern women did not stifle their energy nor silence their tongues. But most pondered the immediate future, probably with some trepidation, sensing that their lives would never be the same again.

Conclusion

One of the most compelling historical debates concerning black and white southern women is how the Civil War ultimately affected them. Did the lives of black women truly change? Did they establish new lives and find opportunities once freedom came? Did four years of war significantly alter the lives of white women and, if so, how? Anne Scott concluded that the Civil War had an indelible effect on plantation wives. Called upon to undertake new and demanding roles, these women discovered their own strength and capabilities. According to Scott's thesis, such experiences helped to shape a more confident, assertive southern woman. More recent scholarship offers a less optimistic view. Suzanne

Lebsock's perspective on the postwar South revealed a white population devastated by loss. The defeated tended to be poor losers and unreceptive to change or major social upheaval. She suggested that southern men returning from war could not handle independent females in the midst of Confederate defeat, freed slaves, and lost fortunes. The men felt that they had not upheld their part of the bargain. Females feeling confident and assertive from their Civil War experiences could threaten the social hierarchy, to say nothing of the male ego. War-weary men needed their confidence and honor restored. Perhaps more than ever before, southern white women realized they had to be outwardly submissive and supportive and help preserve patriarchal authority.

George Rable's study of Confederate women tends to agree with Lebsock's. He feels that white women did not bask in their wartime independence and new roles. They had to deal with ongoing difficulties and tragedies, not glory. Confederate men, unable to defend the region and their families, returned from the war broken in spirit, wounded, or ill. In view of the situation, white women could not challenge male authority or alter the traditional social hierarchy. After 1865, southern women carried on, dealing with poverty, shattered lives, and a changing social order. Formerly wealthy plantation women like Gertrude Thomas and Mary Boykin Chesnut had to hold their family together emotionally and economically. They raised chickens, sold eggs, wrote, and taught school—anything to earn a living. Women in the Petigru family, who would never have considered paid work before the Civil War, now taught school. Family survival and the reality of their situation—not newly discovered ideas of feminist strength and independence—kept them going. Rather than publicly asserting themselves, southern white women learned to hide behind a veil of femininity.

Also less optimistic about the postbellum South are the findings of Drew Gilpin Faust, who sees elite southern women emerging from the war disillusioned and exhausted, but more realistic. They turned inward to meet the needs of their families. In the final months of the war, many privileged women did not care whether the South won or lost—they wanted their men to come home and life to return to normal. Defeat and failure became a part of their vocabulary. Faust suggests that race concerns affected gender relationships after emancipation in 1865. Southern whites saw race, not gender, as the most critical factor in southern society. It was important that all whites adopt a common stance in dealing with their fear of black freedom. Rather than becoming more assertive and independent, southern white women aligned themselves with their men to ensure racial solidarity.

For African American women, 1865 brought hope and the promise of freedom. Some women immediately left their farm or plantation and roamed the South in search of loved ones who had been sold during slavery. Couples legalized their marriages, and everyone dreamed of economic opportunities and a new life independent of white control. Black women who could afford to do so now made choices about work, sometimes remaining in the domestic sphere rather than performing exhausting field labor. Both adults and children began to attend schools established by the Freedmen's Bureau and northern religious organizations. Across the South, black men and women began to organize and attend their own churches, anxious to express their faith free of white dictates. Churches, which during the antebellum period had been the most integrated institution in the South, quickly became segregated by race, a situation that both blacks and whites now apparently preferred.

For a brief period, with the support of the federal government and the passage of new laws and three Constitutional amendments, African Americans saw the promise of freedom. They had the opportunity to become fully integrated into the political, social, and economic life of the South. Reconstruction offered hope that the nation might meet the needs of former slaves and give them full equality. But assuring black men the right to vote in 1870 did not give them land or economic opportunities, nor did it end racism. Neither white southerners at this juncture—nor most white Americans, for that matter—could alter their basic feelings about African Americans.

During the 1870s, white southerners gradually regained political control of the region, and the federal government and courts abandoned the ideals of Reconstruction, leaving the South to fend for itself. State laws throughout the region would eventually legitimize repression and the separation of the races through voting restrictions, Jim Crow laws, and limits on black citizenship. Violence also proved an effective means to keep African Americans in their place.

As they had done throughout years of enslavement, African American women turned inward to their families, churches, and communities for strength. They knew how to support and assist one another in a nation that did not want them. Black women had learned to live under oppression; now they learned how to survive new injustices and live with unfulfilled dreams. Nearly a century would pass before southern women, both black and white, would recognize and attempt to come to grips with racial and gender inequality.

BIBLIOGRAPHICAL ESSAY

Each year, exciting new studies on southern women appear. Early research focused on the records of the most accessible subjects: elite white women and slaves. Newer information reflects the concerns of social historians who are uncovering how laws, health, religion, sexuality, and work affected women's lives. Two bibliographies in essay form on the region's history, published a dozen years apart, indicate the rapid changes in southern women's history. The earlier one, edited by Arthur S. Link and Rembert W. Patrick, *Writing Southern History: Essays in Historiography in Honor of Fletcher M. Green* (Baton Rouge, 1965) included only three citations on women. More recently, John B. Boles's and Evelyn Thomas Nolen's *Interpreting Southern History: Historiographical Essays in Honor of Sanford W. Higginbotham* (Baton Rouge, 1987) has an entire chapter devoted to women. This material already needs updating. A new overview with a chapter on the most significant books on antebellum southern women is forthcoming in the Blackwell Companion to the American South.

The study that fostered initial interest in southern white women was Anne Firor Scott's *The Southern Lady: From Pedestal to Politics, 1830–1930* (Chicago, 1970). Approximately half the book covers the antebellum and Civil War periods and focuses on elite women. Scott argues that slavery affected how women functioned within a patriarchal structure that established women's submissive position in southern society. She describes the enormous difficulties women faced, especially relating to childbearing and the injustices resulting from miscegenation and the double standard. In her article, "Women's Perspective on the Patriarchy in the 1850s," *Journal of American History* 61 (1974), Scott elucidates the level of female discontent as women grappled with a society in which they had little voice and few means to protest.

Catherine Clinton's *The Plantation Mistress: Women's World in the Old South* (New York, 1982) offers a broad overview of the lives of elite southern women. She bases her study on an impressive number of personal writings from the period 1780–1835. Because the study ends a generation before the Civil War, changes during the antebellum period are difficult to detect, although the chapter on female education is detailed and demonstrates the South's commitment to women's schooling. Clinton concludes that white women made valuable contributions to their region but were enslaved by the society in which they lived ("slave of slaves" in her language), enjoying few privileges or rights.

Jane Turner Censer's *North Carolina Planters and Their Children, 1800–1860* (Baton Rouge, 1984), uses manuscript sources to analyze more than one 100 elite families in one southern state. She shows that plantation mothers in the Tarheel state were affectionate, caring, and surprisingly egalitarian toward their children, though they rarely demonstrated such feelings toward their slaves. Censer offers a fairly cheerful picture of family life, finding the planter world of North Carolina less patriarchal than the one described by Scott and Clinton.

Suzanne Lebsock's study, *The Free Women of Petersburg: Status and Culture in a Southern Town, 1784–1860* (New York, 1984) broke new ground when it appeared by focusing on urban black and white women. Using legal documents and personal records in one community, she shows how women's status improved and how their autonomy increased by the Civil War. More women established separate estates, and in their wills, women gave particular items to beloved relatives and friends. Marriage was not always good—or even possible—for free black women or widows. Women's benevolent work provided a meaningful outlet—until men began to interfere and take over.

Elizabeth Fox-Genovese's *Within the Plantation Household: Black and White Women of the Old South* (Chapel Hill, 1988) emphasizes the importance of the household in southern society as the center for productive and reproductive activities. She argues that southern women are best understood in relation to southern men and counters the idea that southern women were feminists or quiet abolitionists. White women receive more attention than slaves in this study.

The difficulties and benefits that women experienced in fulfilling their maternal role are described in Sally G. McMillen's *Motherhood in the Old South: Pregnancy, Childbirth and Infant Rearing* (Baton Rouge, 1990). Using diaries and letters as well as medical accounts and journals, she reveals the sacrifices that women made in bearing and rearing children, the commitment they made to this sacred duty, and the role that the southern medical profession played in assisting them.

A thorough examination of one elite southern marriage is found in Anya Jabour's *Marriage in the Early Republic: Elizabeth and William Wirt and the Companionate Ideal* (Baltimore, 1998). The Wirt relationship was long-lived, revealed in decades of correspondence between the couple. They tried to create an ideal, companionate marriage based upon mutual respect and love, something difficult to achieve considering the demands of childrearing and domestic duties and Wirt's demanding career. The fact that the couple spent so much time apart explains their extensive correspondence and the fact that each operated with a fair degree of independence.

Cynthia Kierner's study, *Beyond the Household: Women's Place in the Early South, 1700–1835* (Ithaca, NY, 1998), focuses attention on the colonial period but also examines women in the early antebellum period. Kierner emphasizes the importance of class status to elite women in Virginia and the Carolinas, arguing that women went to great effort to establish and reinforce the elite culture in which they lived. They sought an education, participated in the public sphere, and fashioned a genteel culture. After the Revolution, perceptions about women altered, and social mores began to emphasize their domestic, maternal role; in the home they could be most virtuous.

Broadening our understanding of southern women and their public role is Elizabeth R. Varon's *We Mean to Be Counted: White Women and Politics in Antebellum Virginia* (Chapel Hill, 1998). Varon challenges the idea that women—at least in Virginia—were apolitical and avoided the public arena. She finds a number of elite women there engaged in a variety of public and reform issues such as colonization, temperance, and—with the rise of the Whig Party—even politics. She insists that at least a few southern white women participated with white men in fashioning a political consensus. Whether her conclusions hold true for other southern states deserves further research.

Adopting a different approach is Joan Cashin's *A Family Venture: Men and Women on the Southern Frontier* (1991) which studies those who moved from the coastal South to the West, including such areas as Alabama, Arkansas, and Texas. Cashin emphasizes gender in analyzing migration, and many of her conclusions parallel those of scholars who have studied migration to the Far West. Southern women were reluctant travelers, not happy about leaving home, family, and community to venture to the unknown. Cashin feels that the frontier experience made southern families even more patriarchal as men took control of their families and exerted more power over their slaves and family members because they no longer were under the influence of extended family and community.

Marli Weiner's *Mistresses and Slaves: Plantation Women in South Carolina, 1830–1880* (Urbana, IL, 1998) presents an overview of South Carolina women and beyond. A strength of her book is its discussion of work roles and the relationship of black and white women in the plantation home. Margaret Ripley Wolfe offers an even more comprehensive approach, presenting an entire history of southern women in her witty and interesting volume, *Daughters of Canaan: A Saga of Southern Women* (Louisville, KY, 1995).

Biographies and autobiographies of southern white women include Gerda Lerner's *The Grimké Sisters from South Carolina: Pioneers for Woman's Rights and Abolition* (New York, 1967) which studies Angelina and Sarah Grimké, who spent their early years as privileged Charleston women but left the South and championed abolition and women's rights. A more typical elite woman was Mary Boykin Chesnut, studied in Elisabeth Muhlenfeld's *Mary Boykin Chesnut: A Biography* (Baton Rouge, 1981) and a brief examination in Mary DeCredico's *Mary Boykin Chesnut: A Confederate Woman's Life* (Madison, WI, 1996). Chesnut enjoyed a privileged childhood, married into a wealthy upcountry South Carolina family, and spent several unhappy years with in-laws until her husband was elected to the Senate. Her journal (see citation below), sketched during the Civil War, has become a classic source for that time period. Avery O. Craven's *Rachel of Old Louisiana* (Baton Rouge, 1975) is a brief biography of Rachel Swayze O'Connor. She was twice widowed and successfully managed a plantation after her second husband died. Daniel E. Sutherland's "The Rise and Fall of Esther B. Cheesborough: The Battles of a Literary Lady," *South Carolina Historical Magazine* 84 (1983) describes this South Carolina literary figure. Adele Logan Alexander looks at women in her family through her study *Ambiguous Lives: Free Women of Color in Rural Georgia, 1789–1879* (Fayetteville, AR, 1991). Jane H. Pease and William H. Pease have written a detailed and fascinating biographical account of one family of privileged South and North Carolina women, *A Family of Women; The Carolina Petrigrus in Peace and War* (Chapel Hill, NC, 1999). Steven Stowe's *Intimacy and Power in the Old South* (Baltimore, 1987) describes the courtship of Bessie Lacy.

Plantation women also come into sharper focus through their letters and diaries. *The Secret Eye: The Journal of Ella Gertrude Clanton Thomas, 1848–1889,* ed. Virginia Ingraham Burr (Chapel Hill, NC, 1990), includes forty years of the thoughts of an introspective and highly literate Georgia plantation woman and reveals how the Civil War affected her privileged life. Robert Manson Myers's *Children of Pride: A True Story of Georgia and the Civil War* (New Haven, CT, 1972) is a lengthy and interesting collection of letters of the Charles Colcock Jones family, written from the 1850s through the end of the Civil War. An extensive kin network and loving relationships created a supportive and affectionate family. Another primary source is Carol Bleser, *Tokens of Affection: The Letters of a Planter's Daughter in the Old South* (Athens, GA, 1996) that contains all the known letters of Maria Bryan of Mt. Zion, Georgia, to her sister Julia Bryan Cumming of Augusta. Others include Mary Curtis Lee DeButts, ed., *Growing Up in the 1850s: The Journal of Agnes Lee* (Chapel Hill, NC, 1984), a diary by a daughter of Robert E. Lee; Fletcher M. Green, ed. *The Lides Go South . . . And West: The Record of a Planter Migration in 1835* (Columbia, SC, 1952) which includes letters about the experiences of women who migrated to the Southwest; *The Pettigrew Papers, Vol. 1, 1685–1818,* and *Vol. 2, 1819–1843,* ed. Sarah Lemmon (Raleigh, 1971–88), letters of a wealthy North Carolina family; and Theodore Rosengarten's *Tombee: Portrait of a Cotton Planter, with the Journal of Thomas B. Chaplin, 1822–1890* (New York, 1986), about a wealthy, troubled Sea Island planter with much information about his invalid wife and stepsister-in-law. Joan Cashin has edited a collection of poignant, revealing thoughts by southern women in *Our Common Affairs: Texts from Women in the Old South* (Baltimore, 1996). Filling a gap that existed on single women is Michael O'Brien's edited collection, *An Evening When Alone: Four Journals of Single Women in the South, 1827–1867* (Charlottesville, VA, 1993).

Journals also have published primary material such as James C. Williams, ed., "Plantation Experiences of a New York Woman," *North Carolina Historical Review* 33 (1956) containing the letters of a lonely woman writing to her parents about life in the South; Ray Holder, ed., "My Dear Husband: Letters of a Plantation Mistress Martha Dubose Winans to William Winans, 1834–1844," *The Journal of Mississippi History* 49 (1987), Harriet R. Holman, ed., "Charleston in the Summer of 1841: The Letters of Harriott Horry Rutledge," *South Carolina Historical and Genealogical*

Magazine 46 (1945), the charming letters of a nine-year-old girl; Caroline Olivia Laurens, "Journal of a Visit to Greenville from Charleston in the Summer of 1825," annotated by Louise C. King, *South Carolina Historical Magazine* 72 (1971); "'Molly Pitcher' of the Mississippi Whigs: The Editorial Career of Mrs. Harriet N. Prewett," by Christopher Olson, *Journal of Mississippi History,* 58 (1996), which focuses on an antebellum newspaper editor who supported slavery and male patriarchy; and James I. Robertson, Jr., ed.,"The Diary of Dolly Lunt Burge," *Collections of the Georgia Historical Society* 44 (1960); 45 (1961); 46 (1962), an interesting account by a New England woman who kept a diary for twenty-seven years.

Biographical articles on white women and their activities include Hugh C. Bailey and William Pratt Dale, II, "Missus Alone in de' Big House,'" *The Alabama Review* 8 (1955), describing an Alabama plantation woman's handling of the household and farm in her husband's absence; Judith N. McArthur, "Myth, Reality, and Anomaly: The Complete World of Rebecca Hagerty," *East Texas Historical Association* 24 (1986), on an interesting woman, part Native American, and successful plantation widow; Berry Stephen, "More Alluring at a Distance: Absentee Patriarchy and the Thomas Butler King Family," *The Georgia Historical Quarterly* 81 (1997) which details the challenges that Anna Page King faced living so much of her life alone; and Clayton Torrence, ed., "Letters of Mrs. Ann (Jennings) Wise to Her Husband, Henry A. Wise," *Virginia Historical Magazine* 58 (1950), written to her husband in Congress and interspersed with biographical commentary.

Other topics dealing with southern white women can be found in a broad selection of journal articles including Harriet E. Amos, "'City Belles': Images and Realities of the Lives of White Women in Antebellum Mobile," *The Alabama Review* 34 (1981); Joan Cashin's "The Structure of Antebellum Planter Families: 'The Tie that Bound Us Was Strong,'" *Journal of Southern History* 56 (1990) which argues for the importance of extended families in southern white society; Cashin's "'Decidedly Opposed to the Union': Women's Culture, Marriage, and Politics in Antebellum South Carolina," *Georgia Historical Quarterly* 78 (1994), on twin sisters who embraced female friendships and initially expressed suspicion toward marriage; Katherine G. Goodwin, "'A Woman's Curiosity': Martha Gaffney and Cotton Planting on the Texas Frontier," *East Texas Historical Association* 24 (1986), about a plucky, determined widow who moved west with her children and successfully ran a plantation; Leah Rawls Atkins, "High Cotton: The Antebellum Alabama Plantation Mistress and the Cotton Culture," *Agricultural History,* 68 (1994) which emphasizes the demanding role of plantation women in one state; William Stanley Hoole, "The Gilmans and the *Southern Rose*," *The North Carolina Historical Review* 11 (1934), describing the founder of a southern ladies' magazine; Guion Griffis Johnson, "Courtship and Marriage Customs in Ante-Bellum North Carolina," *North Carolina Historical Review,* 8 (1931), an interesting article on the happiest and most independent moments in the life of a southern woman; Robert C. Kizer, "Family, Kinship, and Neighborhood in an Antebellum Southern Community," in *A Master's Due: Essays in Honor of David Herbert Donald,* ed. William J. Cooper, Jr., Michael F. Holt, and John McCardell (Baton Rouge, 1985) showing the close ties that developed through kin and neighborhood in Orange County, North Carolina; Conevery A. Bolton, "'A Sister's Consolations': Women, Health, and Community in Early Arkansas, 1810–1860," *Arkansas Historical Quarterly* 50 (1991), focuses on the importance of female networks; Kent Anderson Leslie, "A Myth of the Southern Lady: Antebellum Proslavery Rhetoric and the Proper Place for Women," *Sociological Spectrum* 6 (1986), which includes male thoughts on southern women's proper role; Ann Masson and Bryce Reveley, "When Life's Brief Sun Was Set: Portraits of Southern Women in Mourning, 1830–1860," *Southern Quarterly* 27 (1988); and Anya Jabour's "'Quite a Woman of Business': Elizabeth Washington Gamble Wirt, 1784–1857," *Virginia Cavalcade* 49 (2000).

Valuable additions to scholarship on southern women are found in various edited collections of essays. One by Carol Bleser, *In Joy and In Sorrow: Women, Family, and Marriage in the Victorian South* (New York, 1990) includes Peter Bardaglio's "'An Outrage upon Nature': Incest and the Law in the Nineteenth-Century South;" Carol Bleser and Frederick Heath, "The Clays of Alabama: The Impact of the Civil War on a Southern Marriage"; and Brenda Stevenson's "Distress and Discord in Virginia Slave Families, 1830–1860," which demythicizes slave families by revealing the stresses and pressures they experi-enced. A diverse collection of essays appears in Christie Anne Farnham's, *Women of the American South: A Multicultural Reader*. This includes original work on antebellum women such as Timothy J. Lockley's "A Struggle for Survival: Non-Elite White Women in Lowcountry Georgia, 1790–1830," Alice Taylor-Colbert's "Cherokee Women and Cultural Change," Jean E. Friedman, "The Politics of Pedagogy and Judaism in the Early Republican South: The Case of Rachel and Eliza Mordecai," Johanna Miller Lewis's "Equality Deferred, Opportunity Pursued: The Sisters of Wachovia," and Joan E. Cashin's "According to His Wish and Desire: Female Kin and Female Slaves in Planter Wills." Another edited collection of Catherine Clinton's is *Half Sisters of History; Southern Women and the American Past* (Durham, NC, and London, UK, 1994) which includes essays that have earlier appeared in journals. Patricia Morton's *Discovering the Women in Slavery; Emancipating Perspectives on the American Past* (Athens, GA, 1996) covers both black and white women. Essays on southern women include Wilma King's "The Mistress and Her Maids: White and Black Women in a Louisiana Household, 1858–1868," Marli Weiner's "Mistresses, Morality, and Dilemmas of Slaveholding: The Ideology and Behavior of Elite Antebellum Women," and Lauren Ann Kattner, "The Diversity of Old South White Women: The Peculiar Worlds of German American Women."

Interesting research analyzes changing laws that affected southern women, including Eleanor M. Boatwright's "The Political and Civil Status of Women in Georgia, 1783–1860," *The Georgia Historical Quarterly* 25 (1941); Jane Turner Censer, "'Smiling Through Her Tears': Ante-Bellum Southern Women and Divorce," *The American Journal of Legal History* 25 (1981); Richard H. Chused, "Married Women's Property Law: 1800–1850," *The*

Georgetown Law Journal 71 (1983); Michael B. Dougan, "The Arkansas Married Woman's Property Law," *Arkansas Historical Quarterly* 46 (1987); Sandra Moncrief, "The Mississippi Married Women's Property Act of 1839," *The Journal of Mississippi History* 47 (1985); Marylynn Salmon, "Women and Property in South Carolina: The Evidence from Marriage Settlements, 1730–1830," *William and Mary Quarterly* 39 (1982); and Lawrence B. Goodheart, Neil Hanks, and Elizabeth Johnson, "'An Act for the Relief of Females': Divorce and the Changing Legal Status of Women in Tennessee, 1796–1860," *Tennessee Historical Quarterly* 44 (1985). Donna Elizabeth Sedevie, "The Prospect of Happiness: Women, Divorce, and Property," *Journal of Mississippi History* 57 (1995), assesses how changing divorce laws in the Mississippi territory from 1789 to 1817 affected women.

Little scholarly research is available on southern women and religion. The most comprehensive study is Jean E. Friedman's *The Enclosed Garden: Women and Community in the Evangelical South, 1830–1900* (Chapel Hill, NC, 1985) which argues that the bonds of church and family prevented women from becoming independent and outspoken. Most of the book covers the post–Civil War period, though its examination of church tribunals broadens our understanding of female behavior. Sister Mary Michael Creamer's "Mother Catherine Spalding—St. Catherine Street, Louisville, Kentucky," *The Filson Club History Quarterly* 63 (1989) describes Spalding's benevolence as founder and mother superior of the Sisters of Charity and her active role in establishing schools and orphanages on the frontier; Gwendolyn Gosney Erickson, "Religion, Region, and Community among Quaker Women of North Carolina's Eastern Quarter, 1812–1854," *Southern Friend* 18 (1996), examines a group of women who felt relatively isolated in the slaveholding South; Mark I. Greenburg, "Savannah's Jewish Women and the Shaping of Ethnic and Gender Identity, 1830–1900," *The Georgia Historical Quarterly* 82 (1998) gives a better sense of Jewish women's roles in the region; Steven L. Baker, "Improvising on the Borderlands of Gender: The Friends of Mary at the Foot of the Cross, 1812–1834," *Filson Club History Quarterly* 71 (1997), discusses a community of

Catholic sisters, the Sisters of Loretto; and Joe L. Kincheloe, Jr., "Transcending Role Restrictions: Women at Camp Meetings and Political Rallies," *Tennessee Historical Quarterly* 40 (1981) shows that women who attended camp meetings fell into traditional roles as cooks and mothers but also found a chance to express themselves freely on an equal basis with men. Donald G. Mathew's *Religion in the Old South* (Chicago, 1977) includes some information on southern women's involvement in religion as does Richard Rankin's *Ambivalent Churchmen and Evangelical Church Women: The Religion of the Episcopal Elite in North Carolina, 1800–1860* (Columbia, SC, 1993).

Material on antebellum women's education has begun to emerge. Christie Anne Farnham's *The Education of the Southern Belle: Higher Education and Student Socialization in the Antebellum South* (New York, 1994) draws attention to certain aspects of southern white women's education. She insists that the education offered antebellum southern women was nearly the equal of that enjoyed by southern men and that the South surpassed the North in its commitment to women's higher education. Farnham believes that education helped to reinforce a woman's class standing by emphasizing a classical education and one that offered a variety of genteel arts. Journal articles on women's education include Judith T. Bainbridge, "A 'Nursery of Knowldege': The Greenville Female Academy, 1819–1854," *South Carolina Historical Magazine* 99 (1998), providing a history of this South Carolina women's school; F. N. Boney, "The Pioneer College for Women: Wesleyan Over a Century and a Half," *Georgia Historical Quarterly* 72 (1988), presenting a brief history of Georgia Female College (which later changed its name to Wesleyan College); Daniel W. Harrison, "The Richmond Female Institute, 1850–1868," *Virginia Baptist Register* 37 (1998); and Robert E. Hunt, "Home, Domesticity, and School Reform in Antebellum Alabama," *The Alabama Review* 49 (1996) which argues for concepts of reform and progress in promoting southern women's schooling. Anya Jabour's "'Grown Girls, Highly Cultivated': Female Education in an Antebellum Southern Family," *Journal of Southern History* 64 (1998), examines the education of the daughters of William and

Elizabeth Wirt which prepared them for southern life. Beginning to fill a gap on poor women's schooling is Mary Carroll Johansen's "'All Useful Plain Branches of Education'; Educating Non-Elite Women in Antebellum Virginia," *Virginia Cavalcade* 49 (2000). Mary Carroll Johansen provides an interesting focus on free black women's education in "'Intelligence, Though Overlooked': Education for Black Women in the Upper South, 1800–1840," *Maryland Historical Magazine* 93 (1998).

Until fairly recently, slave women's experiences had been integrated into general histories on slavery. More recent monographs show the importance of gender in understanding the black experience. Deborah Gray White's *Ar'n't I A Woman? Female Slaves in the Plantation South* (New York, 1985) argues that the model for white females had no meaning to slave women, who were the most vulnerable group in antebellum America. Bondwomen had to be aggressive and strong, and they gained respect and worth on a par with black men. White counters the Jezebel and Mammy stereotypes and shows black women's value to the slave community and to their masters.

Jacqueline Jones's *Labor of Love, Labor of Sorrow: Black Women, Work and the Family, from Slavery to the Present* (New York, 1985) is a history of black women, focusing especially on their dual role as laborers and mothers. Two chapters that deal with the antebellum and Civil War periods show how black women struggled against oppression. Their responsibilities to family and work pulled them in opposite directions, but slave women found means to define life on their own terms.

An intriguing, brief study of a slave woman is Malcolm McLaurin's *Celia: A Slave* (Athens, GA, 1991). McLaurin focuses on a Missouri court case involving a slave woman, Celia, accused of bludgeoning her master to death. State law claimed that women had the right to defend themselves. Because Celia was merely property in the eyes of the law, she had no honor to defend and ultimately was found guilty and hanged. Also of interest is Steven Weisenburger's *Modern Medea: A Family Story of Slavery and Child-Murder from the Old South* (1998) about a slave mother from Kentucky who murdered her young child after the family ran away to freedom in Ohio.

Also recent is Brenda Stevenson's *Life in Black and White: Family and Community in the Slave South* (New York, 1996) which studies slave and free black women in Loudoun County, Virginia, between the Revolution and Civil War. She offers a realistic vision of black women and their families, showing the instability of slave families due to the vagaries of a market economy and fluctuating farm prices which forced owners to sell slaves and divide families. Free black women endured a precarious position, facing racial discrimination and limited job opportunities. If they were single mothers, courts sometimes removed their rights as parents.

Leslie A. Schwalm's study of black women, *A Hard Fight for We: Women's Transition from Slavery to Freedom in South Carolina* (Urbana, IL, 1997) emphasizes the important role that slave women played in the rice culture of this wealthy coastal area. Life on these plantations was relatively stable, giving women access to a fairly meaningful family and community life. She claims black women were the "backbone" of the plantation labor force; they made a major contribution to plantation productivity and sometimes comprised a majority of the workers.

A new book, *Born in Bondage; Growing up Enslaved in the Antebellum South* (2000) by Marie Jenkins Schwartz focuses on the experiences of slave children but has important information about fertility and childrearing practices.

Journal articles that deal with more specific concerns of enslaved women include Dorothy Burnham's "The Life of the Afro-American Woman in Slavery," *International Journal of Women's Studies* 1 (1978); Cheryll Ann Cody's "Naming, Kinship, and Estate Dispersal: Notes on Slave Family Life on a South Carolina Plantation, 1786 to 1833," *William and Mary Quarterly* 39 (1982); and Angela Davis's "Reflections on the Black Woman's Role in the Community of Slaves," *The Black Scholar* 3 (1971). Frances S. Foster's "Ultimate Victims: Black Women in Slave Narratives," *Journal of American Culture* 1 (1978) shows that narratives were written to appeal to a particular audience; they emphasized slave women's sexual vulnerability and inability to function effectively as mothers, thus reinforcing stereotypes of African American women and of slavery. Loren Schweninger in

"A Slave Family in the Ante Bellum South," *Journal of Negro History* 60 (1975), describes a bondwoman Sally and her three sons, and his "Property Owning Free African-American Women in the South, 1800–1870," *Journal of Women's History* 1 (1990), counters assumptions that all blacks were poor or strong abolitionists. Thelma Jennings in "'Us Colored Women Had to Go Through a Plenty': Sexual Exploitation of African-American Slave Women," *Journal of Women's History* 1 (1990), carefully examines slave testimony collected by the WPA to show the extent of miscegenation, forced marriages, and slave breeding. Carole Shammas's, "Black Women's Work and the Evolution of Plantation Society in Virginia," *Labor History* 26 (1985), describes the nature and variety of slave work. Catherine Clinton explores the sexual vulnerability of slave women in "Caught in the Web of the Big House: Women and Slavery," in *The Web of Southern Social Relations: Women, Family and Education,* ed. Walter J. Fraser, Jr., R. Frank Saunders, Jr., and Jon L. Wakelyn (Athens, GA, 1985). Wilma A. Dunaway's "Diaspora, Death, and Sexual Exploitation: Slave Families at Risk in the Mountain South," *Appalachian Journal* 26 (1999), uses statistics and slave narratives to argue that slaves in the Piedmont and mountain regions of the South suffered more than did slaves living in the Deep South. Darna L. Raney's "'She Do A Heap of Work': Female Slave Labor on Glynn County Rice and Cotton Plantations," *Georgia Historical Quarterly* 82 (1998) examines the type of labor slave women performed. Collections of essays on black women provide more information, including David Barry Gaspar and Darlene Clark Hine's *More Than Chattel: Black Women and Slavery in the Americas* (Bloomington, IN, 1996).

The health of slaves has generated interesting research. Black women suffered different problems from male slaves due to childbearing and its attendant problems. And because African Americans had different immunities and sensitivities to certain diseases, their health histories contrasted to those of whites. The most comprehensive medical study is Kenneth F. Kiple and Virginia Himmelsteib King's *Another Dimension to the Black Diaspora: Diet, Disease, and Racism* (Cambridge, MA, 1981) which examines diseases and health problems specific to blacks, especially dietary concerns. John Campbell's "Work, Pregnancy, and Infant Mortality among Southern Slaves," *Journal of Interdisciplinary History* 14 (1984), correlates lighter work loads for expectant mothers with more successful deliveries and healthier infants. An interesting comparison between Caribbean and southern slaves' nursing practices is found in Herbert S. Klein and Stanley L. Engerman, "Fertility Differentials between Slaves in the United States and the British West Indies: A Note on Lactation Practices and Their Possible Implications," *William and Mary Quarterly* 35 (1978). Richard Steckel has written several studies on infant slave health that relate to maternal diet and nursing practices including, "A Peculiar Population: The Nutrition, Health, and Mortality of American Slaves from Childhood to Maturity," *Journal of Economic History* 46 (1986), "Birth Weights and Infant Mortality among American Slaves," *Explorations in Economic History* 23 (1986), and "A Dreadful Childhood: The Excess Mortality of American Slaves," *Social Science History* 10 (1986).

More general works on slavery that mention women include Ira Berlin's and Eugene Genovese's *Roll, Jordan, Roll: the World the Slaves Made* (New York, 1974), which argues for a paternalistic relationship between slaves and masters. A newer study is Berlin's *Many Thousands Gone: The First Two Centuries of Slavery in North America* (Cambridge, MA, 1998). John W. Blassingame's *The Slave Community: Plantation Life in the Antebellum South* (rev. ed., New York, 1979) shows the importance of community in creating slaves' strong sense of self and life apart from the master. Herbert G. Gutman's *The Black Family in Slavery and Freedom, 1750–1925* (New York, 1976) disputed the Moynihan Report, arguing for the strength and centrality of the black family. Paul D. Escott's *Slavery Remembered: A Record of Twentieth-Century Slave Narratives* (Chapel Hill, NC, 1979) carefully analyzes responses of former slaves interviewed under the Federal Writers' Project. Supported by numerous tables, the narrative discloses a fascinating tale about life as former slaves remembered it.

Primary source material of black women includes one of the most widely read and dramatic slave narratives, Harriet Jacobs's *Incidents in the Life of a Slave Girl: Written by Herself* edited by

Jean Fagan Yellin (Cambridge, MA, 1987). Jacobs reveals the horrors of slavery, including sexual harassment and the threat of losing her children. Also of interest is Harriet Tubman's recollection of plantation life, *Harriet, The Moses of Her People* (New York, 1886). Documents and personal writings by black women are found in Gerda Lerner, ed., *Black Women in White America: A Documentary History* (New York, 1972); and in Dorothy Sterling, ed., *We Are Your Sisters: Black Women in the Nineteenth Century* (New York, 1984). The most comprehensive primary sources on slave life are the forty-one volumes edited by George Rawick, *The American Slave: A Composite Narrative* (Westport, CN, 1972–79), a collection of interviews collected during the Depression. Charles L. Perdue, Jr., Thomas E. Barden, and Robert K. Phillips, eds., *Weevils in the Wheat: Interviews with Virginia Ex-Slaves* (Charlottesville, VA, 1976) and Octavia V. Rogers Albert, *The House of Bondage: or Charlotte Brooks and Other Slaves* (New York, 1890) provide additional interviews from one state. Primary material covering antebellum free black women is rare. A recent contribution is Virginia Meacham Gould's edited collection of letters, *Chained to the Rock of Adversity: To Be Free, Black, and Female in the Old South* (Athens, GA, 1998), between a mother and her daughter in the Johnson family of Louisiana and Mississippi.

Another perspective on black and white southern women emerges through the writings of travelers to the South. One of the most interesting, especially for its insights on slave women, is Fanny Kemble's *Journal of a Residence on a Georgian Plantation in 1838–39* (Athens, GA, 1984 [1863]). Kemble, a British actress, met and married Pierce Butler, a Philadelphian who owned plantations in the Sea Islands of Georgia. After visiting there, Fanny recorded her activities and insights. Catherine Clinton's "Fanny Kemble's Journal: A Woman Confronts Slavery on a Georgia Plantation," *Frontiers* 9 (1987), describes Kemble's marital problems and how her personal observations and abolitionist feelings enhanced her sensitivity to the plight of slave women. Also of note is Harriet Martineau's *Society in America,* abr. ed. (New York, 1962), originally published in three volumes in 1837.

Martineau came to the United States in 1834 to observe this nation, and she spent some time in the South. Frederick Law Olmsted visited the South in the 1850s and his *Journey in the Seaboard Slave States, with Remarks on Their Economy* (New York, 1968 [1856]) is a classic and filled with perceptive observations.

Fewer studies focus on yeomen farm women, in part because information about their lives is limited. Scholars have had to approach this field by digging into sources other than women's writings, since poor women had little time or inclination to write—and many of them were illiterate. Victoria E. Bynum's *Unruly Women: The Politics of Social and Sexual Control in the Old South* (Chapel Hill, NC, 1992) is the first full-length study of both poor black and white women. The book focuses on three counties in North Carolina. Using court records, newspapers, and other sources, Bynum shows that these women often fell victim to the state, which adopted a paternalistic attitude toward them. Judges often determined that single, poor women were unfit mothers and apprenticed their children. Southern courts exerted coercive control over women and were more concerned about protecting southern society than defending its most vulnerable women.

A provocative book that has generated attention is Stephanie McCurry's *Masters of Small Worlds: Yeoman Households, Gender Relations, and the Political Culture of the Antebellum South Carolina Low Country* (New York, 1994). This book is less about southern women than about gender as a central construct to explain the antebellum South's political discourse and commitment to slavery. As McCurry argues, whatever their status, white men treasured their independence and their position as head of the household. Being even a master of a "small world," with or without slaves, meant that all white males had a stake in the South's social and economic system.

Journal articles add additional perspective on farm women, including Keith L. Bryant, Jr., "The Role and Status of the Female Yeomanry in the Antebellum South: The Literary View," *Southern Quarterly* 18 (1980); and D. Harland Hagler's, "The Ideal Woman in the Antebellum South: Lady or Farmwife?" *Journal of Southern History* 46 (1980) which argues that by the 1850s a different female image that focused on the hardworking farm woman was supplanting the fashionable southern lady. Lauren Ann Kattner's "The Diversity of Old South White Women: The Peculiar Worlds of German American Women," in Patricia Morton's *Discovering the Women in Slavery* begins to address some of the diversity of women in the region.

One of the most exciting areas of recent research on southern black and white women is sexuality. A provocative account that sheds new light on miscegenous relationships is Martha Hodes's *White Women, Black Men: Illicit Sex in the Nineteenth-Century South* (New Haven, CT, 1997). Her evidence comes from court cases of relationships involving black men and white women. Matters of the heart could lead to a transgression of social and racial boundaries, showing the variety of relationships in the Old South. Southerners exhibited some tolerance for these relationships as long as they were not flaunted. Expanding on this subject are Joshua D. Rothman's "'To be Freed from Thate Curs and Let at Liberty': Interracial Adultery and Divorce in Antebellum Virginia," *The Virginia Magazine of History and Biography*, 106 (1998); and Timothy J. Lockley's "Crossing the Race Divide: Interracial Sex in Antebellum Savannah," *Slavery and Abolition* 18 (1997).

Native American women in the South have begun to receive some attention, though their histories are usually included in broader studies that move beyond the antebellum period. Theda Perdue's *Cherokee Women: Gender and Culture Change, 1700–1835* (Lincoln, NE, 1998) examines Cherokee women and their roles in tribal culture, as well as how an exposure to Euro-Americans altered their lives and led to a precipitous decline in their economic and social position. Sarah Hill, in her sensitive study, *Weaving New Worlds: Southeastern Cherokee Women and Their Basketry* (Chapel Hill, NC, 1997) approaches her topic in an innovative manner, using the imagery of basketry to argue a similar thesis to Perdue's. Hill shows how the shapes and materials used in baskets reflected larger changes in tribal history and women's roles.

The study of the Civil War period has benefited from extensive primary material, including diaries and reminiscences of women who found their lives altered forever by war. These sources include *Lucy Breckinridge of Grove Hill: The Journal of a Virginia Girl, 1862–1864,* ed. Mary D. Robertson (Kent, OH, 1979) which includes sensitive, revealing, and somewhat pessimistic reactions to the war she came to despise. Others are Marli F. Weiner's edited volume, *A Heritage of Woe: The Civil War Diary of Grace Brown Elmore, 1861–1868* (Athens, GA, 1997); Elizabeth R. Baer's *Shadows on My Heart; The Civil War Diary of Lucy Rebecca Buck of Virginia* (Athens, GA, 1997); Charles East's *The Civil War Diary of Sarah Morgan* (Athens, GA, 1991); Jean V. Berlin's *A Confederate Nurse: The Diary of Ada W. Bacot, 1860–1863* (Columbia, SC, 1994); Floride Clemson's *A Rebel Came Home: The Diary and Letters of Floride Clemson, 1863–1866,* ed. Charles M. McGee, Jr., and Ernest M. Lander, Jr. (Columbia, SC, 1989 [1961]); and Kate Stone's *Brokenburn: The Journal of Kate Stone, 1861–1868,* ed. John Q. Anderson (Baton Rouge, 1955). Catherine Anne Devereux Edmondston's *"Journal of a Secesh Lady": The Diary of Catherine Anne Devereux Edmondston, 1860–1866,* ed. Beth G. Crabtree and James W. Patton, (Raleigh, NC, 1979), details a privileged North Carolina wife's experiences during the Civil War. *A Rebel Wife in Texas: The Diary and Letters of Elizabeth Scott Neblett, 1852–1864* (Baton Rouge, 2001) is edited by Erika L. Murr. John Rozier's edited volume, *The Granite Farm Letters: The Civil War Correspondence of Edgeworth and Sallie Bird* (Athens, GA, 1988), is a collection of loving letters between a Georgia couple. Sarah Morgan Dawson's *A Confederate Girl's Diary* (Bloomington, IN, 1960), tells of a Baton Rouge family that lost four young members and was exiled from its beautiful home. David J. Rutledge, ed., "Elizabeth Jamison's Tale of the War," *South Carolina Historical Magazine* 99 (1998) prints Jamison's memoir describing her assuming management of her husband's plantation.

Monographs on southern white women during the Civil War have added insight into their experiences. One is George C. Rable's *Civil Wars: Women and the Crisis of Southern Nationalism* (Urbana, IL, 1989), showing the critical role that women played in breaking the spirit of the Confederacy and the central role of yeomen farm wives who were initially silent but became increasingly critical as the war progressed. Rable examines all classes of women on the homefront. Catherine Clinton's *Tara Revisited: Women, War and the Plantation Image* (New York, 1995) gives a compelling overview of southern women's experiences, comparing myth to reality.

A more recent study is Drew Gilpin Faust's *Mothers of Invention: Women of the Slaveholding South in the American Civil War* (Chapel Hill, NC, 1996) which focuses on the experiences of the elite and their complex, contradictory roles. Faust looks at details in women's lives such as the books they read, their social activities, and their forms of mourning. Like Rable, Faust finds elite white women tiring of wartime demands and urging their men to come home.

A lively synthesis of southern women during the Civil War and Reconstruction is Laura F. Edwards's *Scarlett Doesn't Live Here Anymore* (Urbana and Chicago, 2000). Edwards focuses on black and white women, rich and poor, to show their impact on the region and emphasize their active involvement during these critical years.

Although Lee Ann Whites's *The Civil War as a Crisis in Gender: Augusta, Georgia, 1860–1890* moves well beyond the Civil War and focuses on only one southern city, she offers provocative thoughts about the impact of this conflict and women's roles in this urban location.

Other book accounts of women during the Confederacy include Katherine M. Jones, *Ladies of Richmond* (Indianapolis, IN, 1962), a collection of writings by women in the Confederate capital; Frances Butler Simkins and James Welch Patton, *The Women of the Confederacy* (Richmond, VA, 1936), defending women who upheld the rebel cause; Bell Wiley, *Confederate Women* (Westport, CT, 1975) which focuses on three well-known southern women; H. E. Sterkx, *Partners in Rebellion: Alabama Women in the Civil War* (Rutherford, NJ, 1970); Mary Elizabeth Massey, *Bonnet Brigades: American Women and the Civil War* (New York, 1966); and Edward D. C. Campbell, Jr., and Kym S. Rice, editors of the Museum of the Confederacy's *A Woman's War: Southern Women, Civil War, and the Confederate Legacy* (1996).

Journal articles offer similar insights into southern women's war experiences. See David H. McGee, "'Home and Friends': Kinship, Community, and Elite Women in Caldwell County, North Carolina during the Civil War," *North Carolina Historical Review* 74 (1997); Robert E. May, "Southern Elite Women, Sectional Extremism, and the Male Political Sphere: The Case of John A. Quitman's Wife and Female Descendants, 1847–1931," *The Journal of Mississippi History* 50 (1988) which, despite the title, focuses primarily on southern women's support of the Confederacy; Isabel Quattlebaum, "Twelve Women in the First Days of the Confederacy," *Civil War History* 7 (1961); David. J. Rutledge, ed., "Elizabeth Jamison's Tale of the War," *South Carolina Historical Magazine* 99 (1998) including both primary and secondary material; Sarah Woolfolk Wiggins, "Amelia Gayle Gorgas and the Civil War," *Alabama Review* 51 (1998); Catherine Clinton, "Reading between the Lines: Newspapers and Women in Confederate Richmond," *Atlanta History* 42 (1998); John Inscoe, "The Civil War's Empowerment of an Appalachian Woman: The 1864 Slave Purchases of Mary Bell," in Patricia Morton, ed., *Discovering the Women in Slavery*; Tracy J. Revels, "'Grander in her Daughters': Florida's Women during the Civil War," *Florida Historical Quarterly* 77 (1999); Clea Lutz Bunch, "Confederate Women of Arkansas Face 'The Fiends in Human Shape,'" *Military History of the West* 27 (1997); Patricia Dora Bonnin, "The Problem of Relief for the Families of Confederate Soldiers in South Carolina," *Proceedings of the South Carolina Historical Association* (1994); Gordon B. McKinney, "Women's Role in Civil War Western North Carolina," *North Carolina Historical Review* 69 (1992); Darla Brock, "'Our Hands are at Your Service': The Story of Confederate Women in Memphis," *West Tennessee Historical Society Papers* 45 (1991); Drew Gilpin Faust, "'Trying to Do a Man's Business': Slavery, Violence and Gender in the American Civil War," *Gender and History* 4 (1992); Nancy B. Samuelson, "Employment of Female Spies in the American Civil War," *Minerva* 7 (1989); Kreisten L. Forrester, "Disrupting the Domestic Sphere: The Civil War and North Louisiana Women, 1861–1865," *North Louisiana Historical Association*

Journal 26 (1995); Nancy T. Kondert, "The Romance and Reality of Defeat: Southern Women in 1865," *The Journal of Mississippi History* 35 (1973); Janet E. Kaufman, "'Treasury Girls': Working Women of the South," *Civil War Times Illustrated* 25 (1986); Michael K. Honey, "The War Within the Confederacy: White Unionists of North Carolina," *Prologue* 26 (1994); "'Under the Petticoat Flag': Women in the Confederate Army," *Southern Studies* 23 (1984); and Sylvia D. Hoffert, "Mary Boykin Chesnut: Private Feminist in the Civil War South," *Southern Studies* 16 (1977). William A. Strasser, Jr., "'A Terrible Calamity Has Befallen Us': Unionist Women in Civil War East Tennessee," *Journal of East Tennessee History* 71 (1999), examines Unionist women, usually rural and poor, and their wartime experiences; also see Strasser's "'Our Women Played Well Their Parts': Confederate Women in Civil War East Tennessee," *Tennessee Historical Quarterly* 59 (2000), on female Confederate sympathizers.

INDEX

Southern Women: Black and White in the Old South, Second Edition
Developmental editor: Andrew J. Davidson
Copyeditor and production editor: Lucy Herz
Proofreader: Linda Gaio
Printer: McNaughton & Gunn, Inc.